Welcome to

ALL ABOUT
HISTORY
Book of

BRITISH ROYALS

The date is 14 October 1066, and the battlefield at Hastings lies bloodied, littered with the remains of Harold II's ruined army, with Harold himself defeated by an arrow to the eye. William the Conqueror has just earned his now-famous title, and more importantly, the crown of England. This is where our story begins – the fascinating tale of Britain's monarchy. In this book, you'll discover incredible facts about every king and queen of Britain from 1066 to the present day, and uncover the truth behind royal scandals, conflicts and triumphs. From the bloody battles of Hastings, Bosworth and Agincourt, to the treacherous political courts of the Tudors and Stuarts, trace the turbulent history of Britain's royal bloodline from its beginnings right up to the present day, with the current monarch, Queen Elizabeth II.

BRITISH ROYALS

Imagine Publishing Ltd
Richmond House
33 Richmond Hill
Bournemouth
Dorset BH2 6EZ
☎ +44 (0) 1202 586200
Website: www.imagine-publishing.co.uk

Publishing Director
Aaron Asadi

Head of Design
Ross Andrews

Production Editor
Alex Hoskins

Senior Art Editor
Greg Whitaker

Designer
Lauren Debono-Elliot

Printed by
William Gibbons, 26 Planetary Road, Willenhall, West Midlands, WV13 3XT

Distributed in the UK, Eire & the Rest of the World by
Marketforce, Blue Fin Building, 110 Southwark Street, London, SE1 0SU
Tel 0203 148 3300 www.marketforce.co.uk

Distributed in Australia by
Network Services (a division of Bauer Media Group), Level 21 Civic Tower, 66-68 Goulburn Street,
Sydney, New South Wales 2000, Australia Tel +61 2 8667 5288

Part of the

bookazine series

IMAGINE
PUBLISHING

Contents

98

20

162

146

70

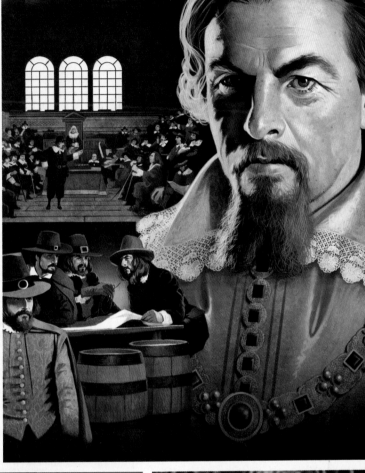

Contents

The birth of the British monarchy

Discover how the union of England and Scotland shaped the line of succession and the modern British monarchy

The United Kingdom of Great Britain has not always been united, or known as Great Britain for that matter. Prior to 1707, this seemingly small island in the North Atlantic had been divided for centuries. England (including Wales) and Scotland were in fact two independent countries, and it wasn't until the passing of the Treaty of Union through both Parliaments in 1707 that the two kingdoms united, officially marking the birth of Great Britain, and as a result, its monarchy.

The first sovereign to rule over Great Britain was Queen Anne. Officially she had reigned as queen of both countries for five years prior to the Treaty, as both the Kingdom of England and the Kingdom of Scotland had shared a monarch since 1603, when King James VI of Scotland inherited the English throne from Queen Elizabeth I through relation. This was known officially as the Union of Crowns. It was the Treaty of Union, however, that united the monarchy under one crown, and then eventually one government.

Due to the treaty, Queen Anne was the first and last monarch from the House of Stuart dynasty to rule over the United Kingdom of Great Britain. Six years prior to 1707, in 1701, it had been decided

through the Act of Settlement that Catholics were to be prohibited from inheriting the throne, and so Sophia of Hanover, a Protestant and the granddaughter of James VI and I, would become Queen Anne's heir. Although Anne had many direct Catholic descendants, she had no surviving children. Sophia of Hanover was her closest protestant relative, which meant in 1714, when Queen Anne died, the House of Stuart dynasty came to an end as the House of Hanover succeeded the throne.

By this time, however, Sophia of Hanover had died aged 83, and so her eldest son George inherited the crown and became King George I of Great Britain. George's succession was controversial, as many people hadn't agreed with the protestant succession that had been outlined in the Act of Settlement, and as a result riots were documented across England in opposition to his coronation. Despite the initial hostility, George I reigned as king up until his death in 1727. During his reign, Britain began to modernise and a cabinet government was formed, which meant that the monarchy held less power over political affairs.

George's son and heir George II succeeded to the throne in October 1727 after his father's death.

Queen Elizabeth II, the current monarch of Great Britain, leaving Westminster Abbey as part of a procession after her coronation on 3 June 1953

Treaty of Union

How England and Scotland united to form Great Britain and the British monarchy

The United Kingdom of Great Britain was officially formed in 1707, when the Parliaments of England and Scotland passed the Treaty of Union agreement. Prior to this date, England (including Wales) and Scotland were independent countries that had two separate governments. The Treaty of Union was designed to merge the Kingdoms of England and Scotland together, creating the United Kingdom of Great Britain.

Negotiations to unite the countries began in 1705 under the reign of the English and Scottish monarch Queen Anne, although there had been several failed tempts prior to this date. 31 commissioners were appointed by each Parliament to negotiate the terms, and talks began on 16 April 1706 at the Cockpit-in-Court in London. After a few days, the Treaty was finalised on 22 July 1706, and two separate acts of union were to be passed through each government before it was put into effect. The first act of union, known as the Union with Scotland Act, was passed by the Parliament of England in 1706, with the second, the Union with England Act, being passed by the Parliament of Scotland shortly after in 1707.

The treaty itself consisted of 25 articles, with two stating that one monarch was to rule over Great Britain and a single unified Parliament of Great Britain was to be formed. In addition to this, agreements regarding trading between England and Scotland were set, alongside the decision to introduce a common currency. On 1 May 1707, England and Scotland officially united.

The union between Great Britain and Ireland, however, did not occur for another 93 years. It was during the reign of King George III that in 1800, Great Britain and the Kingdom of Ireland united to form what is now known as the United Kingdom of Great Britain and Ireland. To signify the union, the Union Flag incorporated the St Patrick's Cross.

The official copy of the Treaty of Union, ratified by the parliaments of England and Scotland in 1907

British Royals

George II's own son and heir apparent, Frederick Louis, Prince of Wales, was next in line to become king. Frederick, however, died unexpectedly in 1751. This mean that in 1760, after King George II's death, Frederick's eldest son George III inherited the crown.

It was during George III's reign that Great Britain and Ireland united, changing his official title to King George III of the United Kingdom of Great Britain and Ireland. George III was also the first monarch of Great Britain since its formation in 1707 to be born and raised in the country he ruled. While sovereign, George saw Britain through many military conflicts, including the Battle of Waterloo in 1815. His early reign was considered successful. However, he is often remembered through history for the mental illness that plagued him in later life, which as a result earned him his nickname 'Mad George'. During his illness, his son and heir apparent, George the Prince of Wales, served as Prince Regent - a position that enabled him to exercise full power as king while his father was incapacitated. This period is known as the Regency in British history, and Regent's Park, as well as Regent Street in London, was named after him. Upon George III's death in 1820, his son, the Prince of Wales, inherited the throne and was titled King George IV of the United Kingdom of Great Britain and Ireland.

George IV reigned as king for ten years, and upon his own passing, had no legitimate issue to inherit the throne. His younger brother, William IV, who was third in line to the throne during George III's reign, became King. William himself reigned for a relatively short period of time (1830-1837), and also had no surviving legitimate children at the time of his death. He was succeeded by his young niece Victoria, Prince Edward, Duke of Kent and Strathearn's daughter, who was only 18 at the time.

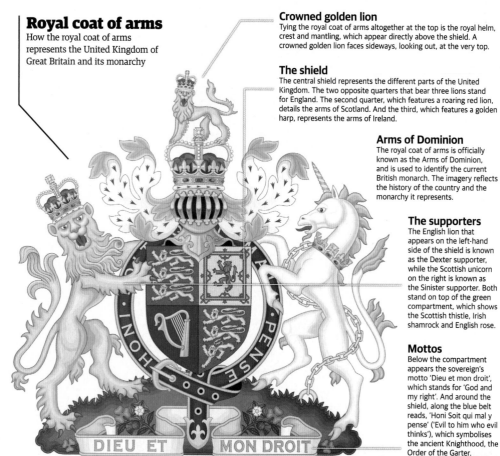

Royal coat of arms
How the royal coat of arms represents the United Kingdom of Great Britain and its monarchy

Crowned golden lion
Tying the royal coat of arms altogether at the top is the royal helm, crest and mantling, which appear directly above the shield. A crowned golden lion faces sideways, looking out, at the very top.

The shield
The central shield represents the different parts of the United Kingdom. The two opposite quarters that bear three lions stand for England. The second quarter, which features a roaring red lion, details the arms of Scotland. And the third, which features a golden harp, represents the arms of Ireland.

Arms of Dominion
The royal coat of arms is officially known as the Arms of Dominion, and is used to identify the current British monarch. The imagery reflects the history of the country and the monarchy it represents.

The supporters
The English lion that appears on the left-hand side of the shield is known as the Dexter supporter, while the Scottish unicorn on the right is known as the Sinister supporter. Both stand on top of the green compartment, which shows the Scottish thistle, Irish shamrock and English rose.

Mottos
Below the compartment appears the sovereign's motto 'Dieu et mon droit', which stands for 'God and my right'. And around the shield, along the blue belt reads, 'Honi Soit qui mal y pense' ('Evil to him who evil thinks'), which symbolises the ancient Knighthood, the Order of the Garter.

DIEU ET MON DROIT

Scottish royal coat of arms
Scotland has its own version of the royal coat of arms. This features two representations of Scotland as apposed to one, and the unicorn appears as the Dexter holding the Scottish flag, while the lion is the Sinister holding the English flag. A red lion, as opposed to a gold one, appears on top holding a banner that reads 'In Defens' ('In defence'). The motto of the Order of the Thistle sits along the compartment and reads 'Nemo me immune lacessit' ('No one attacks me with impunity').

Defining moment
Monarch 1 1707
Regnal name: **Queen Anne**
Name: **Anne**
Birth/death: **6 February 1665 – 1 August 1714**
Reign: **1 May 1707 – 1 August 1714**
Dynasty: **House of Stewart**
Queen Anne had reigned as Queen of England and Scotland since 1702. However, the signing of the Treaty of Union in 1707 meant she became the first monarch of the United Kingdom of Great Britain.

Defining moment
Monarch 4 1760
Regnal name: **King George III**
Name: **George William Frederick**
Birth/death: **4 June 1738 – 29 January 1820**
Reign: **25 October 1760 – 29 January 1820**
Dynasty: **House of Hanover**
George III became King of Great Britain in 1760, after inheriting the throne from his grandfather King George II. During his reign, Great Britain and Ireland united to officially form the United Kingdom of Great Britain and Ireland, and in 1815, Britain defeated Napoleon at the Battle of Waterloo.

● Monarch 6
Regnal name: **King William IV**
Name: **William Henry**
Birth/death: **21 August 1765 – 20 June 1837**
Reign: **26 June 1830 – 20 June 1837**
Dynasty: **House of Hanover**
King William IV was the third son of King George III; he inherited the throne from his eldest brother King George IV, who had no legitimate issue at the time of death. Upon William's death in 1837, his 18-year-old niece Victoria inherited the throne.

Timeline

1707

● Monarch 2
Regnal name: **King George 1**
Name: **George Louis**
Birth/death: **28 May 1660 – 11 June 1727**
Reign: **1 August 1714 – 11 June 1727**
Dynasty: **House of Hanover**
King George I was the first monarch from the House of Hanover. He inherited the throne from Queen Anne, due to the Act of Settlement in 1707, which stated only Protestants could reign. By the time of Queen Anne's passing in 1714, George I was her closest protestant relative.

● Monarch 3
Regnal name: **King George II**
Name: **George Augustus**
Birth/death: **30 October 1683 – 25 October 1760**
Reign: **11 June 1727 – 25 October 1760**
Dynasty: **House of Hanover**
George II was the last British monarch to be born outside of Great Britain. He ascended the throne upon the death of his father George I. His eldest son and heir apparent Frederick died, leading to his grandson George III inheriting the throne.

● Monarch 5
Regnal name: **King George IV**
Name: **George Augustus Frederick**
Birth/death: **12 August 1762 – 26 June 1830**
Reign: **29 January 1820 – 26 June 1830**
Dynasty: **House of Hanover**
King George IV inherited the throne from his father George III after serving as Prince Regent for nine years previously, due to his father's mental illness. George IV's only legitimate issue, Princess Charlotte of Wales, died in 1817.

A portrait of King George III. He reigned from 1760-1820, but suffered from mental illness, resulting in a regency being established in 1811

William the Conqueror

William the Conqueror was the first Norman King of England and is often referred to as William I of England. After successfully invading the country in 1066, he reigned as sovereign up until his death in 1087.

Prior to this, William's cousin, Edward the Confessor, ruled as one of the last Anglo-Saxon kings of England from 1042 until his death in 1066. Although Edward was married, he had taken a vow of celibacy, which meant he had no heirs to the throne. On his deathbed, Edward declared that the English earl Harold Godwinson was to succeed him. William, however, refuted Harold's claim to the throne, and so in 1066, he gathered a fleet and invaded England, famously killing King Harold during the Battle of Hastings. Upon William's own death in 1087, his lands were divided among his sons. His second son, William II, inherited the throne.

The modern British monarchy we know today descends from William the Conqueror. In fact, he is Queen Elizabeth II's 22nd great grandfather. Since William I's death in 1087, most reigning monarchs of England, and later Great Britain, come from the same line of senior descent. Only 23 ruling monarchs have not been direct descendants of William I, including sovereigns from the House of Lancaster, Tudor and Stuart.

Defining moment
Monarch 7 1837
Regnal name: **Queen Victoria**
Name: **Alexandrina Victoria**
Birth/death: **24 May 1819 – 22 January 1901**
Reign: **20 June 1837 – 22 January 1901**
Dynasty: **House of Hanover**
Queen Victoria remains the longest reigning monarch in British history, reigning for over 63 years up until her death in 1901.

Defining moment
Monarch 10 1936
Regnal name: **King Edward VIII**
Name: **Edward Albert Christian George Andrew Patrick David**
Birth/death: **23 June 1894 – 28 May 1972**
Reign: **20 January 1936 – 11 December 1936**
Dynasty: **House of Windsor**
Edward VII was the only British monarch to abdicate, after Parliament opposed his intent to marry Wallis Simpson.

Monarch 11
Regnal name: **King George VI**
Name: **Albert, Frederick Arthur George**
Birth/death: **14 December 1895 – 6 February 1952**
Reign: **11 December 1936 – 6 February 1952**
Dynasty: **House of Windsor**
George VI reigned as King of Great Britain until his death in 1952. During his reign, Great Britain went to war with Nazi Germany, Ireland declared itself a republic, and the British Empire transitioned into the Commonwealth of Nations.

1926

Monarch 8
Regnal name: **King Edward VII**
Name: **Albert Edward**
Birth/death: **9 November 1841 – 6 May 1910**
Reign: **22 January 1901 – 6 May 1910**
Dynasty: **House of Saxe-Coburg and Gotha**
Queen Victoria's eldest son and heir inherited the throne after her death, becoming King Edward VII. Due to his mother's long reign, he was the longest serving heir apparent in British history, until 2011 when Charles, Prince of Wales, surpassed it.

Monarch 9
Regnal name: **King George V**
Name: **George Frederick Ernest Albert**
Birth/death: **3rd June 1865 – 20th January 1936**
Reign: **6th May 1910 – 20th January 1936**
Dynasty: **House of Windsor**
During George V's reign, the First World War broke out. While other empires fell, he was able to expand the British one. In 1917, due to ill feeling as a result of the war, he changed the German House of Saxe-Coburg Gotha to House of Windsor.

Monarch 12
Regnal name: **Queen Elizabeth II**
Name: **Elizabeth Alexandra Mary**
Birth/death: **21 April 1926 – present day**
Reign: **1952 – present day**
Dynasty: **House of Windsor**
Queen Elizabeth II is the current monarch of Great Britain and Head of the Commonwealth. She is set to be the longest reigning monarch of the United Kingdom, after over 60 years on the throne.

The House of Windsor

Why did the monarchy change its royal house name to Windsor?

Historically, monarchs do not have surnames; they are known by the countries they rule over and the royal house name that they inherit from their fathers when they succeed the throne.

Queen Victoria was the last British monarch to reign under the House of Hanover dynasty. Her successor and heir apparent Edward VII inherited the throne after her death in 1901, under his father's royal house name the House of Saxe-Coburg and Gotha. Edward was the first and last monarch of Great Britain to reign under this name, as upon his death in 1910, his son George V inherited the throne and subsequently changed the name to the House of Windsor in 1917.

George's decision to change the German dynastic name was a result of World War I, which occurred between 1914-1918. Due to anti-German sentiment at the time, the English name Windsor was adopted and was to be used as both the new royal house name and

as a family surname. This officially marked the start of the House of Windsor dynasty.

Following George VI's death in 1952, his eldest daughter and the current monarch of Great Britain, Elizabeth II, inherited the throne, continuing the House of Windsor line. Queen Elizabeth II still reigns under this royal house name, as will her direct heirs and descendants. In 1960, however, under an Order in Council, Elizabeth II adapted the personal Windsor surname to incorporate her husband's heritage (Philip Mountbatten). The new surname, Mountbatten-Windsor, can be used by some of her descendants who do not carry the styles 'Royal Highness', 'Prince' or 'Princess'.

Although the surname has changed, the official royal house name of Windsor remains the same. As of today, many British royals use the Mountbatten-Windsor surname for official documents, including those that have styles.

Queen Elizabeth II and her husband Prince Philip, Duke of Edinburgh, stand side by side on her coronation day in 1953

The official royal portrait of Prince George's Christening. (Back row, L-R) Prince Phillip, the Duke Of Edinburgh, Charles, Prince of Wales, Camilla the Duchess of Cornwall, Prince Harry of Wales, Pippa Middleton, James Middleton, Carole Middleton and Michael Middleton; (Front row, L-R) Queen Elizabeth II, Catherine, Duchess of Cambridge carrying Prince George Alexander Louis of Cambridge and Prince William, Duke of Cambridge

Queen Victoria is currently the longest reigning monarch of Great Britain. After inheriting the throne in 1837, she reigned for 63 years until her death in 1901. As a result, she is one of the most famous British monarchs in history. During her reign, also known as the Victorian era, Great Britain modernised, thanks to the industrial revolution and changes to politics, the military, science and culture. Victoria was also the last monarch to reign from the House of Hanover. Her son and successor King Edward VII reigned (1901-1910) customarily under his father's dynastic name, the House of Saxe-Coburg and Gotha. In 1917, however, seven

years after Edward VII's son George V inherited the throne, the house name was changed to Windsor as result of World War I (1914-1918) and anti-German sentiment at that time.

The current British monarchy still reign under the House of Windsor name today, and it was first inherited by George V's son and successor, Edward VIII, in 1936. As the only monarch since the union of Great Britain in 1707 to abdicate the throne, Edward VIII reigned under the House of Windsor for less than a year. His decision to abdicate was a result of his wish to marry the divorced American socialite, Wallis Simpson, which at the time would

"Edward VIII's wish to marry a divorced American socialite caused outcry across Britain"

have caused outcry across Britain and conflicted with his role as the Head of the Church of England. Upon Edward's abdication, his brother Albert ascended to the throne, and was formally styled King George VI.

Due to George VI's succession, his eldest daughter Elizabeth became heir apparent to the throne. And in 1952, she officially became Queen Elizabeth II upon her father's death. Elizabeth II is the current monarch of Great Britain and is set to become the longest reigning sovereign in British history. In 2012 she celebrated her Diamond Jubilee, marking 60 years as reigning monarch.

GVLIELM

1066-1087

William I

From the illegitimate son of a duke to the holder of the English crown, William I conquered detractors, kings and even the odds to become one of Britain's most memorable rulers

In 1028, William was born into a period rife with violence and disorder. Despite every nobleman owing fealty to the King of France, many duchies and fiefdoms were in constant flux as political alliances chopped and changed at a moment's notice. France itself had been at war with its rival Flanders for years, creating an intense air of conflict across much of Western Europe.

William's social status was also of some contention. His father, Robert I, Duke of Normandy, never married his mother, Herleva of Falaise, so the young Norman was born a bastard. However, William would be Robert's only child, so the presence of his father's blood was strong enough for the duke to name him as his heir. So serious was he about it that he gathered a group of Norman magnates in January 1034 to swear fealty to William as Robert's true successor. Soon after, Robert left on a pilgrimage to Jerusalem. Over a year later, Robert fell ill on his return from the Holy Land and died in Nicaea, Greece. And so, at the age of eight, William inherited one of the most powerful political positions in France.

The first few years of William's tenure as Duke of Normandy were surprisingly smooth, mostly due

to two considerably powerful supporters - namely his great-uncle Archbishop Robert and the king of France, Henry I. Such influential allies enabled William to retain the fealty over the Norman nobles he'd inherited from his father, but such support was not meant to last. With the king preoccupied with the costly conflict with Flanders, and Archbishop Robert passing away in March 1037, William's duchy soon descended into chaos.

Eventually a group of William's detractors formed an uneasy alliance and led a revolt against him. Led by his cousin, Guy of Burgundy, the revolters attempted to capture the duke at Valognes, a commune in northwestern France - however, the duke escaped and sought refuge with the French king. The duke may have been young, but the title of king was quite the trump card to play.

William returned to Normandy in the early months of 1047 with King Henry at his side and their armies consolidated into one considerable force. The rebel army outnumbered William's, but it lacked the leadership provided by the king's own elite. The Battle of Val-ès-Dunes descended into a number of skirmishes, but the rebel army soon

> Blood ties were common in the royalty at the time. Edward the Confessor was William's first cousin, once removed

William I

CONQISTER .

Despite his influential position in the history of the monarchy, no authentic portrait of William is in existence

During his reign, William crossed the Channel about 19 times

15

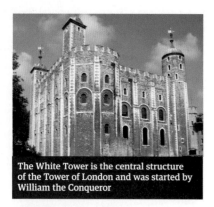

The White Tower is the central structure of the Tower of London and was started by William the Conqueror

Life in the time of William I

A nation divided

When William became king, he discovered a government far more complicated than Normandy's own. The country was divided into shires and counties, with these territories further divided into wapentakes (an old Norse word that refers to small meeting places).

Strength in stone

During his early reign, William commissioned a number of castles, keeps and mottes (a wooden or stone structure erected on raised earth). One of the most memorable of these was the White Tower, which remains the central structure of the Tower of London.

The hunting king

According to the medieval chronicler William of Malmesbury, William depopulated large swathes of land in the south of England in 1079 (36 parishes to be precise), to create the royal New Forest for hunting.

Forging ties

With his alliances and political standing in Normandy, William forged long-lasting ties between England and France that lasted for much of the Middle Ages (despite political and military clashes). His Viking roots also created a closer bond with Scandinavia.

The royal family

William had nine legitimate children with his wife, Matilda of Flanders. His sons were Robert, Richard, William and Henry, his daughters were Adeliza, Cecilia, Matilda, Constance, Adela and Agatha.

"William's forces were able to rout Harold's men like cattle. And after nine or so hours of battle, the fight was over"

broke apart and William finally established his authority over the Duchy of Normandy.

When William finally turned his attention to the kingdom across the Channel, his claim held more merit than most. The English monarch at the time, King Edward I, had named William as his successor (they were, in fact, distant cousins) and a chance meeting with the most powerful earl in England, Harold Godwinson, in 1064/5 also secured his support should the duke move to inherit the throne. According to William of Poitiers, a French priest who served as the official chronicler of William's invasion, the duke had the backing of almost all the lords and earls in Normandy as well as the backing of the Holy Roman Emperor, Henry VI. He even had the support of the pope, if Poitier's claims are to be believed. Either way, over a period of around seven months, he gathered a fleet of 600 ships with roughly 7,000 men (2,000-3,000 of these were cavalry). It was an impressive force designed for one thing: to conquer a kingdom.

William finally made landfall on 28 September 1066. They had arrived at Pevensey in the south of England, but William soon sent an envoy to London to speak with the Anglo-Saxon king.

Harold had just returned from repelling another invasion by the King of Norway, Harold Hardrada, and had rushed back to the capital after hearing of the Norman incursion. William told Harold that his claim to the throne was invalid and that he should relinquish the throne immediately or allow the pope to make an absolute decision. Harold, unsurprisingly, declined and the two leaders met in Hastings on 14 October 1066.

The Battle of Hastings was a bloody affair. Reports and speculations from historians differ on the size of Harold's army but a majority agree that it was roughly the same size as William's. The only real differences? Diversity and exhaustion. Despite a brief stop in London, Harold had marched a great deal of the army he used to defeat Harold Hardrada in the north down to the south in just two weeks. Despite their training, the men were fatigued and in no state to face a fresh Norman contingent. Harold's forces were almost entirely made up of infantryman, which was likely the deciding factor in the battle. With plenty of archers and cavalry, William's forces were able to rout Harold's men like cattle. And after nine or so hours of battle, the fight was over. Harold was dead and William was now the de facto King of England.

> Reports state that William was around 5'10", which was incredibly tall for a man of this time

Defining moment
William is double-crossed
January 1066

In the years leading to his death, Edward the Confessor named William, the Duke of Normandy, as his future successor. However, although William did visit England a couple of times in Edward's final years, it was difficult for him to leave the delicate political ecosystem back in Normandy. When the king died, Harold Godwinson (sometimes simply referred to as Henry Godwin) took advantage of William's absence and, against the late king's wishes, claimed the crown for himself. The Godwins were one of, if not *the*, most powerful and influential families in England at the time. Henry would be the last Anglo-Saxon king of England.

Timeline

1028

William is born
While the exact date of his birth remains an issue of contention among historians, we do know that he was born in Falaise. He was the only son of Robert I and Herleva of Falaise.
1028

Inheriting the duchy
When he was round the age of seven or eight, William's father Robert passed away. With his death, the title of duke and its political responsibilities fell to the young boy.
1035

William and Godwinson meet
Harold Godwinson, who later became King Harold II of England, was shipwrecked off the coast of Normandy. William and Henry met during this time and Henry endorsed William's claim to the English throne.
1064

The invasion begins
After assuring his affairs were in order in Normandy, William arrived at Pevensey in the South of England with a large invasion force. Once all of his troops had disembarked, William led his force into Hastings.
28 September 1066

Following his coronation on 25 December 1066, William discovered that presiding over a duchy was a world away from ruling a kingdom. Defeating Harold at Hastings and taking the capital should have cemented his position, but William's arrival was more than just the ascension of a new king - it was the end of the Anglo-Saxon era.

William was careful not to upend the social equilibrium of England's nobility, but a backlash was inevitable. William fought to contain a series of revolts in Dover, Exeter, Hereford, Nottingham, Durham and York, but it was the revolt led by Edgar the Atheling that was the most severe – not only in its potential threat, but also for how aggressively William dealt with it.

The revolt centred on Edgar the Atheling, the only remaining individual with a legitimate claim to William's seat of power. And when Sweyn II, King of Denmark, offered his support in 1070, the Norman grip on the north was broken. The region began to destabilise with revolts and civil unrest, and Edgar and Sweyn's forces soon took the key stronghold of York. William immediately marched from Nottingham with his own forces to settle the rebellion, but by the time he got there the revolt had all but dissolved. Edgar fled to Scotland and Sweyn left suitably paid off by the king. However, William was far from a mood to grant clemency.

He and his troops scoured the land from York to the borders of Scotland in Northumbria. So severe was the devastation that William enacted on the north that the Domesday Book (which was conducted in 1086) revealed that around 100,000 people died from starvation alone following William's 'harrowing'. Considering the census revealed the population to be 2.5 million, such a figure shows just how far the new king would go to burn his legacy into England's history books.

The Harrowing of the North, as it came to be known, was just one of the many conflicts William had to deal with throughout his 21-year reign. He was continually dealing with issues with his neighbours (such as his clashes with the king of Scotland in 1072), rebellions among his own gentry (namely the Revolt of the Earls in 1075) and even quarrels with his own children. Between his native duties as Duke of Normandy, and as King of England, William was forced to solidify his legacy with political marriages, truces and military force.

By the time of his death on 9 September 1087, William had maintained his authority over both Normandy and England for over two decades. He built over 50 castles and fortifications during his reign, determined not only to remind the people of the land who their monarch was, but to protect the nation from the very act he'd taken the throne with. While his acts of domestic growth and merciless violence have been largely overshadowed by his invasion, the man himself remains a defining figure on those storied pages.

Even though King Harold's forces had defeated one invasion and marched hundreds of miles from Newcastle to the south, they still fought valiantly in the face of William's superior cavalry and archers

The Domesday Book

In the years that followed the taking of the English crown, it became clear that official records relating to population and landholding were nearly nonexistent. Almost 19 years after his invasion, while spending Christmas in Gloucester with his advisors, William decided a census was needed. It seems likely it was planned as a way to determine how to restructure taxes across the nation. The Domesday Book (or The Great Survey as it was known then) was split into two documents; the 'Little Domesday' (which covered Suffolk, Essex and Norfolk) and the 'Great Domesday' (a larger document that covered the rest of the country). Interestingly, these documents did not cover the entire nation. This was for many reasons – for example, Westmorland and Cumberland were absent as both formed part of the Kingdom of Strathclyde until they were conquered by his son, William II, in 1092. Elsewhere, London and Winchester were left out because of their special tax status, while the County of Durham was omitted because the Bishop of Durham held ecclesiastical rights to tax that county.

Defining moment
The Battle of Hastings 14 October 1066
Prior to the main battles with the invading Normans, King Harold had already exhausted his military forces defeating *another* invading force led by Norwegian monarch Harold Hardrada at Stamford Bridge. Interestingly, King Harold knew that William was coming before Hardrada's Scandinavian force arrived, however, the Norman forces remained moored off the coast for almost seven months before disembarking. Accounts relating to the size both forces differ greatly, but it's assumed they were leading armies of between 7,000 and 10,000 men. William's forces are ultimately successful, using the considerable number of cavalrymen and archers to wear down the English contingent. King Harold died on the battlefield after taking an arrow to the eye.

Defining moment
Harrowing of the North 1070
William had defeated or outlived most of the legitimate claimants to the English throne, but one still remained. Edgar the Atheling had a great deal of support in the north of England and when Sweyn II of Denmark landed in 1069, Edgar's claim became a real threat. In 1070, he paid the Danes to leave and began to attack the land around Edgar's supporters. Over the next few months he destroyed livestock and farmland, and killed (according to reports) thousands of men, women and children. William's aim was to ensure they would never, ever revolt again.

● **The Great Survey**
In order to determine the true worth of his English kingdom (and to unravel the holdings and lands of his earls) William commissioned a countrywide consensus. While not every part of the nation was covered, it still serves as the most detailed record from the Middle Ages.
1086

1087

● **William takes London**
Despite defeating the king and the remainder of his standing army, England was far from won. Earls and lords loyal to the English king barred William's entry into Winchester and London but the Norman usurper soon overwhelmed them and took control of the royal treasury.
October-November 1066

● **Crowning a new king**
With most of Harold's supporters either dead or in flight, William was crowned King William I of England. One of his first actions was to reaffirm the titles and lands of many earls but strip those of Harold's supporters.
25 December 1066

● **Returning to Normandy**
After his coronation, William returned to Normandy to ensure his lands were intact. While there, he had a number of new monasteries built. He also met with most of his nobles and earls, all of whom were eager to learn of possible new wealth and holdings.
1067

● **Hereward the Wake**
Despite promising to leave England for good, Sweyn II of Denmark returned a few months later and joined the growing uprising led by northern theign Hereward the Wake. William forced Sweyn to leave yet again and soon brought this, the last of the northern revolts, to an end.
1070

Death of a king ●
Despite the relative military success of his reign, his final days were remarkably uneventful. While on a military expedition against France, William either fell from his horse or became ill and died soon after.
9 September 1087

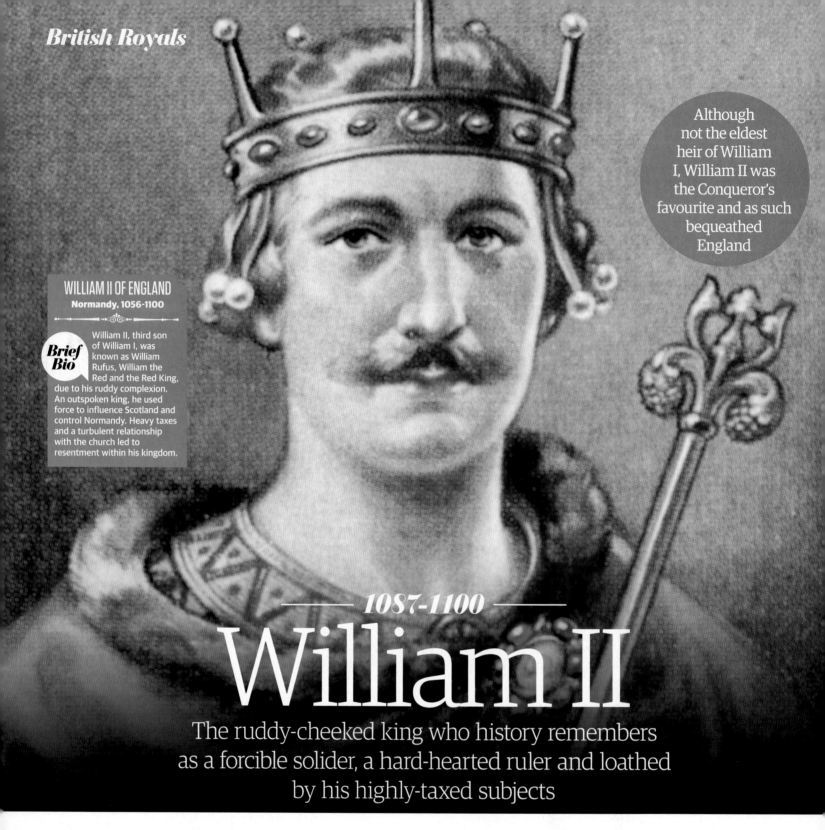

Although not the eldest heir of William I, William II was the Conqueror's favourite and as such bequeathed England

WILLIAM II OF ENGLAND
Normandy, 1056-1100

Brief Bio

William II, third son of William I, was known as William Rufus, William the Red and the Red King, due to his ruddy complexion. An outspoken king, he used force to influence Scotland and control Normandy. Heavy taxes and a turbulent relationship with the church led to resentment within his kingdom.

1087-1100

William II

The ruddy-cheeked king who history remembers as a forcible solider, a hard-hearted ruler and loathed by his highly-taxed subjects

Blond, red-cheeked and well-set, William II, born in Normandy in 1056, was the third son of William I (William the Conqueror) and Matilda of Flanders. His ruddy complexion was the focus of the various nicknames inspired during his 13-year reign, most notably William Rufus, William the Red and the Red King.

William II's ascent to power in 1087 is perhaps one of the most flagrant displays of favouritism ever practised by a sovereign, as before his father William I (William the Conqueror) died, he arranged for his third and favourite son, William II, to succeed him as King of England. This was a decision the Conqueror felt was his right as he had won the country by war. William I's eldest son and William II's only surviving

older brother, Robert, who'd previously rebelled against his father, was bequeathed the Duchy of Normandy as tradition dictated.

William I's decision to effectively divide his kingdom in two might have seemed like a good idea at the time, but it troubled many nobles who owned land on both sides of the channel. They were all too aware of the bitter rivalry between the brothers, which began in, and had snowballed since, childhood. Knowing it impossible to keep favour with both rulers, the lords followed the leadership of Bishop Odo of Bayeux (half-brother of William I) and sided with Robert, who was the more amiable and perceived weaker of the two, in the hope of uniting the kingdom once again. The rebellion collapsed in

The Rufus Stone in the New Forest marks the place of William's death

1088, less than a year into their respective reigns, when Robert failed to show up to support the English rebels, so William won them over with silver and promises of a better government. William, ever the firebrand, laid claim to Normandy in 1091 and waged war against the sibling who he defeated, forcing him to cede a portion of his land. After the conflict, the pair were able to kiss and make up, and William even agreed to help Robert regain control of areas of his land lost to France.

It wasn't only in the south that William was forced to engage in battle during that year, as later in 1091 he successfully stopped a Scottish invasion led by King Malcolm III, who was then finally forced to pay homage to the English King and accept his overlordship. A year later William decided to annex Cumbria from Scotland and ordered the construction of Carlisle Castle. In 1093 Malcolm retaliated by invading and ravaging Northumbria, but met his end, along with his son Edward, at the Battle of Alnwick after being overpowered by William's stronger and better organised army. William was then free to wield his influence in Scotland unrestricted by using the succession of subordinated Scottish kings as vassals. In 1095 Robert de Mowbray, the man who had helped lead William to victory against the Scots, sparked a rebellion with an

assortment of other barons to depose the king in place of Stephen of Aumale. Robert was defeated and imprisoned, whereas his co-lead conspirator, William of Eu, was castrated and blinded.

As well as his conflicts with his brother and nobles, as well as France and Scotland, William was also vilified for his discord with the church. Among other quarrels, he left bishop positions vacant so that he might take the revenues for himself, and his turbulent relationship with the very popular Anselm Archbishop of Canterbury, who was considered one of the greatest theologians of his generation, led to a long period of animosity between the church and state, souring public opinion against the king.

Resentment continued to fester across William's kingdom, a problem he seemed not too bothered about. In 1096, he remained unaffected as he made it a whole lot worse. The king's brother Robert had become inspired to join the First Crusade, a military expedition by Roman Catholic Europe to regain the Holy Lands taken in the Muslim conquest of the Levant (632-661). Finding himself without the funds to raise an army, Robert mortgaged the Duchy of Normandy to his bemused younger brother, who became regent in Robert's absence. To pay for this exchange, William levelled a heavy and much-resented tax on his English subjects, helping to cement his legacy as a cruel and unpopular leader.

> William died in mysterious circumstances, when a rogue arrow killed him while out hunting in the New Forest

The king, who was a huge fan of hunting and feasting, met his end on 2 August 1100 (aged 43/44). While out hunting deer in the New Forest, a rogue arrow pierced his chest. It is claimed that his body was abandoned by the nobles in his hunting party, and was later stumbled upon by peasants who took it by cart to Winchester Cathedral, where it would go on to be buried.

It was accepted as an accident, but some theorised of an assignation as Sir Walter Tyrrell, who was considered an accomplished bowman, immediately fled to France. William's younger brother Henry was also with the hunting party and rode straight to Winchester to seize the treasury. He had himself elected the following day.

The nicknames Red King and Rufus referred to William's ruddy complexion and red cheeks, not his hair which was blond

Life in the time of William II

Fabulously flamboyant
The court of the Red King, who was rumoured to be homosexual, was described by 12th Century historian William of Malmesbury (1095-1143) as being "filled with 'effeminate' young men in extravagant clothes mincing about in 'shoes with curved points'". As well as curved-toe shoes, fur-lined cloaks and long, ornamented and embroidered tunics were popular among men of money at this time.

Take him to the Tower
In 1078 the White Tower, (at the Tower of London), was built. Commissioned by William the Conqueror, the monument was seen as a symbol of oppression by London's residents, and acted as a constant visual reminder of their country's defeat to the Normans.

Learning and literacy in the 12th Century
While the majority of people living in England during William II's reign were illiterate, education took a dramatic leap forward at this time. Although Oxford University has no known date of foundation, there is evidence that shows teaching took place at Oxford in some form during 1096. This makes the institution the oldest English-speaking university and the second-oldest surviving university in the world.

Medieval yellow pages
The first widespread compilation of land and property took place across England after William the Conqueror's successful invasion, resulting in the 1086 Domesday Book. It was commissioned so the new ruler could astutely assess all his new possessions. Interestingly, some towns, such as London and Winchester, were not included in the Domesday Book due to their tax-exempt status.

It's all about the Crusades
Anyone who was anyone with a burning loyalty to the Roman Catholic church joined the First Crusade. This was a widespread pilgrimage that saw tens of thousands of Europeans travel to the Middle East to regain the Holy lands taken by the Muslim conquests of Levant some 400 years earlier.

The curse of the New Forest
The curse of the New Forest didn't just claim William II's life; in fact, three descendents of the New Forest's 'creator' William the Conqueror died in its leafy glades. The first was his second eldest son Richard who is said to have become sick from the foggy 'pestilent' air. The next was William II in a hunting "accident". The third was Richard, William I's grandson, who accidently hanged himself when his horse ran under a low hanging tree branch. At the time many suggested it was a form of karmic retribution or curse, as the king had razed entire villages across Hampshire to create his new hunting forest "Nova Foresta" at the expense of more than 36 parish churches, 20 small hamlets and several isolated farmsteads, leaving hundreds of people homeless.

William was killed in the New Forest

HENRY I 'BEAUCLERC'
England, 1068-1135

Brief Bio Henry I, fourth and youngest son of William I, is celebrated as the most effective of all the Conqueror's sons. He righted the wrongs of his brother by strengthening the crown's executive powers, modernising royal administration and establishing a professional bureaucracy on both sides of the channel.

1100-1135

Henry I

Despite proclaiming himself king while his brother's body was still warm, Henry I proved himself a worthy monarch

Whether King William II died as the result of a mistimed or a well-timed hunting arrow is a mystery. What we know is that just moments after it happened, his younger brother Henry raced to Winchester to seize the treasury and declare himself king, over his oldest brother Robert.

The Norman brothers Robert, William and Henry were renowned for their rivalry, but the real trouble began when their father, William the Conqueror, died and left Normandy to his oldest son, Robert, and England to his next surviving son, William. Henry, the fourth and only other remaining son, was simply given money to buy land and he chose Cotentin in Western Normandy, where he established himself as the count.

When Robert decided to challenge William's claim to the English throne, he neutralised further threat by imprisoning Henry. After the conflict Henry was released and allowed to return home - albeit stripped of his title. So when William invaded Normandy in 1091, Henry made sure he pledged allegiance to Robert, but later lost his favour when he out-shadowed him in combat. Consequently, both sovereign brothers overlooked Henry when they reconciled and drew up a treaty that saw the other as their rightful heir of their respective kingdoms. Deciding he was better off on his own, Henry fought against both brothers in the years that followed, taking land for himself in Normandy. Sensing an opportunity for conspiracy, William sent money to his younger brother to strengthen his campaign against Robert. Henry visited William often at court and fortuitously was present when he died, making him able to claim the throne for himself.

Henry knew that, while claiming it had been relatively straightforward, holding on to the throne would be a great deal more challenging. As the youngest son, Henry was not expected to become ruler, so had been permitted time and opportunity to invest in his education. Henry used his sharpened mind to secure the barons as allies by granting favours, promising a better-orchestrated government and pledging to restore peace to England. In a show of respect for his new people, a few months after he came to power, Henry married the Saxon Princess Edith, daughter of King Malcolm III (who was killed by his brother's army during the Scottish invasion in 1093). The union also helped to soothe tensions between the two neighbouring countries. Edith became known as Matilda, Henry's mother's name, to please the Norman Barons, and together the pair had two children, Matilda in 1102 and William in 1103.

In 1101, Robert resurfaced from the First Crusade and attempted to seize the crown yet again. The invasion was thwarted and the brothers compromised, signing the Treaty of Alton, in which Robert recognised his younger sibling as the true King of England in exchange for Norman territories. Peace didn't last long and just five years later news of Robert's chaotic reign reached Henry's court, prompting him to invade. The war ended in Henry's favour at the Battle of Tinchebrai. Henry decided to stop Robert once and for all, imprisoning him in Cardiff Castle for the rest of his life, which turned out to be nearly three decades.

With Normandy now under his control, Henry was proving himself a powerful and decisive leader on both sides of the channel. In England he strengthened local government, sent judges off around the country to reinforce the law and created institutions such as the Royal Exchequer. In Normandy, Henry governed through a growing system of justices and an exchequer. His preference to promote 'new men' who were intelligent and had risen through the ranks, as opposed to those of high status, proved the administration's making. Henry reversed many of William's less popular policies, making wide-ranging concessions in his Charter of Liberties and returning to the gentler customs of Edward the Confessor. He was able to soothe the wounds inflicted on the church by his older brother, restoring a sense of peace.

While Henry's professional life went from strength to strength, his personal life suffered a tragic blow. In 1118 his wife died, followed two years later by their son, William. Prince William was on-board a vessel known as The White Ship, travelling back to England, when it hit some rocks outside a Norman harbour and sank. Some 300 crew members and passengers, including an illegitimate son and daughter of Henry's, also drowned.

Finding himself without a legitimate son, Henry's thoughts turned to the succession and he married Adelicia of Louvain. When the union proved childless, Henry summoned his only legitimate child, Matilda, and his grandson Henry (later Henry II) back to England and willed his barons to accept her as his heir. The problem wasn't only that Matilda was a woman; those at court were upset that Matilda, who was the widow of Henry V, Holy Roman Emperor, had married George Plantagenet of the House of Anjou, rivals of the house of Normandy. Although the barons swore their allegiance in 1131, they weren't convinced. When Henry died after a week of food poisoning in Normandy in 1135, the throne was seized by Henry's nephew, Stephen of Blois. This sparked a succession crisis and a civil war known as The Anarchy.

> Henry, the fourth and youngest son of William the Conqueror, was the only heir to be born in England

Historical biographers refer to the raven-haired king as short, stocky and barrel-chested

Life in the time of Henry I

A friendly Viking invasion
During the autumn and winter months of the year 1107, Norwegian King Sigurd the Crusader and his army travelled through, and stayed in, England during their southward journey to Palestine. They were on their way to join the pilgrimage of Roman Catholic fighters in the First Crusade.

Joined at the hip, literally
In 1100, supposedly the world's first recorded conjoined twins were born, sparking interest in the pair. Mary and Eliza Chulkhurst, known as the Biddenden Maids were joined at the shoulder and the hip. According to legend Mary died suddenly aged 34, followed by Eliza six hours later after refusing to be separated.

Family of sinners
Throughout his reign, Henry I went to great lengths to right the wrongs his family had inflicted on the church, including ordering the construction of new churches and abbeys. At the founding of Reading Abbey in 1121 (which was to become his final resting place), Henry said "for the salvation of my soul, and the souls of King William, my father, and of King William, my brother."

Best-selling novels
During this period, William of Malmesbury, the most respected historian of the 12th Century, finished his first version of his historical accounts of England *Gesta Regum Anglorum* (Deeds of the Kings of the English) and *Gesta Pontificum Anglorum* (Deeds of the English Bishops) in 1125.

Cathedral set backs
Work on St Paul's Cathedral began at the end of Henry's father's reign in 1087 and took over 200 years to complete. In 1035 a fire delayed construction. The cathedral was formally finished in 1314 but was completely gutted in during The Great Fire of London in 1666.

William Clito: the true heir?
When Henry imprisoned his older brother Robert in Cardiff Castle for attempting to take the English crown for the umpteenth time, Robert's son William Clito was understandably resentful. So like father, like son, William decided to rebel, once in 1116 and again in 1119, supported by several Norman barons who disliked Henry's 'new men' officials and high taxes. Henry proved victorious at the Battle of Bremule and a peace settlement was agreed upon in 1120 with the French king's backing, accepting Henry's son, William Adelin, as Duke of Normandy. Dispute over the throne reignited when Prince William drowned, resulting in more quarrels and rebellions. William Clito died without an heir when a wound he received from a foot soldier turned gangrenous.

William Clito, Count of Flanders, mortally wounded during the siege of Alost

Stephen rebuked the slur of 'oath-breaker' by saying that he only swore to protect the stability of the kingdom

KING STEPHEN (OF BLOIS)
France, 1097-1154

Brief Bio King Stephen's reign is a tale of one-upmanship, double-crossings, promises and broken promises that ultimately divided and destroyed much of the kingdom he had sworn to protect. The Anarchy civil war, which became synonymous with his time at the helm, played out like a game of chess against his powerful opponent Empress Matilda, daughter and heir of Henry I, for nearly two decades.

1135-1154
King Stephen

King Stephen's usurpation tore the country apart with a 19-year civil war. But with little gained and Henry I's succession restored, was it worth it?

Born in Blois, central France, at the end of 11th Century, Stephen was the fourth son of the Count Stephen-Henry of Blois and Adela, daughter of William the Conqueror. Adela, who was incredibly politically astute, allied with Henry I during his military campaign in Normandy to quash their brother Robert's son William Clito and his rebellion. Stephen, who had shown great promise as a swordsman, accompanied his uncle in the ensuing battles. To reward his courage, Henry later gave Stephen a knighthood and invited him to the English court, where he rose through the ranks at great pace, receiving notable land and honours (estates). The king also arranged a great marriage for Stephen with the incredibly wealthy Matilda of Boulogne, which saw him inherit yet more land in Kent and Boulogne,

making the couple one of the wealthiest in the whole of England.

Before his death, Henry I made his nobles, including Stephen, swear an oath to ensure that his daughter Matilda, the former Holy Roman Empress, succeeded him. It wasn't just because Matilda was a woman that they were reluctant to observe this oath: the Anglo-Norman elite also resented the Empress's second marriage to Angevin ruler Geoffrey, Count of Anjou, a long-standing enemy whose lands bordered the Duchy of Normandy. At the time of his death, Henry was deep in the Duchy attempting to thwart an attack by rebels supported by his daughter and her husband, who resented not having the land prematurely. Henry's death put the empress in a tricky situation as she was effectively now supporting rebels against her

Henry and Stephen agree a truce across the Thames

own crown, which left her now scheming cousins - Stephen, who was in Boulogne, and his older brother Theobald, in southern Blois - to make a play for the throne.

Stephen, who was well liked and - perhaps more importantly - incredibly wealthy, was the first to reach England. His younger brother Henry of Blois had become a powerful ecclesiastic in England thanks to his uncle, King Henry I, who had blessed him with the richest abbey and bishopric. This gift had made him one of the wealthiest men in the country. Stephen, supported by Henry, was therefore in a prime position to pay many powerful barons for their fealty, get the church and eventually the Pope onside and sway public support to proclaim himself king. Meanwhile, across the Channel, the Normans were busy declaring Theobald king, but when news came of Stephen's coronation, support for the older brother dissolved at the prospect of yet another divided and warring kingdom.

The early years of Stephen's reign were a relative success; he created a new royal charter confirming his earlier promises to church, and reversed some of Henry's less popular policies. He held good relations with the church and his barons, stabilised the northern border (thereby halting an invasion by the Scottish King David I), contained Geoffrey of Anjou's attacks on Normandy, and made peace with France through Louis VI.

Harmony was short-lived, however, and in 1136, cracks started to show. First, Owain Gwynedd of Wales defeated the English, rapidly taking a

succession of bordering strongholds and territories. Geoffrey of Anjou reignited his campaign to take Normandy, and at home, many hard-done-by barons began to play with the idea of defecting to the empress's side. The first of these was Robert, Earl of Gloucester, one of Henry I's illegitimate sons, attributed with giving the civil war momentum, so that when the empress landed in England in 1139, she had fledgling support from a growing number of allies. Stephen surrounded her at Arundel, but foolishly escorted her to Bristol where she caught up with her ally Robert. From there, they rallied support and took control of western England.

The next chess-like move saw the empress declared queen after her forces captured Stephen at the Battle of Lincoln in 1141, imprisoning him in Bristol Castle. He was released in exchange for Robert of Gloucester, who was captured by the king's wife and forces at the Rout of Winchester. The war dragged on with more sieges and rebellions in both England and Normandy, creating long periods of stalemate, and it wasn't until 1145 that the empress was defeated at the Battle of Faringdon, abandoning her cause and fleeing England. Two years later her son Henry (later Henry II) took up the campaign but after running out of money had to return home, paid for by King Stephen. Far from giving up, he returned to England in 1149 and subsequently 1153, capitalising on new support in north and east England. A truce was called during a bout of bad weather, and Henry levied support in the Midlands and Southwest. The two rivals later met on opposite sides of the river Thames at Wallingford, but avoided engaging in open battle.

The sudden death of Stephen's son and intended heir Eustace, later in the year, hastened negotiations. Peace was restored when Stephen agreed to the Treaty of Winchester, which allowed him to remain as king for the rest of his life in exchange for acknowledging Henry as his rightful heir, renouncing his surviving son William's claim. Stephen had less than a year to finally enjoy being king. He died in Dover of a stomach complaint, during a tour of England where he had been resolving conflicts caused by the civil war.

> After Stephen was freed from Bristol Castle by his wife and William of Ypres in 1141, he threw himself a second coronation to celebrate

Stephen was imprisoned in Bristol Castle in 1141

Life in the time of King Stephen

The White Ship disaster
In 1120, Stephen narrowly escaped death when he disembarked the doomed White Ship at the last minute, reportedly due to concerns of overcrowding or illness on board. Moments later the vessel hit rocks outside the harbour, taking 300 people, including Henry I's only legitimate son William, to a watery grave.

Two queens
After Stephen was imprisoned in Bristol Castle in 1141, England was effectively ruled by two queens: Empress Matilda with the chief support of Robert of Gloucester and, on the other side, King Stephen's wife Matilda, Queen Consort of England, and her advisor William of Ypres. The two camps bargained relentlessly with nobles to strengthen their support.

For money, not love
To help win his wars, Stephen paid an army of Flemish mercenaries to campaign on his behalf in Normandy. Eventually, however, there was a great deal of infighting between the supposed allied forces of the Flemish and Normans, which caused the latter to defect, forcing him to sign a truce with Geoffrey of Anjou.

Temper, temper
In 1152 during a lull in combat, Stephen, perhaps devastated by his wife Matilda's death, reached a low point with the church. Stephen decided to imprison Archbishop Theobald after he was refused permission by the Pope to crown his son Eustace early.

So close, but so far
Despite finally gaining the upper hand in 1141 when her forces captured Stephen, Empress Matilda was never crowned Queen of England. On the way to her planned coronation, she faced a surprise uprising of citizens, forcing her to flee to Oxford.

Stephen's early life and family members
Stephen's father died when he was a young boy, and had earned the reputation of being a coward during the First Crusade, while his mother was considered a pious, strong, brave and intelligent woman. As well as one older sister, Stephen had three older brothers: William who is thought to have been intellectually disabled, Odo who died in his adolescence and Theobald. Five younger sisters, plus brothers Philip and Henry followed Stephen. Breaking with tradition, the close-knit family were raised in their mother's household rather than being sent away to be mentored by relatives.

HENRY PLANTAGENET
England, 1133-1189

Brief Bio

The grandson of Henry I, Henry II spent his entire 35-year reign hoping to rule his kingdom with the same political pragmatism as his namesake. Ruthless and driven, Henry II was one of the most proactive monarchs in history. He succeeded in re-establishing royal administration in England and Wales, gaining control over large provinces in France and making changes to the legislation that would later form the foundations of Common English Law.

1154-1189
Henry II

Fiery yet shrewd, the first of the Plantagenet kings helped rebuild a tattered realm while defying rulers, popes and even his own heirs

Born in Le Mans, France, in the spring of 1133, Henry was the eldest child of Geoffrey the Fair, Count of Anjou, and Empress Matilda, daughter of Henry I of England. Thanks to her ties to the English crown (as well as her former marriage to the Holy Roman Emperor, Henry V of Germany), Henry's mother was one of the most powerful women in Europe. However, when the English king's eldest son and heir, William Adelin, died at sea in 1120, it threw the line of succession into turmoil. In the confusion, Matilda's cousin, Stephen of Blois, installed himself as the sovereign, which succeeded in plunging the country into a civil war.

While the conflict raged in England, the young Henry was fast taking to the life of a French nobleman. Tough and resilient, yet intelligent and pragmatic, Henry had already gained a vital understanding of building political relationships - he was already on good terms with the normally prickly bishops of Normandy and understood the importance of paying homage to those in higher positions of power (despite the fact that Anjou had become almost entirely independent of France).

When his father passed away a few months later, Henry became the Count of Anjou, a position that was further bolstered by the lands of Eleanor of Aquitaine, whom he married on 18 May 1152.

"By the time of his in 1189, Henry had laid the groundwork for a new age of law"

Eleanor had been the wife of King Louis, but she had failed to provide any sons, so the zealous French monarch had had the marriage annulled. Henry and Eleanor unified the houses of Aquitaine and Plantagenet eight weeks later, a move that sent her ex-husband into fits of rage.

In retaliation, Louis organised an alliance between Stephen, Eustace, the Counts of Champagne and Perche (both of whom saw the potential benefits of splitting Henry's lands between them), as well as Henry's own young brother, Geoffrey (who believed that his older sibling had cheated him out of rightful lands and titles). The borders of Normandy were suddenly at war as Henry moved to defend his lands. The conflict could have been incredibly bloody, but Louis VII later withdrew from illness and the campaign fell to pieces soon after.

Back in England, King Stephen had been fighting his own civil war for years, a conflict that only served to diminish his position as monarch. He was keen to bring the conflict to a close, but would defend his own claim to the crown to the bitter end. Upon landing on English soil in 1153 intent on taking the crown for himself, Henry wisely chose to form an alliance with Robert de Beaumont, Earl of Leicester. With Leicester's considerable northern support - and the timely death of Stephen's son, Eustace - the two would eventually broker a truce that saw Stephen recognise Henry as his heir.

Henry was crowned Henry II of England on 19 December 1154. With Queen Eleanor at his side, Henry set about repairing the damage of Stephen's six-year reign and the civil conflict that had characterised it. He was also driven by a furious desire to return his ancestral homeland to the glory days of his grandfather, so he began reclaiming lands and castles lost during his predecessor's reign, destroying those erected by his enemies, and reforming the political strength of the kingdom. In the turmoil of the civil war, the Scottish king, Malcolm, and a number of the Princes in Wales had taken lands outside their borders. With Henry now reaffirming his lands in England and Normandy, those territories were soon returned.

While Henry had enjoyed successes reaffirming his kingdom elsewhere, he faced a far more difficult challenge bringing the clergy to heel. With the death of the Archbishop of Canterbury, Henry appointed his childhood friend Thomas Becket in the role, intending to use this ally as a proxy in his relationship with the church. However, Becket had no intention of being Henry's whipping boy and refused to change ecclesiastical law to meet the king's will. Henry did not react well. In 1163, Henry had charges of royal contempt drawn up against him and Becket fled the country. When he returned in 1170, he sought to make peace with the fiery king but ended up being murdered soon after by four knights who wished to curry favour with Henry.

Despite such overwhelming odds against him, Henry's powerbase was stronger than ever. The French king had been cowed and England was once again an imposing military and political beast. But for his victories in rebuilding his kingdom, Henry's refusal to recognise his own children with titles of worth would finally be his undoing. His cold relationship with son Richard saw the disgruntled heir form an alliance with Philip Augustus, the new French king. With a new powerful ally at his side, Richard began claiming Henry's continental lands as his own. Henry attempted to form a treaty with his disenfranchised child, but the shock of his betrayal would prove too much for the aging monarch.

By his death on 6 July 1189, Henry had laid the groundwork for a new age of law and the judicial process by having an army of sheriffs enforce the king's laws across the land. Legislation was drawn up to provide greater clarification on ownership of property and the punishment of civil crimes. And while his son Richard would eventually ruin many of his father's achievements, Henry II remains one of history's most progressive monarchs.

> Much like future monarch Henry VIII, Henry II was a redhead with a hellish temper to match

Following clashes with his son Richard, Henry eventually collapsed from fever and was buried in Fontevraud Abbey in France

Life in the time of Henry II

Money, money, money
Once Henry had ascended to the throne in 1154, he was determined to improve the dire state of England's finances. Decades prior, his grandfather, Henry I, had helped invigorate the kingdom with a fresh influx of trade and commerce. While Henry II's efforts weren't quite as successful, he did make a positive impact on England's financial welfare.

Church and crown
Under the rule of his predecessor Stephen of Blois, relationships between the crown and the papacy were at an all time low. In his early years as a duchy in France, Henry enjoyed a relatively peaceful relationship with the bishops. However, his appointment of friend Thomas Becket as Archbishop of Canterbury would backfire causing an even greater divide.

The effects of war
When Henry took the throne in 1154, England had suffered greatly from the civil war between its usurping leader Stephen of Blois and the supporters of his rival, Empress Matilda (Henry's mother). Known as The Anarchy, it had nearly bankrupted the economy and devastated much of the land.

Public opinion
Despite the reforms he ultimately made to legislation and the positive position he left England in on his death in 1189, Henry II proved to be a relatively unpopular king. This was less of a reflection on him as an individual monarch, but of the civil unrest the country had endured following the death of his grandfather Henry I.

Law of the land
Under Henry II's reign, the legal system saw something of a renaissance. Henry was keen to resolve the disputes that remained from The Anarchy and pushed through legislation that gave more power to local courts. He cracked down on crime and civil unrest, which led to the creation of General Eyre, a group of justices who travelled each part of the country to resolve cases.

The Great Revolt
In 1153 King Henry faced one of the greatest threats to his entire reign: the Great Revolt of 1173-1174. It was masterminded by some of his own sons, his wife and a group of rebellious barons, as well as having the full support of Scotland, Flanders and France. It saw invading forces clashing with Henry's army, but it would be an act of public humility that would finally dismantle the uprising. On the grave of Thomas Becket, his once trusted ally, Henry proclaimed the revolt to be divine penance for his past actions. The forces attempting to invade both England and Normandy remarkably fell apart soon after and the kingdom was safe once more.

1189-1199

Richard I

Born to royalty but educated in the charnel gutter of war, King Richard brought the religious fanaticism of the Christian West on the Muslim East in a quest to claim the fabled Holy Land

For almost a year the mighty city of Acre held firm. Despite wave after wave of Christian knights pouring all their religious fervour and military might into its ancient walls, it had held back the tide and somehow halted the progress of the foreign hordes that now threatened to overrun the entire Near East.

More and more men came, though - the attacks were relentless. When the first army had been held at bay, the city's inhabitants thought they were safe, that the invasion was defeated. However, then yet another army landed and the city's main artery, its port, which provided passage in and out of its walls, was taken. The city's defences were tested once more, with an even more ferocious attack battering at the doors and calling for blood. Luckily for those within, once more the city held off the mass of warriors, its infidel leaders repelled.

Then, with the new year's sailing season, another invader arrived by sea with a fresh bloodthirsty army. He was followed in May by yet another, with tens of thousands of soldiers joining the infidels' camp outside the walls, swelling their numbers to terrifying proportions. They attacked again and the losses on both sides were massive. The lack of food and supplies in the city, and the spread of disease within the invaders' camp drove both sets of warriors to extremes, stoking the fires of faith that lay within their hearts to pursue bolder and bolder acts of violence.

Today is the eighth day of June 1191 and, as Acre slowly suffocates in the oppressive heat of the Levant's summer months, yet another fleet is landing in the city's once-prosperous port, this time with one of the biggest forces the city has ever seen. If the ruler of Acre, the noble and great Saladin, doesn't send meaningful reinforcements soon, then the city will fall and the gates to the Holy Land will be brutally wrenched open to the Christian hordes.

They call this one, this man-mountain stepping off his ship onto the dusty dry shore, the Lionheart, and he is here to kill them all in the name of his god and glory. The passage had been long and painful, featuring storms, shipwrecks and a mad despot who threatened to derail the Third Crusade before it had even begun. No matter, King Richard the Lionheart and his army had survived the trip across the Mediterranean Sea and reached the Holy Land. After months of pursuit and planning, they were primed to fulfil their mission, Richard's mission, God's mission, to take the Holy Land by storm and cut a direct path to the holiest of all cities, Jerusalem.

RICHARD THE LIONHEART
English, 1157-1199

Brief Bio

King of England from the 6 July 1189 until his death, Richard I was the third of five sons of King Henry II of England and Eleanor of Aquitaine. At 16, Richard took control of his own army and thanks to a series of victories over rebels threatening his father's throne, developed a reputation as a great military leader. Following his father's death and his own coronation he launched the Third Crusade.

"To the disgrace of all of Christendom, Jesus's city had fallento the Saracens"

Crusaders

NUMBER OF TROOPS:
20,000

LEADER
RICHARD THE LIONHEART
Excellent on the battlefield, Richard the Lionheart was a brutal killer and a gifted tactical thinker, leading an army of religious fanatics with ruthless efficiency.
Strength Amazing warrior and powerful military leader.
Weakness Politically and economically reckless as king.

KEY UNIT
TEMPLAR KNIGHT
The most skilled Christian fighting unit to take part in the Third Crusade, the Knights Templar were wealthy, well-trained and fanatical fighters, driven by a holy purpose.
Strength Well-equipped and trained in hand-to-hand combat.
Weakness Few in number and fanatically religious, leading to recklessness.

KEY WEAPON
BROADSWORD
The most popular hand-to-hand weapon of all Christian knight orders, including the Knights Templar and Knights Hospitaller, the broadsword was a well-balanced and deadly weapon capable of stabbing and cleaving.
Strength Great all-round weapon that also allowed shield use.
Weakness Could be out-ranged with two-handed swords and spears.

Battle of Arsuf
A major battle in the Third Crusade, Arsuf saw Richard and Saladin face off

01 The Wood of Arsuf
After taking Acre, Richard set out for his next target, Arsuf. To get there, he had to move south along the coast of the Mediterranean Sea and then traverse the Wood of Arsuf, one of the few forested regions in all of the Levant. Saladin knew this and after tracking and harassing Richard's slow-moving baggage train and infantry, decided the woods would be the ideal position to strike.

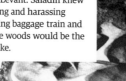

02 A narrow plain
Richard, wary of an assault on his convoy, proceeded slowly through the Wood of Arsuf, making the first 10km (6mi) without incident. Saladin had already identified a striking point however - a narrow clear plain in the forest approximately 9km (5.5mi) from Arsuf. Saladin intended to engage in skirmishes along the length of the convoy and then hit its rear with a decisive attack.

03 Scouts at dawn
Moving out of their camp at dawn on 7 September 1191, Richard's scouts reported Saladin's scouts could be seen. Richard realised that this meant Saladin's full army was nearby and started to arrange his army. Men were deployed at the fore and rear of the convoy column, with the van - the foremost division - made up of the Knights Templar under the command of their 11th grand master, Robert de Sable.

04 Saladin attacks
As soon as Richard's convoy reached the plain Saladin's forces attacked. At the front, Saladin sent a dense swarm of skirmishers, while behind them streamed squadrons of heavy cavalry and foot and horse archers, splitting so that the army attacked from the centre, left and right.

05 Crusader flanks hold
Saladin's chief tactic was to break the flanks of the crusader column and ordered incursions of javelin throwers and mounted archers to perform lightning strikes along their flanks and retreating before crusader crossbowmen could retaliate. The flanks held, though.

To the disgrace of all of Christendom, Jesus's city had fallen four years previous to the Saracen Ayyubid hordes, which was now not only ruled by Christianity's arch-nemesis Saladin, but also defiled by their very presence within its hallowed walls. The city, which had been safely held in Christian hands for almost 100 years since the First Crusade had established the Kingdom of Jerusalem in 1099, had been ordered to be retaken by none other than the Pope in Rome. Richard, a devout and deeply religious king, had heeded the call. Here he now stood, ready to do his duty to the one true god. Conquering Acre was merely the first step in wrestling Jerusalem from Saladin's grip.

So far the city's capture and wider crusade had been in the hands of a number of other leaders. These included Guy of Lusignan - a proud Poitevin knight and the supposed rightful king of Jerusalem through his marriage to Sibylla of Jerusalem - and King Philip II of France, who had helped raise the 'Saladin tithe' to pay for the crusade. The Duke of Austria, Leopold V, had overall command of the imperial forces. There had been yet more leaders at the siege's instigation the summer previous

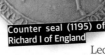
Counter seal (1195) of Richard I of England

10 Ayyubid army scatters

Its right wing smashed, the Ayyubid army soon routed, scattering back into the hills and forests south of Arsuf. Richard, realising the pursuing knights could be ambushed in a surprise counterattack, drew the warriors back into an orderly formation at Arsuf and ordered them to pitch camp at the now-secure fortress. Saladin was forced to retreat with his reputation as an invincible leader tarnished.

09 Templars let loose

Freed from the tactical order to defend and maintain discipline, the crusader knights took the fight to the Saracens, unleashing their hatred and combat prowess in one brutal wave of death. The right wing of Saladin's army couldn't sustain the assault and collapsed almost immediately, with Richard himself weighing into the heart of the fighting. As a bloody revenge for the day's attacks was complete, the Knights Templar set off in pursuit of the fleeing Saracens.

08 Counterattack slams home

Garnier de Nablus disobeyed orders in counterattacking, but with the Hospitaller charging, Richard knew they needed support and ordered his army to engage with them. The full weight of the crusader army therefore suddenly switched emphasis from defence to attack, ramming into the Ayyubid army with immense ferocity.

06 Hospitallers come under attack

Saladin shifted the focus point of his army to the rear of column, engaging the Knights Hospitaller. Saladin joined the assault along with his brother to inspire his men to make a breakthrough. Richard held the convoy together despite some losses and edged them toward Arsuf.

07 Knights break rank

Richard reached Arsuf in the middle of the afternoon, with the besieged Hospitaller vanguard retreating into the fortress city. Line discipline was finally lost and a melee began. Seeing his men in trouble, the grand master of the Knights Hospitaller, Garnier de Nablus, broke ranks and charged the Saracens.

---

but illness and disease had claimed many over the winter months, with Frederick of Swabia and even the holy Patriarch Heraclius of Jerusalem all passing from this mortal world into the next.

The siege itself had stalled, so every passing week threatened to allow Saladin to outmanoeuvre the crusaders. Richard, being the honed and experienced military leader that he was, realised this and gave orders for vast siege engines to be built, ones that could bring down the city's walls. These engines, once completed, towered over the Christian knights and, when unleashed, brought the siege into a deadly endgame.

Colossal boulders rained down upon Acre's walls, smashing against them with thunderous brutality.

Corpses of animals and Muslim soldiers littered the city's streets, spreading disease and sapping the morale of the terrified residents. Most fearsome of all though, flaming balls and arrows set ablaze anything that wasn't made out of stone, causing panic to quickly spread among Acre's populace. The surviving Muslim soldiers defended bravely, but the sheer carnage and chaos the machines and men of war now levied on the city was too much and, after a month of death and destruction, the remaining Muslim garrison within the city surrendered, which was a direct violation of Saladin's orders.

On receiving the news of Acre's fall, Saladin immediately set out for the city. On his way he received news that Richard had taken the

---

Muslims

NUMBER OF TROOPS: 25,000

LEADER
SALADIN

He attained his exalted position as leader of the Ayyubid army and founder of the Ayyubid dynasty and was a wise and experienced military commander.
Strength Respected tactical thinker and powerful politician.
Weakness Hands-off leader with little personal combat prowess.

KEY UNIT
MOUNTED ARCHER

The light cavalry of Saladin was feared throughout the world due to its acute ability to strike quickly and at range, with skilled marksmen riding the world's fastest horses.
Strength Fast units that excelled in ambush and hit-and-run attacks.
Weakness Easily cut down by knights in hand-to-hand combat.

KEY WEAPON
SHORT BOW

Saladin's mamluk infantry and his light cavalry units excelled in bowmanship, with their short bows used to swarm arrows on crusader forces at every opportunity.
Strengths Fast to fire and reload with good stopping power.
Weakness Could be outranged by the longbow and all-but-useless in hand-to-hand combat.

Due to its position of strategic importance Acre was often the scene of violence

Lionheart's crusade

The Third Crusade faced challenges even before reaching the Holy Land

04 Battle of Arsuf
Arsuf - 7 September 1191
Richard and the crusaders move out to capture Jaffa. However, Saladin intercepts Richard near the fortress city of Arsuf, pursuing him right up to the city, but Richard wins the engagement.

05 Richard bows out
Jaffa - 8 August 1192
After taking Jaffa and then launching two failed advances on Jerusalem, the crusaders split in two, leaving neither capable of taking the city. Richard finds Jaffa back in Saladin's hand, but reclaims it in battle.

Vezelay

Genoa

Marseilles

01 **Rome**

Tripoli

Acre

Jerusalem

01 A papal decree
Rome - 29 October 1187
Pope Gregory VIII decrees the fall of the Kingdom of Jerusalem is punishment for Christian sins, before issuing a papal bull calling for the Third Crusade. France and England heed the call, imposing the 'Saladin tithe' to fund the mission.

02 The mad despot
Cyprus - 8 May 1189
On his way to the Holy Land, Richard's fleet is hit by a storm and runs aground on Cyprus. The island's despot ruler seizes the ships, cargo and occupants. Richard takes Cyprus by force, freeing the enslaved subjects.

03 Acre under siege
Acre - 28 August 1189
The prolonged siege of the Muslim-held city and port of Acre sees thousands of crusaders and Saracen soldiers killed. Following the Lionheart's arrival at the siege on 8 June 1191, the city's prolonged defence falters.

The city of Acre as it looks today

"They call this one the Lionheart and he is here to kill them all in the name of his god and glory"

surrendering Muslim garrison of 2,400 men captive and was offering their return for a ransom. Saladin, known for his loyalty to his men and his wisdom, agreed to the ransom, which not only included monetary compensation but also the release of all of his Christian prisoners.

In Acre the banners of the Kingdom of Jerusalem, France, England and the Duchy of Austria fluttered in the light breeze. With Acre down, Richard knew that only the city of Jaffa to the south stood in their way of making a direct assault on Jerusalem, so he began making preparations for the continued crusade, as well as for the reparation of the sacked city. These preparations were swiftly interrupted by an argument that developed between the conquering leaders as to how the city should be divided up

£70,000 was raised by the 'Saladin tithe' to fund the rather expensive Third Crusade

and to how the spoils of their victory should be apportioned. This quarrelling led Richard to strike down the Austrian standard from above the city's walls, slighting Leopold, as the king of England sided with Guy of Lusignan rather than Philip and Leopold over who should become king of Jerusalem when the city was taken. Philip and Leopold preferred fellow crusader and Italian nobleman Conrad of Montferrat, with Phillip so angry he threatened to return to Europe.

This cauldron of scheming and disagreement was tipped over the edge when Saladin delayed in paying the garrison's ransom. An already irate and disgruntled Richard deemed the lateness a massive slight and ordered every single one of the garrison to be executed. Saladin reached the city just as the decision was

made, but could only watch as man after man was publicly executed, their heads lopped from their shoulders atop the city walls. Thousands died. The enraged Saladin replied like-for-like, executing the 1,000 Christian prisoners in his custody. Whatever deal could conceivably have been reached between the rival leaders now lay in ruins, seemingly as dead as the unfortunate prisoners.

Angered and frustrated with Richard and Guy, Philip and Leopold finally decided that their participation in the Third Crusade was at an end, leaving in late August for their European homes.

Anatomy of a Templar knight

The key kit and weapons carried by the most elite of Christian warriors

Helmet
Decapitation resistance
The great helm was the mainstay of the Templar Order and offered excellent protection against blows, as did the sugarloaf helmet. Due to narrow viewing corridors and high temperatures experienced in the Holy Land, many opted for more lightweight alternatives with open faces.

Jerkin
A guaranteed chafe-free experience
Unseen, however often critical in keeping a Knight Templar breathing, was the haubergeon, a padded jerkin that sat against his skin. The jerkin extended over much of the upper body and was the last line of defence from enemy blows. In colder climates, it also helped keep the warrior warm – not an issue in the Holy Land.

Broadsword
Designed to hack and slash
As standard for western knights, the typical Knight Templar was armed with a broadsword, however when fighting on horseback spears were also used. Sometimes, two-handed broadswords were opted for while fighting on foot, but while they granted extra reach and cleaving power, they left the knight shieldless.

Surcoat
It ain't half hot in the Holy Land
Above the knight's chainmail sat the visible surcoat. This white garment not only kept the Sun off their metal armour, also displayed the symbols of the Order.

Chainmail
Thy enemy's blade shall not pass
The primary form of defence against enemy strikes, the hauberk, a long-sleeved shirt of chainmail fitted with chain covers for the hands and a chain coif hood for the head, was a knight's armour. The chainmail would be partnered with iron chausses to protect their legs.

Shield
The first and best line of defence
Adorned with the Christian cross of their order, the Templar shield was large and long, with a teardrop design protecting their entire torso and upper legs. It was constructed from wood and had a metal rim, the latter helping to protect against it splitting under the weight of sword blows. It had a leather handgrip at the rear.

Around 8,000 English knights and soldiers journeyed to the Holy Land for the Crusades

For Richard, though, such betrayal of faith was unimaginable, and after calling on the Philip to do right in the eyes of god, managed to persuade him to leave behind 10,000 French crusaders along with the necessary funds to pay for their upkeep. The Lionheart was now the central remaining commander of over 20,000 crusaders, knights and soldiers alike and, burning with glorious purpose, ordered the continuation of the crusade, with the bulk of the crusading army marching out of Acre in August's final days. This was no doubt who was now leading this holy crusade.

The next city on the crusaders' relentless march to Jerusalem was Jaffa, an important port that provided passage into the southern Mediterranean Sea. As long as Jaffa remained untaken Saladin had a natural avenue to pour more of his troops into the region from his impregnable stronghold of Egypt, but if it fell to the crusaders Saladin would be forced to move men over land, a far less effective and more time-consuming proposition. The city also lay a mere 65 kilometres (40 miles) from Jerusalem, making it the ideal coastal base for crusaders. Before it could be taken, though, the crusaders needed to get there in one piece. Richard knew Saladin was somewhere in the nearby area and, aware of his enemy's skill in arranging ambushes, ordered his troops to march down the Mediterranean coastline, with the baggage train protected by being nearest to the coast. This tactic prevented Saladin from attacking on one flank, as Richard also got his fleet to sail down the coast in parallel with them, shutting off the sea as an avenue of possible attack.

However, to the north of Jaffa lay the Wood of Arsuf, one of the only forested areas in all of the Levant. The woods ran parallel to the coastline for over 20 kilometres (12 miles) and had to be traversed by Richard's army if they were to reach Jaffa. After harassing Richard's troops with small hit-and-run attacks within the woods, Saladin sanctioned a full-scale assault on the crusaders, which led to the largest pitched battle of the Third Crusade. Saladin knew the battle would be decisive, but couldn't possibly have foreseen how disastrous

"Saladin could only watch as man after man was publicly executed, their heads lopped from their shoulders atop the city walls'" for him it would be. As the Sun went down on 7 September 1191 the Saracen army had been routed in a decisive counterattack led by Richard's Knights Hospitaller. Saladin retreated to regroup what was left of his battered army and lick his wounds.

The crusaders made a beeline for Jaffa, swiftly besieging and taking it. Despite some disagreement with the other crusader leaders, Richard - with Jerusalem almost in sight - decided to open negotiations with his enemy. Saladin, who was being questioned by some of his subjects following the defeat at Arsuf, agreed to the negotiations and sent his brother, Al-Adil to Jaffa to lead the talks. Despite headway being made - at one time Richard's sister Joan was being talked about as a potential bride for Al-Adil with Jerusalem as a wedding gift - the talks ultimately broke down.

The breakdown of the talks caused unrest in the crusader ranks, with arguments arising about the best way to proceed toward their goal. Richard, growing tired of the constant in-fighting, acted decisively and ordered the army to move on Jerusalem in November, first moving through Ascalon and then Latrun. The Christian army was soon at Beit Nuba, a mere 20 kilometres (12 miles) from Jerusalem. The news quickly spread of the crusaders' progress and the morale in the Muslim garrisons within the city crumbled. Saladin's forces had been crushed, Acre, Arsuf and Jaffa taken and Jerusalem looked set to be next. Victory for the Third Crusade seemed inevitable.

At this vital point hesitation crept into the crusader ranks, though. Saladin had proven himself a worthy and tricky foe and, not knowing the extent to which his forces had been depleted, Richard feared that a retaliation attack, most likely another large-scale ambush, was very near. In addition, the weather in the winter months had

The number of Muslim prisoners Richard had executed in the city of Acre totalled around 2,700

Know thy enemy: Saladin
The main features and kit of the most respected Muslim warrior of all

Swords
Straight and deadly
The swords the Saracens used in the period of the Crusades were generally straight, unlike the curved blades often depicted in films of the period.

Armour
For the high-ranking
While the lower ranking Saracens wore little or no armour higher ranking warriors and leaders such as Saladin would often wear mail coats or other armour under their robes.

Horseback rider
Warfare on the move
The Saracen army in the Third Crusade had a good number of cavalrymen – more than their Christian counterparts. The soldiers on these horses were normally archers and could be very effective when harassing their enemy.

Physical appearance
Slight, not scary
Most accounts of Saladin make reference to him being quite slight and frail – he did not have the imposing physical stature of Richard but was well respected for his wisdom and piety.

The modern day city of Jerusalem

Salāh ad-Dīn Yūsuf ibn Ayyūb (Saladin) was the first sultan of Egypt and Syria and the founder of the Ayyubid dynasty. He was elevated to this lofty position through a series of military victories, first under the Fatimid government and then his own leadership, with him overseeing the decisive Battle of Hattin in 1187. It was due to Saladin himself that the Third Crusade was instigated, with the fallout from the Battle of Hattin and the fall of Jerusalem leading to the famous 'Saladin tithe', a tax levied in England and some parts of France to finance an army that was capable of reclaiming the holy territory.
Despite Saladin and Richard's armies clashing multiple times during the Third Crusade, the two men famously shared a more complicated relationship than would have been expected, with great respect reported on both sides. After the Battle of Arsuf - a battle in which Saladin's army was soundly beaten - Saladin sent Richard two excellent horses as Richard had lost his own in the battle. The two men never met in person, though, and Saladin died a year after the Third Crusade, struck down by a fever while staying in Damascus.

taken a marked turn for the worse, with heavy rain and hail leading to poor conditions under foot. These factors caused Richard to pause for thought rather than make straight for the holy city and he consulted his fellow crusaders. It was agreed that if they started besieging Jerusalem and were hit with a relieving force from Saladin, the poor conditions would lead to a massacre. As such, Richard ordered a retreat back to the coast. The attack would have to wait.

The invading army spent the rest of the winter months in Ascalon before continuing hostilities in the spring of 1192. Saladin, who had been forced by his emirs (commanders) to disband much of what was left of his army - the emirs favouring consolidation rather than open hostilities - launched no major attack. However, bands of Saracen troops constantly plagued the crusaders, with a series of small fights and skirmishes slowly eroding the crusader army's numbers and morale. This came to a head on 22 May when the fortified town of Darum fell to the crusader forces after five days of bloody fighting. The crusaders had won great battles in the Holy Land but no more armies were journeying across the Mediterranean to bolster their forces; those men who fell in battle weren't going to be replaced. Richard's crusade was faltering, its primary purpose slipping away like sand in an hourglass.

The crusading king of England managed to marshal his remaining forces together for one last advance on Jerusalem, marching inland in June of that year. This time, far from being checked at Beit Nuba, the crusaders actually came within sight of the hallowed city. The time, it appeared, had finally come. Richard was to return Jesus's city to its rightful owners and reinstate Christianity as the dominant religious and military power in the Holy Land. However, as the tired, dusty and bronzed warriors stood there watching the distant city from afar, once more the poison of dissent started to seep among its leaders.

Despite standing before the city, months of resentment over the course the Crusade had taken boiled over among the military commanders, with debate over the best military course of action descending into personal attacks and squabbles. The majority of the leaders, including Richard, believed the best way to take Jerusalem was not besiege it but to attack Saladin directly in Egypt, thereby forcing him to relinquish it of his own free will as a bargaining chip to prevent his own fall. However, the leader of the surviving French crusaders, the Duke of Burgundy Hugh III, believed the only course of action was an immediate and direct assault on the city. News of the split in the leaders' plans filtered down to the crusaders themselves, with the knights and soldiers now breaking previous allegiances and siding with either one side or the other, splitting the crusader army in two.

Some 2,000 Christian soldiers fought as part of the Third Crusade's last battle at Jaffa

Crusading king or bloody murderer?

Historian Douglas Boyd gives his verdict on the Lionheart

Despite Richard's leading role in the Third Crusade, the opinion of Victorian historian Bishop William Stubbs was that this king was "a bad ruler, whose love of war effectively disqualified him from being a peaceful one; his utter want of political common sense from being a prudent one." Stubbs called him "a man of blood, whose crimes were those of one whom long use of warfare had made too familiar with slaughter, and a vicious man."

Respected historian of the crusades Sir Steven Runciman balanced the two sides of Richard's character: "He was a bad son, a bad husband and a bad king, but a gallant and splendid soldier." While Richard consistently displayed supreme physical courage, gallant and splendid are not adjectives one would use today of the man who slaughtered 3,000 prisoners at the siege of Acre and nearly bankrupted the kingdom twice in his ten-year reign. The enduring legend of Richard as a heroic Christian warrior is due to the brilliant public-relations campaign of his mother, Eleanor of Aquitaine, to raise the ransom when he was taken hostage returning to England after the events of the Third Crusade.

Douglas Boyd is the author of *Lionheart: The True Story Of England's Crusading King*, published by The History Press.

"Richard believed the best way to take Jerusalem was not besiege it but to attack Saladin directly in Egypt"

Neither of the two forces were now powerful enough to assault a city, let alone Jerusalem, and as such Richard was forced to order a retreat. While progressing back toward the coast, angry with the French, Richard decided to return to England. However, just as he was approaching Jaffa, news arrived via a scout that the city had fallen to Saladin, who had personally overseen the assault. Furthermore, the scout reported that the lives of all the people there were under a very real threat as the Muslim ruler had lost control of his army, the thousands of Muslim soldiers driven berserk due to the massacre at Acre.

With the lives of the surviving crusaders very firmly in his hands - after all, it had been Richard who ordered the Acre executions - a return to England would have to wait. With a band of 2,000 surviving knights and soldiers, Richard launched one final assault on Saladin, approaching Jaffa by sea in a surprise attack. The Ayyubid soldiers who had only just taken the city were completely unprepared for the attack and were soon overrun, with a combination of knights and crusader crossbowmen decisively breaking their resistance. The attack was so brutally effective that Saladin was forced to flee from Jaffa to the south.

This would be the final battle of the Crusade for Saladin and Richard. Following Jaffa's second fall, the region entered a limbo-like stasis, with the Christian crusaders and Muslim Ayyubids

Richard the Lionheart's forces on the march toward Jerusalem

Why was Jerusalem so sought after?

The geographical region of Palestine, between the River Jordan and the Mediterranean Sea, was referred to as the Holy Land by Christians and Muslims alike. Both religions claimed ownership due to their faith, with the city of Jerusalem held in particular esteem. Both Islam and Christianity were Abrahamic monotheistic religions and as such, both sides considered the other to be unbelievers in the one true god and considered their presence heretical.

By the Third Crusade, Jerusalem and large parts of Palestine and the Levant region had changed hands again and again, with conflicts destabilising the region. Richard, coming from the Christian West, therefore perceived the fall of Jerusalem to Saladin's forces in 1187 as a direct attack on his faith. From Saladain's point of view he was merely taking back the spiritual heartland of his own faith; one that had previously rested in the hands of infidels.

sapped of any further willpower for bloodshed. The fighting had gone on for three years and large parts of the historic area lay in ruins. Tens of thousands of men, women and children had lost their lives and, despite some areas of the Levant changing hands, nothing had really changed. Jerusalem remained under Muslim control, Saladin was ruler of the Ayyubid Empire and Richard the Lionheart was still the fierce warrior king with a renowned reputation in Europe without a firm foothold in the Holy Land. What had changed, though, was Saladin and Richard's desire for more war and bloodshed, and so a treaty soon followed. Jerusalem would remain under Muslim control but from now on, Christian pilgrims and traders would be permitted to visit the city, with their rights protected by law.

Richard the Lionheart remained in the Holy Land for a grand total of 17 months during the Crusades

For Richard, the treaty was to be his last act in the Holy Land and the final curtain for the Third Crusade, with the king setting out on his return to England immediately after. His return journey, though, would not be as straightforward as the one over, with a series of events leading to his own capture, temporary imprisonment and yet more battles. However, the war he would go down in history for was his quest for the Holy Land - a journey full of bloodshed, plunder and religious fanaticism, but relatively little territorial success.

It ensured his legacy would forever be debated between those who see him as a crusading Christian king and others who view him as an amoral, cold-blooded killer, a debate that still rages on today.

1199-1216
King John

Revolt, treachery, excommunication: how the last Angevin king, born to inherit nothing, won and lost an empire

Standing upon the banks of the Thames in the water-meadow at Runnymede on 15 June 1215, it would have been difficult for King John, brother of Richard I and inheritor of the Angevin Empire, to not reflect upon the events that had led him there. With lands lost in France, civil war dividing the kingdom, London fallen to rebel barons and a damaged relationship with the church, John was forced to sign a treaty that would reduce the crown's power and grant new rights to church and state.

The fifth and youngest son of Henry II and Eleanor of Aquitaine, John was nicknamed "Lackland" by his father as the chances of him inheriting significant lands seemed slim. This was a nickname that would gain an ironic twist towards the end of his reign. John's fortunes changed in 1173, however, when three of his brothers, "Young" Henry, Richard and Geoffrey, revolted against their father in protest at Henry's proposed distribution of lands among his sons. The rebellion failed and John became the favoured son, a status that led to his appointment as Lord of Ireland in 1177 and opened up the possibility of becoming heir to his father's throne.

But it was not to be; attempts to alter the plans for succession in the wake of Young Henry's death in 1183 angered brother Richard, who refused his father's request to pass the Duchy of Aquitane to John. Though forced to reconcile at the time, the

> Often portrayed as a tyrant, modern opinion suggests John was actually a capable ruler brought low by the treachery of others

hostility between Richard and his father remained, and Richard ultimately went on to seize the throne six years later.

Richard left England to join the Third Crusade, buying John's loyalty in his absence with lands and titles. John used this time to develop his own power and influence, taking advantage of growing tensions between Richard's appointed officials by brokering promises of support with England's nobles and proposing an alliance with King Philip II of France. A failed attempt to seize the crown for himself in 1193 resulted in John losing many of his titles upon Richard's return. Fortunately for John, Richard forgave him, seeing the attempted rebellion as little more than a youthful indiscretion. The final years of Richard's reign saw an outwardly loyal John work hard to reclaim favour in his brother's court and win back much of the power he'd lost.

Following Richard's death in 1199, John was favoured over Arthur, John's nephew and Richard's stated heir, and crowned king. Arthur withdrew to France, swearing fealty to Philip II, while John settled into his new role as king.

The Angevin Empire, established by his father and maintained by Richard, now comprised the Kingdom of England, parts of Ireland and around half of France, including the duchies of Normandy, Gascony and Aquitane; this was territory that Philip intended to bring back under French rule.

John's second marriage produced five children, though he is believed to have fathered as many as a dozen illegitimate children

The Magna Carta, written in medieval Latin and agreed to and sealed by King John in 1215

The Magna Carta

The Magna Carta was a document written to satisfy the grievances of England's barons and the church by clearly defining their rights and responsibilities, as well as those of the king. The agreement covered such topics as the giving of heirs in marriage and a widow's right to choose not to re-marry, the handling of debts following a debtor's death, and the introduction of standard weights and measures for wine, ale, corn and cloth.

Of particular note though were the promises that no free man would be imprisoned except by lawful justice, nor would they be denied the right to justice. There were also restrictions placed on the use of taxation by the king and his barons, including the formation of a council that could approve or reject proposed taxes and monitor the king's compliance with the terms of the charter. Although the charter was ultimately rejected by both John and the rebel barons, it would later be revised and reinstated after the king's death. Many of its edicts still remain intact in English law to this day.

"With England and Aquitane secured against possible French attack, John focused on building his forces"

In 1200, John's 11-year marriage to Isabella, Countess of Gloucester, was annulled so that he could marry Isabella of Angoulême, sparking a dispute that would define the rest of his reign. Conflict erupted along Normandy's eastern border between John and Hugh de Lusignan, Isabella's then-fiancé. de Lusignan's subsequent appeals to Philip II over John's actions, and John's refusal to answer Philip's summons left the French king with little choice but to punish John. He seized Normandy and reassigned John's lands in France (of which Philip was recognised as feudal overlord) to Arthur. The loss of Normandy, and with it the majority of England's continental territory, was unacceptable, and John was determined to take it back, whatever the cost.

With England and Aquitane secured against possible French attack, John focused on building his forces ready to recapture the lost lands in France. This required money, and John put more and more pressure on the English barons to provide the finances he needed, breeding increased discontent among the barons, particularly those in the north who felt far removed from John's campaigns in France. Baronial unrest delayed John's attempt to mount an expedition to Normandy in 1205, forcing him to depart for France with a much smaller military

presence than he had hoped for. Further funds were needed to forge alliances with Renaud of Boulogne, Count Ferdinand of Flanders and Otto IV, John's nephew and aspirant to the crown of the Holy Roman Empire in Germany. With these allies, John hoped to push forward with his attempt to retake Normandy from Philip, but in 1212 once again his progress was halted by unrest in England.

Seeing an opportunity, Philip sent his son Louis to invade Flanders, with the aim to push on to England's shores. Redeploying his forces to meet this new threat, John destroyed Louis' fleet, but again his plans had been disrupted and further taxes were levied to keep John's campaign in France viable. The whole series of events pushed tensions back home closer and closer to breaking point.

John's final French campaign began in 1214, though it was with significantly diminished support from many English barons, who refused to supply soldiers for John's war effort. In their place, mercenary regiments were hired to strengthen John's armies. The initial stages of the campaign progressed well - John pressed Louis' forces and retook Anjou, but was forced to retreat when the local Angevin nobles, whose loyalty lay with their feudal lord Philip II, refused to advance with him. The final blow to John's hopes of retaking Normandy came

> Signing the treaty of Le Goulet in 1200 earned John the nickname "Softsword" for his willingness to bow to Philip II

Defining moment
Rebellion against Richard I
1193-1194
John takes advantage of Richard's capture and imprisonment by Emperor Henry VI while returning from the Third Crusade by allying with Philip II of France and attempting to take Richard's crown for himself. Opposed by the forces who were loyal to Richard, John's rebellion is unsuccessful and he is forced to surrender upon Richard's eventual return.

Richard forgave John's attempted rebellion, but stripped him of much of his power as punishment

Timeline

1166

● **Birth of a king**
John, fifth and youngest of Henry II's sons, is born on Christmas Eve at Beaumont Palace in the city of Oxford.
24 December 1166

● **First Lord of Ireland**
Henry II grants lands captured in Ireland to John, naming him Lord of Ireland at just 10 years old, and temporarily alleviating the problems Henry faced in providing suitable lands and titles to all his sons.
1177

● **An unhappy union**
John marries his betrothed, Isabella, Countess of Gloucester. However, as cousins, the laws of consanguinity lead the Pope to forbid them from having children together.
1189

● **A king against the odds**
John is crowned at Westminster, supported by English nobles and denying his nephew Arthur's claim to the throne.
1199

● **Treaty of Le Goulet**
John and Philip II sign a treaty recognising Philip II as suzerain of John's lands in France. This is in return for Philip's recognition of John as Richard's heir and King of England.
1200

● **Wedding bells and death-knells**
Conflict erupts in Normandy with John's decision to marry the already-engaged Isabella of Angoulême. The Le Goulet peace treaty, which lasts just two years, ends in open war.
1200

at the battle of Bouvines in July, in which Philip defeated John's allies under the leadership of Otto IV. Otto was deposed, Renaud and Ferdinand were captured, and Philip took control of Brittany and Normandy. John was forced to concede defeat, sign a peace treaty and return to England.

News of the failed campaign did little to settle the growing tensions in England, and soon barons in the North and East were organising resistance to John's rule. John arranged discussions with the rebels, though whether this was born from a genuine wish to reconcile, or an attempt to stall any potential conflict until he had received official support from Pope Innocent III, was unclear. By the time Innocent's letters arrived, the rebels were ready to act, marching on London. The capital fell, as did Lincoln and Exeter, and the rebels' successes prompted more barons to throw their lot in against the crown. John's position was desperate, and with his only option being to agree to peace talks, a meeting was arranged. The date was 15 June 1215. The place, Runnymede.

The peace agreement created by Stephen Langton, Archbishop of Canterbury, would later be known as the Magna Carta, and it would shape English law for years to come. In addition to resolving baronial complaints, the charter defined the rights and freedoms of the barons, the citizens, the church and the king. The king's ability to impose taxation was restricted, the church would be allowed to appoint its own officials without interference and a council of barons would be formed to monitor the king's adherence to the charter. In return, the rebels were to surrender London to John and withdraw their forces.

> John rarely took communion and was said to have made blasphemous remarks and jokes about the church

The charter failed. The rebels, believing John would not abide by the agreement, refused to stand down. In turn, John, claiming to have signed the charter under duress, sought help from Pope Innocent III, who declared the charter to be "shameful, demeaning, illegal and unjust" and excommunicated the rebel barons. The stage was set for the First Baron's War.

Faced with the strength of John's armies, the English barons sought assistance from another quarter - Prince Louis of France. The rebels had early successes, taking the castles at Rochester and Canterbury and gaining control of much of Kent. John enjoyed similar success against the northern barons and Alexander II of Scotland and won control of many of the disputed northern territories. With the north contained and rumours of Louis' imminent arrival in the south, John turned back to meet the coming threat.

Louis landed in Kent in May 1216 and marched on London unopposed, though his attempts to take Dover and Windsor by siege proved unsuccessful. John withdrew to Winchester before pushing towards Cambridge and north in an attempt to divide the rebels of Lincolnshire and East Anglia. With Alexander II marching south to pledge his support to Louis, John turned west once more, enduring a disastrous crossing of the Wash's estuaries, which saw much of his baggage train, including the crown jewels disappear.

By the time John reached Newark Castle, he was suffering from dysentery and could go no further. He died there on 18 October 1216. His kingdom, a pale reflection of the empire it had been 16 years earlier, passed into the hands of his heir.

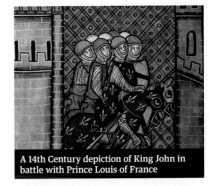

A 14th Century depiction of King John in battle with Prince Louis of France

Life in the time of King John

Soldiers of fortune
John made extensive use of foreign mercenaries. Though more expensive to employ, mercenary contingents could fight year-round. By comparison, feudal troops were restricted by fixed-term service, providing greater tactical flexibility.

Scutage
Scutage was a form of taxation that allowed a knight to buy his way out of military service. John's use of scutage as a legitimate form of taxation at times when the threat of military conflict was not apparent was one of many sources of discontent among his barons.

Dysentery
Dysentery thrived in the Middle Ages, aided by a lack of proper sewage control, poor understanding of hygiene and an abundance of spoilt food. Doctor-approved treatments for dysentery at the time included consuming barley water, eggs and even lead.

The Feudal System
Feudalism was a tiered order of governance, from the king down. Instigated by William I in 1066, when he divided the freshly-conquered Saxon lands among his barons, the system would last until the 17th Century.

Persecution of the Jews
Many Jews of the Middle Ages held significant wealth and acted as money lenders. They were widely disliked by the nobility and their protection under the king left them vulnerable to heavy taxation whenever the crown needed to raise emergency funds.

Defining moment
Excommunication
November 1209
Following a dispute with Pope Innocent III over the church's appointment of the new Archbishop of Canterbury, John is excommunicated. Although John reacts by seizing English lands and money held by the church in England, he ultimately reconciles with the Pope in 1213, fearing the possibility of a Papacy-backed French invasion. Innocent becomes one of John's greatest supporters, discouraging the French from attacking and providing official support during the Barons' Revolt in 1215.

Defining moment
Laying down the law
15 June 1215
Forced into conciliatory action by both the church and England's rebel barons, John signs the Magna Carta at Runnymede, agreeing to abide by its restrictions on royal power and the freedoms it grants to the church and the citizens. These covenants would shape England's laws for centuries to come. John would go on to claim the charter was unlawful and signed under duress, prompting the barons to revolt in protest and leading to the First Barons' War.

A broken empire
War with King Philip II and Arthur in France results in the loss of the majority of the ancestral Angevin territories John had inherited from his brother and father.
1202

A son and heir
John's wife Isabella gives birth to their first son, Henry III, who would inherit his father's kingdom nine years later.
1207

Battle of Bouvines
John's final attempt to reclaim Normandy ends with the destruction of his allies at Bouvines in Flanders. John and King Philip II agree to peace and he returns home defeated.
1214

The First Barons' War
Civil war erupts in England as Pope Innocent declares the Magna Carta unlawful, releasing John from its rules. The barons revolt.
1215

Death of a king
Suffering from dysentery, John dies at Newark Castle. Rumours at the time attribute his death to many things, such as poisoned ale, plums and an indulgent "surfeit of peaches".
1216

1216

Henry was crowned twice – first in 1216, and again in 1220 to reaffirm his right to rule and strengthen efforts to rebuild the kingdom

1216-1272
Henry III

How a boy king whose reign was plagued by rebellion went on to become one of England's longest-reigning monarchs

Upon King John's death in 1216, his nine-year-old son, Henry III, inherited a kingdom in chaos. The First Barons' War was still in effect, with rebel barons in open conflict with supporters of the crown, and Prince Louis of France occupying London. With Henry too young to reign, John had appointed a council of nobles to help him reclaim the kingdom, and this regency government would steer Henry's rule for much of his first 20 years as king, bringing the First Barons' War to a close in 1217 and working to reinstate royal authority for many years after. All the while, foundations were being laid for parliamentary institutions that are still in place today.

As a man, Henry was a marked contrast to his father; where John was considered to be scandalously impious, Henry was renowned for his religious conviction, holding lavish religious ceremonies, giving generously to the church (particularly during his wife Eleanor's five pregnancies) and adopting Edward the Confessor as his patron saint. Henry believed that he should rule England in a dignified manner through peace and order, just as Edward had before him. As a king, though, his rule would mirror that of his father a great deal more than most would have liked. Conflict in France over the remaining English-held territories there led to Henry reissuing the failed Magna Carta agreement in 1225 in return for the financial support of his barons in raising an army, a 1230 invasion to reclaim the contested territories ended in failure, and conflicting political ambitions

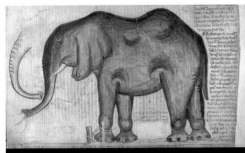

A drawing of an elephant gifted to Henry for his menagerie by Louis IX of France, by Matthew Paris, a Benedictine monk and contemporary chronicler

among his advisors led to discontent from many nobles at their treatment by Henry's government.

The greatest parallel to his father's reign came with the Second Barons' War in 1264, a result of years of financial pressure placed on the barons by their king. Funds raised to support a planned crusade were spent instead quelling revolt in Gascony in 1252 when the populace rebelled against the king's lieutenant, Simon de Montfort. An agreement in 1254 with Pope Innocent IV that would have seen Henry's second son Edmund crowned as King of Sicily turned sour after Innocent was succeeded by Alexander IV. The deal involved Henry financing the papacy's wars in Sicily in return for the crown. By 1258, Alexander threatened to excommunicate Henry for failing to meet his financial obligation towards the Sicilian campaign. Unable to convince Parliament to supply all the funds he needed, Henry turned to the senior clergy, forcing them to sign over thousands to help settle the debt. Earlier attempts to influence the Holy Roman Empire's elections, in order to have his brother Richard crowned King of the Romans, only added to Henry's debts. With the barons and the church dissatisfied at being constantly asked to foot the bills for Henry's continued spending, conflict was inevitable and building pressure on Parliament to reform led to the passing of the Provisions of Oxford. This plan of reform, decided by a royal commission, resulted in Henry being forced to accept the formation of a new baronial council of 15 members. The new council would supervise

> **Henry kept a menagerie of exotic creatures at the Tower of London, including a lion, leopards, a polar bear and an elephant**

ministerial appointments, local administration and the custody of royal castles, and would be monitored in turn by Parliament. Henry initially agreed to the Provisions, but, like his father before him, sought papal assistance to release him from the agreement, assistance that came in the form of a papal bull in 1261 absolving Henry of his responsibility to uphold the Provisions. Simon de Montfort and Richard de Clare, radical reformists and key figures amongst those that had forced Henry to accept the Provisions, formed their own parliament, installing a rival system of government to Henry's, but the rebels backed down in the face of a mercenary army raised by Henry in case of open war. De Montfort fled to France, and de Clare joined the loyalists. Royal order was restored, albeit briefly with Henry's influence weakening once more under the combined effect of Welsh unrest on the borders and the papacy reversing its decision on the Provisions of Oxford.

By 1263, civil war was a threat once more, with de Montfort returned from France and quick to gather the unhappy barons under a coalition banner against the crown in the Midlands. The Second Barons' War officially began in April 1264, with Henry and Edward, his heir, marching on de Montfort's Midlands power base before turning southeast. De Montfort gave chase, defeating Henry at the Battle of Lewes, capturing the king and forcing him to pardon the rebels and reinstate the Provisions of Oxford. Disorder reigned in the wake of de Montfort's victory, however, and Edward was able to form a new army in May, eventually bringing de Montfort to battle near Evesham in August 1265. The rebel forces were outnumbered, outmanoeuvred and subsequently massacred, with de Montfort killed and his body mutilated by the royalists. Henry was freed by his son, and the restoration of royal power brought with it hard justice - all those that had taken part in the rebellion were disinherited at the next meeting of Parliament. With baronial opposition ended, Henry was able to spend his remaining years delivering a largely peaceful and orderly rule of which his idol, Edward the Confessor, might have approved.

Upon his death, Henry's reign had lasted for 56 years and 29 days, the fourth longest in English history

Life in the time of Henry III

A short and brutal life?

Average life expectancy at birth in the 13th Century was just 30 years, largely due to high incidences of infant mortality, though making it to 20 years old vastly improved an individual's chances of surviving to see their 40th, and even perhaps 50th birthday.

A parliamentary affair

During Henry's reign, the role of parliament in the country's governance evolved a great deal, growing from a nominal council able to exercise a degree of restraint upon the king's proposals, to a formal and independently powerful entity whose support could be essential to a successful reign.

Population boom

From the 11th to 13th Centuries, England's population is thought to have grown from around 1.5 million to between 5 and 7 million, a considerable increase as there were no medical breakthroughs or major immigration occurring. During Henry's reign, the population may have grown by as much as 1.2 million, though reliable contemporary sources are rare.

Friends in high places

Papal support was a valuable resource throughout the Middle Ages, and making an enemy of the church inevitably also meant making an enemy of those countries that supported the church. The threat of excommunication was a powerful tool for bringing an unruly baron, or even king, to heel.

A French connection

The official language at Henry's court was French: Henry's Angevin heritage and family traditions were important to him, and he hoped that his court would help bring his English and continental nobles together.

A lost inheritance

Henry considered the Angevin lands in France, lost during his father's reign, to be legally his and reclaiming these territories was an important concern for the young king. Following the death of Louis VIII and the coronation of 12-year old Louis IX, Angevin nobles in France revolted against the French crown, pledging their support to Henry if he would take back the Angevin provinces. Henry invaded in the summer of 1230, marching south to Poitou, but the guidance of his advisors resulted in an ineffectual and costly military campaign. The lost territories remained under French rule, and Henry returned home defeated.

Edward I wasn't the first Edward to rule England but the third. Kings were only numbered after the Norman conquest of 1066

EDWARD I
England, 1239-1307

Brief Bio Remembered primarily for his brutal conquests of Wales and Scotland, Edward I – also known as 'Longshanks' and 'Hammer of the Scots' – was a master statesman and unlikely reformer who enshrined the Magna Carta in law and paved the way for a representative English parliament.

1272-1307
Edward I

Conqueror of Scotland and Wales and unlikely father of democracy, Edward I was the savage warrior king who laid down the bloody foundations of the United Kingdom

One of the greatest monarchs of the Plantagenet dynasty, Edward I – also known by his forbidding nickname, the 'Hammer of the Scots' – proves that a great king isn't necessarily a good person. Very much his father's son, he inherited from Henry III not only a drooping left eye and unpredictable Plantagenet temper, but also a series of life lessons that shaped his reign. Over a reign of 34 years and seven months, Edward I brought order to a chaotic political system, created a uniform system of justice for his entire kingdom, and led an orgy of conquest into Wales and Scotland. Edward I was indeed one of the fathers of modern Britain, but a stern one

who was at times capable of great cruelty and even self-destructive obsession.

Henry III ensured that his son had the best possible education available to a European prince – giving him England's French domain of Gascony in 1254, along with other territories, to rule and hone his skills – but the real life lessons came from the old king's weak and indecisive rule. His religious conviction had made him too biddable to the pope in Rome and his secular power too had been usurped by a snake pit of powerful English barons.

Already more comfortable solving problems with a mailed fist, aged 24 the hot-headed prince got his first taste of blood – and of the true extent of

Henry III's failings - at the Battle of Lewes on 14 May 1264. In one of the key engagements of the Second Barons' War against the crown, Edward had successfully routed the rebel cavalry and chased them miles off the battlefield. The thrill of victory was short-lived; returning to the field, he discovered that the king's forces had surrendered to the upstart earl, Simon de Montefort, and Edward was held hostage. The humiliation wouldn't stand, and after escaping captivity he defeated his tormentor at the Battle of Evesham, leaving the traitorous earl mutilated on the battlefield.

Edward had entered the Second Barons' War as the loyal son to a weak king, and emerged one of the most powerful men in England - a clear monarch-in-waiting - as the weak king got even weaker with age. Still enthralled by the taste of blood and the lure of chivalry, Edward joined the Ninth Crusade in June 1268, although his passage was delayed by lack of money until 1270. Chalking up victories - not least of which was the seizure of Nazareth, the Biblical birthplace of Jesus Christ - Edward's blaze of holy glory was cut short when he was attacked by an assassin with a poisoned dagger. Scarcely had he begun to recover when he discovered that his father had died on 16 November 1272. Returning home at a leisurely pace thanks to his injuries, Edward was crowned Edward I on 19 August 1274.

An invasion of Wales followed with campaigns in 1277 and then 1282-3, ending the independence of the nation. What began with sword and shield ended with bricks and mortar as new castles - built in the oppressive Crusader style - sprung up and English settlers moved into fortified towns that cracked apart Welsh resolve and identity like hammer blows.

Just as Wales had seen England grow from overbearing neighbour to occupying power under the reign of Edward I, so too would Scotland. After a dispute over succession to the Scottish throne arose, Edward was asked to mediate over the 13 hopefuls and picked the easily pliant John Balliol as King of Scots in 17 November 1292. From thereon Edward I behaved as though Balliol were another cringing courtier and Scotland another rural estate.

Resistance to English interference arose in the form of the charismatic William Wallace and on 11 September 1297 the Scottish rebels trounced a larger English army at the Battle of Stirling Bridge. As if stung by this defeat, Edward I assembled an army of 15,000 men. Heavily outnumbered, Wallace led his forces in a gruelling guerrilla war amid the heather, but was eventually forced to engage in open battle at Falkirk on 22 July 1298. Wallace's rebel army was crushed, leaving Edward in control of southeast Scotland.

In the castles and palaces, the clash was no less unpredictable thanks to the shifting loyalties of the Scottish nobility. Robert the Bruce sided with the English in 1302, William Wallace was betrayed and executed in 1305 and then, just as all seemed peaceful, Robert the Bruce declared himself King of Scots in 1306 and turned against England. Edward I, despite his increasingly poor health, responded as he knew best - with war. He drove Robert the Bruce from his throne and into hiding with a series of thunderous assaults, but on 10 May 1307 Robert the Bruce delivered his first major victory against the English at the Battle of Loudoun Hill. Two months later, weak with dysentery, Edward I died in the arms of his pages at his camp near the Scottish border. Once so powerful, ferocious and sharp of claw, this old lion had choked on his final meal.

Various legends swirled around his dying wish - that his heart should be carried to the Holy Land with the Crusaders to rage against the infidel one last time, or that his bones should accompany all further wars with Scotland.

His son, Edward II, did neither. As Edward I had been to Henry III, Edward II wasn't blind to his father's faults and in August the young king abandoned the campaign against the Scots, returning to London for his coronation and to lay the old warlord to rest in a sarcophagus of Purbeck marble.

"I am more afraid of the bones of the father dead," admitted Robert the Bruce, "than of the living son; and, by all the saints, it was more difficult to get a half a foot of the land from the old king than a whole kingdom from the son!"

> Following his invasion, the title of Prince of Wales was conferred to Edward I's son Edward Caernarfon in 1301, starting the long tradition

Life in the time of Edward I

Mother of parliaments
With its origin in the word 'parlay', the Parliament was traditionally an infrequent consultation between nobles and the king. Edward I held them more frequently and summoned not just lords, but two knights from each county and two representatives from each borough.

Law and order
Edward I created statutes to process everything from settlement of debts to land ownership and released travelling judges - eyres - across the country to review the rights and holdings of nobles. He also held inquests into the abuses of power in the Second Barons' War.

Magna Carta
Edward I restored the Magna Carta (and the Charter of the Forest, which covers the use of public land), limiting the power of the king. It is this version of the document that remains in statute today, underpinning the political system of the United Kingdom.

Return to Camelot
Edward I was a great believer in the ideals of chivalry - even if his campaigns in Wales and Scotland didn't always live up to them - and he built castles in Wales to correspond with locations in Arthurian legend. He even held Round Table festive banquets to celebrate his conquests.

Assassins
The *Hashāshīn* - or Assassins - were a secret order based in Syria and Persia who undertook assassinations during the Crusades. Edward I was just one of many Crusader leaders to feel the prick of their daggers.

Edward the romantic
For all his fearsome reputation, Edward I was devoted to his wife, Eleanor of Castille, whom he married in 1254. Unlike other kings, Edward had no affairs or illegitimate children and she even accompanied him on his military campaigns - reportedly sucking the poison from his wound when he was attacked by an assassin during the Crusades.

After her death in 1290, Edward I planted 12 stone crosses marking her funeral processions from Lincoln to London, from which Charing Cross takes its name.

In 1291 he wrote to a French abbot seeking prayers for the "dead we cannot cease to love."

He succeeded Edward I as king because his three older brothers John, Henry and Alfonso had died in childhood

1307-1327
Edward II

This much-loathed king had an equally hated favourite, saw Scotland slip from his grasp and ultimately met a murderous end

Edward I had proven himself to be a very effective king, suppressing numerous rebellions and waging a good many bloody wars. He had become one of Scotland's greatest adversaries and he had annexed Wales in a bid to bring stability and control to his realm. But when he died in July 1307 and his son, Edward of Caernarfon, became king at the age of 23, there was a real danger that much of that hard work would be undone.

For while Edward II had accompanied his father on his campaigns and had, in 1301, been bestowed the title of the first Prince of Wales, he was a more cultured man who did not share the same appetite nor aptitude for battle. His father had noted this and hoped, in assigning Piers Gaveston to the

young Prince Edward's household, some of the English nobleman's martial skills would rub off. It didn't. Instead, Edward II became very attached to Gaveston who, as a consequence, was exiled to France for being a bad influence.

So when Edward II became king - his three elder brothers having died - he was left in a difficult position. The war with Scotland was still ongoing, debts were running high and relations with France were hostile. Yet rather than gather together the best possible people to help him sort these issues, one of his first moves was to recall Gaveston and give him the earldom of Cornwall. Since this was a title that had always been given to royalty, it caused an uproar. Gaveston had become Edward II's favourite and the barons did not like it one bit.

In a bid to resolve long-running tensions between the French and English crowns which had been a legacy of his father, Edward II married the daughter of the French King Philip IV, Isabella of France in 1308. It led to Gaveston being banished to France for a second time on the insistence of both the barons and the French royals in an attempt to put distance between the two men. The exile didn't last long and Gaveston was brought back in 1309.

With tensions continuing to run high and opposition to the king barely diminishing, the nobles issued the Ordinances of 1311. They sought to restrict the king's power over finances and appointments. They also ordered Gaveston be banished for a third time. Edward II agreed - but it was a bluff. Gaveston was brought back again,

Edward II, as depicted in Cassell's *History of England*, published around 1902

with the king not only insisting that it had been unlawful to banish him but restoring his own power. This angered the barons, who gathered their own armies.

In 1312, Gaveston was besieged in Scarborough Castle. After surrendering, he was taken to Deddington in Oxfordshire, but he was then seized by the Earl of Warwick, Guy de Beauchamp. Paraded through the streets of Warwick and imprisoned in the castle, Edward II's favourite was tried, taken to Blacklow Hill outside of the town and beheaded. The king vowed revenge.

Two years later, Edward II sought to resolve the ongoing war with Scotland. Edward Bruce, the brother of Robert the Bruce who had seized the Scottish throne in 1306, had besieged Stirling Castle and this forced England's hand. Around 2,000 cavalry and 15,000 infantry were assembled against the Scots, but the resulting Battle of Bannockburn in June 1314 proved too much. Over two days, Robert the Bruce's men put up a fierce fight and pushed the English back. Humiliated, Edward II was unable to prevent subsequent Scottish raids in the north of England, nor the invasion of Ireland.

It was a terrible time for the king. A shortage of food caused by terrible weather that devastated crops caused support for him to fall further. Edward's cousin, Thomas of Lancaster, was

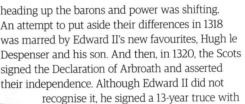

His 19-year reign came to an end when he was betrayed by his own wife, forced to abdicate and murdered

heading up the barons and power was shifting. An attempt to put aside their differences in 1318 was marred by Edward II's new favourites, Hugh le Despenser and his son. And then, in 1320, the Scots signed the Declaration of Arbroath and asserted their independence. Although Edward II did not recognise it, he signed a 13-year truce with Robert the Bruce who, by this point was seriously ill.

Not that it solved any of the king's problems. Civil war had broken out in 1321, triggered by tensions between the Despenser family and the barons. Lancaster led a group of the Despensers' enemies into battle, seizing land. He was joined by Roger Mortimer of Wigmore, who led the Marcher lords in a revolt. Edward II's men fought back and Lancaster was defeated at Boroughbridge in 1322. Lancaster was executed, but Mortimer escaped from the Tower of London and fled to France.

At the same time, tensions with France began flaring again and in 1325, Isabella was sent across the sea to help resolve them. Instead, she refused to return and allied herself with Mortimer, who also became her lover. Together, they led an army to capture Edward II, forcing him to become the first English royal to abdicate, in his case in favour of his 14-year-old son, Edward III. Imprisoned and tortured in the most grotesque of manners, he was murdered in Berkeley Castle in 1327.

War of Saint-Sardos

A conflict between the kingdoms of England and France ran from October 1323 to September 1335 and it proved to be a bitter blow for Edward II's reputation. Edward was the Duke of Aquitaine in France, but a dispute in the ancient region with King Charles IV of France flared. The French were interfering in the governing of Aquitaine and had agreed to build a royal bastide in Saint-Sardos. When a French sergeant looked to seize the site, he was hanged by a local landowner. The French believed Edward II had ordered the killing, something he denied. But the diplomatic gloves were off. Charles IV would go on to conquer the Duchy of Guyenne in a battle that lasted six weeks. It was a precursor to the Hundred Years' War.

King Charles IV of France

Life in the time of Edward II

Medicine was positively medieval

Becoming severely ill during the time when Edward II reigned was almost a direct route to the grave. Only the wealthy had access to trained doctors and even they would tend to diagnose on the basis of examining blood, stools and urine. Poor people had to rely on passed-down traditional 'cures', accompanied by a pleading prayer.

People were more cultured in those days

Although Edward II enjoyed the company of the lower classes, he loved music, sailing, dancing and plays, and the time in which he lived was certainly cultured. In 1308, Italian poet Dante began to write his epic *The Divine Comedy*, which has come to be seen as one of the greatest works of literature.

Food was rather scarce

Poor harvests took their toll throughout the early part of Edward II's reign, leading the masses towards hunger, but things got worse when crop failures between 1315 and 1322 led to famine. Peasants even feasted on seeds that were intended for planting in the spring and tens of thousands of starved to death.

Death was an obsession for many

One of the most popular stories of the day was a tale that most likely came from France. It told of three corpses meeting three living princes, warning that life would soon come to an end for them. Death was a regular plot driver in stories of the early 1300s.

Inflation reached its greatest ever rate

The pound sterling was established as England's main currency, but there was trouble ahead. Inflation rocketed to a staggering 100.4 per cent in 1316. With half of the pound's value lopped off, great hardship was caused among an already embattled population. 20 shillings made up a pound, with 12 pence equalling one shilling.

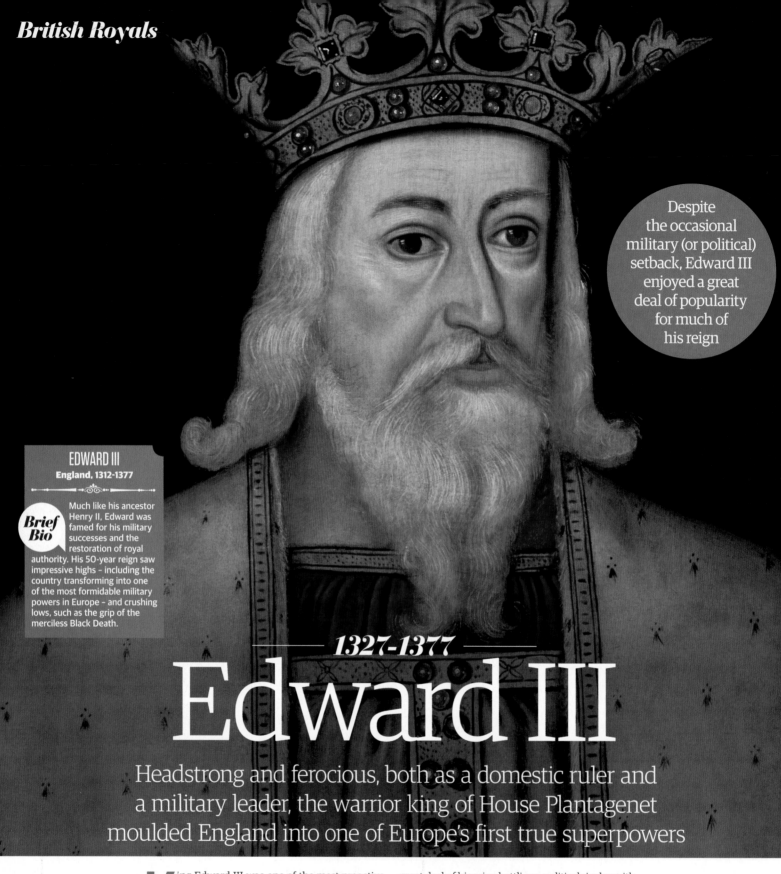

Despite the occasional military (or political) setback, Edward III enjoyed a great deal of popularity for much of his reign

EDWARD III
England, 1312-1377

Brief Bio

Much like his ancestor Henry II, Edward was famed for his military successes and the restoration of royal authority. His 50-year reign saw impressive highs – including the country transforming into one of the most formidable military powers in Europe – and crushing lows, such as the grip of the merciless Black Death.

1327-1377
Edward III

Headstrong and ferocious, both as a domestic ruler and a military leader, the warrior king of House Plantagenet moulded England into one of Europe's first true superpowers

King Edward III was one of the most proactive and - more importantly - successful rulers England and its surrounding realms have ever known. His half-century of rule saw plague, wars, political intrigue and judicial upheaval that collectively transformed our small island into a military powerhouse. It was quite the dramatic period of English history and Edward's road to kingship was just as theatrical.

Born at Windsor Castle on 13 November 1312, Edward was the only child of King Edward II and his wife, Isabella of France. His father had spent a great deal of his reign battling a political rivalry with his own gentry and the birth of a strong male heir helped fortify his position, at least for a time. In 1325, Edward II was required to pay homage to the French king, Charles IV. Uneasy at leaving the country during an ongoing and costly war with Scotland, the king sent his 13-year-old son and his wife Isabella on behalf of the crown. However, Isabella conspired with the exiled Roger Mortimer (a former earl who had led the unsuccessful Despenser War against Edward four years earlier) to usurp the king and set up Prince Edward in his place.

While the young Edward was now king, he was really nothing more than a political pawn for his mother and Mortimer. In order to gain French military backing for an invasion, Isabella organised an engagement to the 12 year-old Philippa of Hainault and soon Mortimer arrived on English soil with an army behind him. Edward II stood down as king, with Mortimer ruling as the de facto leader while the young Edward came of age. Mortimer was monarch in all but name and his unpopularity grew as he gathered titles and lands for himself. The situation reached a head on 19 October 1330 when the young king and a group of his most trusted allies entered Nottingham Castle through an underground passage and arrested Mortimer. Finally, the time for Edward's personal reign had begun.

Edward's rule started the way it would continue for 50 years: at war. His father had continued to pay homage to the French king for most of his reign, but all that was about to change. As a man, Edward was headstrong and direct; as a monarch, this made him very dangerous indeed. Edward decided to make a claim for the French throne, citing his blood connection to Philip IV. The French responded by rejecting the claim under Salic Law (a manuscript from the Middle Ages that defined the foundations of French legislation, including the rules of succession). This butting of political heads would form the origins of the Hundred Years' War, a conflict that would draw most of Europe into its numerous battles.

While the conflict would ultimately go England's way, funding a rebuilt navy and constant military campaigns placed considerable strain on England's economy. Edward needed cash to keep pressing the French, but he found the coffers had almost run dry. Edward would eventually gain the funding he needed, but it came at a price: in April 1341, Parliament drafted a new grant of taxation, but in return Edward had to accept certain limitations on his spending. Such rules irked the

Edward III is one of only five monarchs to have reigned for over 50 years – also including his great-grandfather Henry III

king, but it served as one of his first tastes of a parliament willing to stand up to the absolute rule of its monarch.

Edward was steadfast in his desire to expand England's hold over French territories. Victories over King Philip VI at the Battle of Crécy (as well as putting down a campaign by King David II of Scotland) rocked France, and it wasn't until the Treaty of Brétigny that Edward finally renounced his claim on the French throne. So dominant was England at this time that Edward claimed full sovereignty over the lands he'd conquered in France (which amounted to almost a third of the country).

The decade of the 1350s saw something of a boom in legislative activity. Edward's frustration with the murkiness of England's judicial system was just the impetus he needed to streamline the political landscape. This was especially important in light of the Black Death, a bubonic plague which killed more than a third of the country's population. He initially attempted to deal with the shortages of labour with legislation that made work more palatable, but it wasn't enough to settle the problem. However, his removal of papal benefices, his reformation of laws surrounding treason and the increased power provided to the roaming justices of the peace had a profound effect that echoed long after his death.

Upon his death on 21 June 1377, Edward was succeeded not by his son, but his ten-year-old grandson Richard II

While the majority of Edward's reign was energetic and filled with military conquests, the latter part of his rule strayed into the opposite. Bored by the machinations of domestic kingship, the aging Edward relied more and more on his most prominently active children, Edward the Black Prince, Lionel Duke of Clarence and John Duke of Lancaster. In the hands of his sons, England lost a significant amount of its lands in France, a fact that made them very unpopular with the English public. Ironically, while he lived through most of these disasters until his death in 1377, Edward's descent into obscurity only served to preserve the legacy of his earlier reign.

Such was Edward's impact and legacy on the kingdom that his tomb – and this bronze effigy – remains in Westminster Abbey

Life in the time of the 50-year king

Death, triumphant
While Edward III did many things to put England back on the political map, nothing could have prepared the nation for the Black Death. It ravaged Europe from 1346 to 1353, killing between 75 and 200 million people across the continent. In England, the disease wiped out over a third of the population.

A new form of government
During Edward's reign, the English Parliament began to take a very familiar shape. The institution became bicameral in nature, which meant that Parliament divided into two separate assemblies, the House of Lords and the House of Commons. Such features as the role of speaker and Parliament's ability to impeach were also introduced in this period.

Order of the Garter
Edward had planned to introduce a setup similar to Arthur's symbolic Round Table, but the idea soon fell through. In its place, the English king established the Order of the Garter, an honorary cabal reserved only for the most chivalrous gentleman (and ladies) in the land. New appointments are always announced on St George's Day.

Laws of the land
The substantial loss of population caused by the infamous Black Death caused a crisis within England's economy, with a dramatic decrease in the supply of labour. This resulted in the Statute Of Labourers 1351 being passed in order to suppress the workforce. The new law prohibited increases in wages and the movement of workers from their home areas in search of better conditions.

Keeping the peace
Justice of the peace – a role created during the time of Henry II – saw its most formative years under Edward III. Justices were the eyes, ears and word of the king and these men travelled to the kingdom's far corners to enact the law in his name. Under Edward's influence, justices could not only make arrests but also try suspects for felonies.

The Hundred Years' War
Despite its title, the Hundred Years' War lasted far longer than a century – in fact, it lasted for another 76 years after Edward's death in 1377. The conflict began with the breaking of a centuries-old agreement that began with William the Conqueror's accession to the English throne. As ruler, Edward held the Duchy of Normandy and the lands of Aquitaine, but these lands came with the stipulation that homage be paid to the French king. When Edward refused to respect this deal, Philip VI of France declared war and the Houses of Plantagenet and Valois became embroiled in a brutal military struggle comprising a series of conflicts.

RICHARD II

France , 1367-1400

Brief Bio

Richard became king aged ten and early on in his reign displayed bravery to help end a rebellion, but his policy of giving patronage to his own men caused friction with the nobles and he briefly lost control of the country. A fragile peace followed, but he had not forgotten those who opposed him and his desire to bring them down ultimately led to him losing his crown.

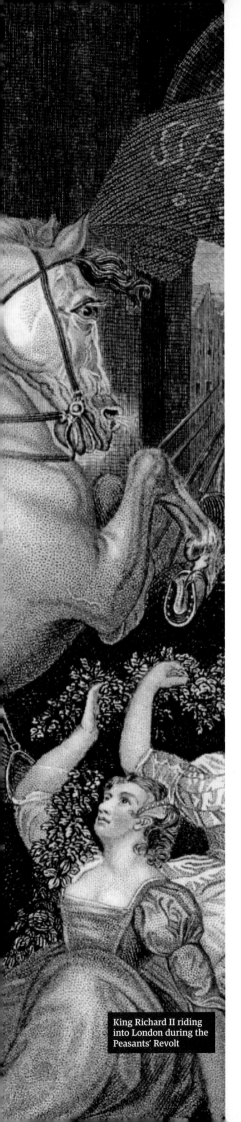

King Richard II riding into London during the Peasants' Revolt

1377-1399

Richard II

The king whose thirst for revenge led to him losing his crown and his life

Soldiers barged into the house where the former chief justice of England, and one of the monarch Richard II's favourites, Robert Tresilian, had been hiding and arrested him at sword point. Tresilian had already been judged guilty of treason in absentia and his poor disguise didn't fool the soldiers; they had their man. This key player in the government of Richard II, a man upon whom had been bestowed much royal patronage, was hanged on 19 February 1388. With the former chief justice executed along with Sir Nicholas Brembre - another man of the king - and others fleeing overseas in exile sentenced to a similar fate if they ever again stepped afoot on the land of their birth, it seemed that the power base of King Richard II had been eradicated.

After this cull, the king - in public at least - seemed to adopt a conciliatory position. He claimed the problems that had led to such divisions between himself and his leading nobility that caused many of his leading figures in government being executed or exiled was the result of bad advice from councillors. He would now rule with the men that his nobles suggested as being key parts of the apparatus of the English government and peace could return to England. In private, though, Richard neither forgave nor forgot.

Born in Bordeaux in 1367, Richard inherited the throne from his grandfather Edward III - since his father, Edward 'the Black Prince' had already died in 1376 - when he was just ten years old. As such, for the early parts of his reign the country was effectively run by a series of councils, but by the early 1380s the king was becoming increasingly involved. Richard would prove himself to be a capable king early on in his reign with his response to a situation that all high-born and of power feared - a peasants' revolt. Led by Wat Tyler, the 1381 revolt was triggered by the crown's demands for a poll tax to help pay for the costly Hundred Years' War with France. With many in England struggling to feed themselves, the demand for even more money was the tipping point and a large group of dissenters actually entered London where they looted, damaged buildings and killed anyone associated with the government.

Richard II, then aged 14, initially retreated for safety to the Tower of London, but with many of the royal forces in northern England or abroad he knew he needed to end the rebellion. As he didn't have the military strength to do this, diplomacy would have to suffice. The young king met with the rebels and agreed to their demands (which included abolishing serfdom) and the following day

> His uncle, the Duke of Gloucester, had a key role in sentencing many of Richard's favourites to death

"After an altercation broke out, Wat Tyler was stabbed to death by the lord mayor of London, William Walworth, who feared for the safety of the king"

spoke with Wat Tyler just outside the city's walls. However, after an altercation broke out, Tyler was stabbed to death by the lord mayor of London, William Walworth, who feared for the safety of the king. Seeing their leader killed, the rebels seemed likely to storm the city again, but Richard rode over to them and managed to defuse the situation. This gave the city's militia time to organise themselves and 'persuade' the rebel forces to disperse. Other rebellions occurred throughout the country - notably in East Anglia - and the king mobilised around 4,000 troops to restore law and order. The revolt's aims, which Richard had only agreed to in order to buy time, were studiously ignored and by the end of the

year, some 1,500 rebels had been killed. The king had passed his first test and proven himself to be a brave and intelligent ruler, but in just six years' time he would lose control of his kingdom.

The crown that Richard inherited in 14th Century England, and the power that came with it, was different to that of his predecessors. The Magna Carta of 1215, signed by King John, had put into law the rights of the nobles and barons and by the late 1300s it was no longer possible for a king to govern solely by himself with no consideration as to the thoughts and feelings of his leading citizens. Of course, the king was still the pre-eminent figure in the land and had the most power, but it was necessary

> Richard was buried in a church in Hertfordshire, but his bones were later moved to Westminster Abbey as a sign of respect

to rule with the nobles - or at least give them the impression that the king was doing so.

Rather than rule with his nobles, though, Richard preferred to bestow patronage and power to a small group of men, many of whom were in his royal household. To these figures, mostly knights and minor nobility, he gave land, money and positions of influence in government. Michael de la Pole, the son of a merchant, rose to become chancellor of England, one of the most important and influential positions in the whole land, while the minor nobleman Robert de Vere became Duke of Ireland. These were positions that the nobility of England, the great men with their own land and armies and ancient history, believed were theirs by right.

The king's military failures in France and Scotland only added to the bubbling resentment felt by the barons and earls at their marginalisation from power. The Hundred Years' War was a conflict that Richard inherited, but his policy of seeking peace not only robbed the nobles of potential glory and riches but failed; France regained territory previously held by England and even threatened invasion of the island nation. While Richard looked - unsuccessfully - for peace in France, closer to home he was no such pacifist and military campaigns in Scotland and Ireland brought little tangible rewards for the money and effort they cost.

Described as handsome, tall (when his grave was dug up he was discovered to be over six feet tall) and refined, Richard may have looked the part but his actions were leading the country steadily towards crisis. Money was raised through Parliament for an army to attack Scotland to break one half of the 'auld alliance' between that nation and France. Richard led this force of 14,000 men himself, but the Scots refused to meet in battle and the king returned having achieved little. The threat of a French invasion continued to loom ominously in the background and matters weren't helped for Richard when his uncle, John of Gaunt, left the country to pursue his claims to Castile in modern-day Spain. The king had an uneasy relationship with his uncle, who was one of the most powerful men in the kingdom, but John had always been loyal. In his absence Richard had lost his most influential and respected supporter and when the chancellor de la Pole demanded more money from Parliament, the fragile accord between the king and the leading men of the country shattered into tiny fragments; Parliament refused and insisted on the removal of de la Pole from his position and even demanded his impeachment.

After initially dismissing Parliament's request out of hand - Richard initially said he would not dismiss so much as a scullion (a servant) from his kitchen on Parliament's command - he soon realised that he had been outmanoeuvred and he had to give into the demands of the 'Wonderful Parliament' of 1486. He grudgingly relieved de la Pole of his position and slinked, full of resentment, out of the capital to embark on a tour of the country. While he no doubt wanted to get far away from the men who had humiliated him, the tour

King Richard II of England rides over to placate the rebels after Tyler's death

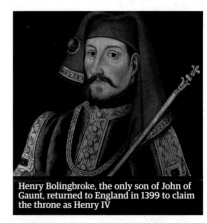

Henry Bolingbroke, the only son of John of Gaunt, returned to England in 1399 to claim the throne as Henry IV

Life in the time of Richard II

Duelling for honour

Honour among knights and noblemen was extremely important and often the way that disputes wold be settled was by a duel. In 1398 a remark made by Bolingbroke, the future Henry IV, was believed to have been treasonous by the Duke of Norfolk so the two agreed to a duel, but Henry was banished to France to avoid bloodshed.

Two popes

In 1378 a papal schism began that would split the catholic church and see two rival popes; Urban VI in Rome and Clement VII in Avignon. Both these popes were supported by different countries and the conflict was eventually resolved in 1418 with the Council of Constance which saw the election of Pope Martin V, although tensions continued afterwards.

A peasant's life

In England during the Middle Ages, most peasants held very few rights and lived in serfdom – this is where they worked a lord's lands for the right of protection and to farm it themselves. Following the Black Death, many peasants had been paid to work on the land and seen their status improved, but they were worried these new rights would be taken away and were prepared to fight to keep them.

The Hundred Years' War

This conflict, which actually lasted 116 years, began in 1337 when Edward III declared himself king of France. Richard did not win any major battles in the conflict and the taxation required to pay for the war was one the reasons for his unpopularity. In 1396 he signed a 28-year truce with Charles VI and married his seven-year old daughter to forge an alliance.

Great men

While the king was the ultimate authority, during Richard II's reign there were many great men who had considerable land, power and access to troops. Five of these men – the Duke of Gloucester and Earls of Arundel, Warwick, Derby and Mowbray – formed the Lords Appellant and effectively ruled England for a brief period in 1388.

also had a more practical purpose: to try to shore up his support throughout the nation and ensure that, if it came to it, plenty of nobles and barons would offer him military support.

A battle between these two opposing sides did take place in 1387 but, for Richard at least, it was as an anticlimax. The king had instructed one of his favourites, Robert de Vere, to raise an army and come to his aid, but this force was met by men loyal to Parliament on one of the bridges of the river Thames in what is called the Battle of Radcot Bridge; in truth, it was barely a skirmish. The men who had been summoned to Richard's aid found they would be unable to cross the bridge and had no hope of winning against the troops commanded by Henry Bolingbroke (this would not be the last time that he played a key role in Richard's life) and so their options were to surrender or flee. The 16th Century chronicler Raphael Holinshed wrote that only three people were killed at the battle and de Vere escaped and went into exile in France.

The king now had no choice if he wanted to keep his crown but to agree to Parliament's

> Richard was born on the religious feast day of Epiphany – thought to be a good omen, so great things were expected of him

demands and it was around this time that Robert Tresilian, the chief justice, was found hiding in a house in a ramshackle disguise and was taken to be hanged. Many of the king's men were either killed or exiled as his circle of favourites was ruthlessly broken up in what was called the Merciless Parliament of 1388. Despite having his power base shattered, the authority the King of England wielded was still strong and when, in 1389, the steadying hand of John of Gaunt returned and Richard declared himself old enough to rule without advisors and secured a peace treaty with France, the signs were positive. It looked as if the conflict that had disturbed the country could just be a blip in Richard's rule, but this was a mere illusion – Richard believed that God had placed him on Earth to rule and he never forgot how Parliament had challenged his authority or executed and exiled his chosen men. He would bide his time before he reminded them of the supreme authority of the king.

This fragile peace was built on a house of cards and by the end of the 1390s came crashing down

William Shakespeare's Richard II

The great bard is believed to have written his play *Richard II* in 1595 when Queen Elizabeth I was the monarch of England. The work only encompasses the last two years of Richard's reign, from 1398 to 1400, and is loosely based on the actual events, with the main source believed to be Raphael Holinshed's *Chronicles*. As with all Shakespeare plays, it is primarily a work of fiction and the context of when it was created is important. The play was written towards the end of Elizabeth I's life and reign and so was influenced heavily by the idea of succession and the authority of rulers. It has been claimed that the queen complained that the play was being performed numerous times in streets and houses, which would indicate that she thought that the people were already preparing for the next ruler while she was still on the throne.

Shakespeare's interpretation of Richard II is perhaps the most widely known as he is a monarch not often studied or examined. The play depicts him as a king who believes that God put him on the throne, and a man who went too far by taking land that didn't belong to him and seeking revenge on those he thought had wronged him. So, it isn't actually too far removed from the truth.

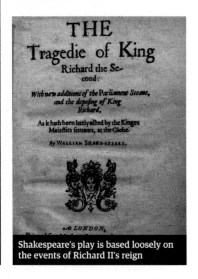

Shakespeare's play is based loosely on the events of Richard II's reign

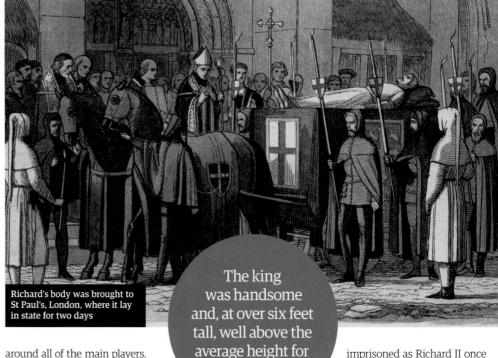

Richard's body was brought to St Paul's, London, where it lay in state for two days

> The king was handsome and, at over six feet tall, well above the average height for the time

around all of the main players. The king began to rule in an increasingly tyrannical manner, abusing his power to grab land for himself and his followers and, in 1397, he had three of the leading men arrested - officially it was because of a plot, although no evidence was found, but in reality this was all about revenge; the three men - the Duke of Gloucester and the Earls of Arundel and Warwick - had been key components of the parliament that had dared to take him on. They and others who had opposed him were either executed, exiled or imprisoned as Richard II once again began to build up a power base of those whose loyalty lay exclusively with him.

The king finally went too far when on 3 February 1399 John of Gaunt, his uncle and one of his most loyal supporters, died. John's son, Henry Bolingbroke, had been banished to France, in part because Richard saw him as a threat. Henry was from the house of Lancaster and his father had controlled some of the largest landholdings in the country. However, rather than let Henry return to England and inherit what was his, Richard decided

Defining moment
Peasants' Revolt 1381

Heavy taxation, partly caused by the Hundred Years' War, and a general dissatisfaction with living standards, leads to a serious popular uprising known as the Peasants' Revolt. A large body of people led by Watt Tyler and others march on the capital and kill those associated with the government, including the archbishop of Canterbury and the treasurer of England. Richard's actions during this crisis are brave, as he rides out to meet the rebels and calm them by agreeing to their demands. When the immediate crisis has been averted, the rebels are dealt with severely and none of their requests is met.

Timeline

1367

● **Birth of a king**
Richard is born in Bordeaux, France to Edward – a skilled military commander known as the Black Prince – and Joan of Kent, described as "the most beautiful woman in all the realm of England."
1367

● **Passing of the Black Prince**
Richard's father Edward dies after contracting an illness while on a military campaign in modern-day Spain, meaning that Richard is now the heir to the throne.
1376

● **A new monarch**
Edward III dies aged 65 after a long illness which had left him inactive for a number of years. His grandson is crowned Richard II.
1377

● **The king weds**
Richard marries Anne of Bohemia, daughter of the Holy Roman Emperor Charles IV. The marriage is for diplomatic reasons, but Richard appears to have genuine affection for his wife.
1382

● **Wonderful Parliament**
Not wonderful for Richard, Parliament had grown tired of the king giving patronage to his own men and the high levels of taxation and so refused a request from the chancellor to levy more money.
1386

● **Tour of the country**
Richard leaves London to travel the country to shore up his support after his defeat to Parliament and to ensure that, if required, the nobles would provide him with military support.
1387

to seize the land for himself and his supporters. This showed to the nobility of England that if the king would do this to such a powerful family then none of them was truly safe.

Henry returned to England with a small force while Richard and most of his knights were in Ireland and, while at first Henry insisted that he was only interested in reclaiming his birthright, it soon became clear that Richard had little support and Henry's campaign was gathering momentum. When the king landed in Wales in July it was clear his kingdom had been lost; neither the nobles nor the people would fight for him. Richard met with Henry and promised to abdicate if his life was spared; he was soon transported to the Tower of London and Henry Bolingbroke was crowned Henry IV on 13 October 1399. The country had a new king.

The man who had once been ruler but had thrown it all away by pursuing vengeance was transported to Pontefract Castle in Yorkshire and placed under close guard. Richard may well have eventually been allowed to live out the rest of his days in exile but when a plot to reinstate him to the throne by his closest supporters was discovered, it was clear he was too dangerous to be left alive. Historians disagree on the exact nature of his death, with opinion being divided as to whether he was starved to death or murdered in his cell, but it is thought that he died in early 1400. Richard had believed in the ultimate authority of the king, but this very belief led to him eking out his final days in a dank, dark cell far away from the throne.

Richard had no children with his first wife and his second wife was only seven years old when they married

A depiction of the dramatic death of Richard II

Defining moment
Battle and defeat 1387

All trust between Parliament and Richard has now evaporated and so the king instructs Robert de Vere to raise troops and march to London. This small force is met on one of the bridges crossing the river Thames by some men commanded by Henry Bolingbroke, who will later become Henry IV. When the force loyal to the king sees that they will not be able to cross the bridge, most of them refuse to fight. De Vere manages to escape to France, but the defeat for Richard leads to control of the county briefly passing to five great magnates known as the Lords Appellant, and the Merciless Parliament where many of the king's key men are killed or exiled.

Defining moment
Losing a kingdom 1399

After the death of John of Gaunt, one of the country's most powerful landowners, Richard takes the estate of the duchy of Lancaster. Following his actions in the Revenge Parliament, many of the nobles are wary of the king and they see that if he can take the land of one of the country's most prestigious estates then the same thing could happen to them. John of Gaunt's son Henry Bolingbroke has previously been in France, but returns with a small force to claim what is rightfully his. Henry receives support from other nobles and, with the king and most of his knights in Ireland, is able to claim the crown for himself.

1400

A new dawn?
Now aged 21, Richard declares himself to be ready to govern in his own right without advisors and blames the problems on the past in the bad advice he had been given. A fragile domestic peace emerges.
1389

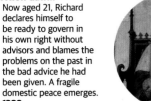

Peace with France
The English king meets with Charles VI of France and they agree to a 28-year truce. Anne, Richard's first wife, died in 1394 and as part of the accord he marries Charles's daughter Isabella.
1396

Revenge Parliament
Proving that he has not forgotten Parliament's actions in the Wonderful and Merciless Parliaments, Richard exiles and murders many leading nobles who had previously opposed him. Their lands and wealth go to the king and his leading men.
1397

Surrender
Richard gives himself up while staying in Flint Castle in Wales and is imprisoned at the Tower of London on 1 September. Henry Bolingbroke is declared king and the fourth of his name.
1399

Ignominious end
Richard is taken to Pontefract Castle as a prisoner, but when a plot by his supporters to kill Henry and restore him to the throne is uncovered it's clear he is too much of a threat. There is still debate as to the exact manner and date of Richard's death.
1400

Rebel sigil
Much of Hotspur's forces - most noticeably the archers - were recruited from Cheshire, an area hostile to King Henry due to its loyalty to the former king Richard II.

Royal forces
The victory at Shrewsbury was a decisive one for King Henry, marking the end of the biggest challenge to his reign and giving his rule a welcome degree of credibility.

Ruthless fighting
The fighting between the two sides was brutal and fierce, with former allies being forced into battle with each other. Amid a near constant hail of arrows, the death toll was heavy on both sides.

Hotspur

Hotspur was killed after being brought down in a last-ditch charge aimed at killing the king. In the melee that followed, no one knows who struck the decisive blow.

HENRY IV
England, 1367-1413

Brief Bio

The tenth king of England from the House of Plantagenet, Henry seized control from Richard II but found his own reign plagued by other upstarts, eager to do for him what he had done for the previous king: depose him, preferably violently. In the Battle of Shrewsbury he saw off a challenge from the fiery young Henry Hotspur, son of Henry Percy, the First Earl of Northumberland.

1399-1413
Henry IV

The story of a king on an unstable throne, and how the close-fought Battle of Shrewsbury eventually legitimised his rule

Perhaps ironically considering that his reign began with the seizure of the crown from the sovereign monarch, Henry IV of England's kingship was an insecure one. He was beset by rebellions from those who were either dissatisfied with his rule, believed themselves to be more credible claimants to the throne, or who saw the precedent that he started as part of a new status quo; one that allowed for the strongest to seize power, with birthright having been reduced - by virtue of Henry's original rebellious act - to a mere technicality.

The event that came the closest to putting a premature end to Henry's rule was the Battle of Shrewsbury, the culmination of a rebellion by the Percy family: chiefly Thomas Percy, the Earl of Worcester; his elder brother Henry Percy, the Earl of Northumberland; and his nephew, Henry 'Hotspur' Percy. Having assisted Henry with his successful overthrow of Richard II in 1399, the Percys found themselves increasingly dissatisfied with Henry's rule, in large part to his refusal to lend them sufficient funds to defend their lands against the Scots in the north (due to the parlous state of the royal treasury) or to grant them additional titles or lands, with one noteworthy sticking point being when the king gave the justiciarship of Wales - previously in the possession of Northumberland and Hotspur - to his son, Prince Henry, the future Henry V.

Allying themselves with Owen Glendower, the Welsh leader who was in open rebellion against English rule at the time, Hotspur gathered his forces from nearby Cheshire - including a large force of archers - and marched south towards Shrewsbury, where he planned to meet forces led by Northumberland and Glendower. However, Henry heard about the attack, and immediately mobilised his forces, sending a small force ahead to hold the town, along with a group led by Prince Henry, while the rest of his army marched towards Shrewsbury from the east. When Hotspur arrived, not only did he find the town held against him, but with the king coming from the east, he was caught between the town, the nearby river and an army, effectively cutting him off from Glendower's reinforcements and leaving him with little choice but to choose a place of attack.

With the primary aim of the rebels being to kill Henry himself, he disguised two knights in his own attire as diversions. Even with this clever precaution, however, the battle was closely fought, with the rebels getting the better of the early stages thanks to the devastating attacks from their archers, which decimated and scattered the royal vanguard. Despite this, a two-pronged attack from father and son turned the battle in their favour, forcing Hotspur into a desperate last-ditch charge at the King that resulted in his own death.

With the rebel leader dead and his surviving forces fled, the most serious challenge to Henry's rule was at an end. His rule had been legitimised, and his son's military prowess, later to achieve legendary status at the Battle of Agincourt, became clear for everyone to see. The Earl of Northumberland would later make another attempt at rebellion in the Battle of Bramham Moor in 1408, which also resulted in his defeat and death.

Royalists

TROOPS	14,000
INFANTRY	12,000
ARCHERS	2,000

HENRY IV OF ENGLAND
LEADER

Having usurped Richard II as king of England, Shrewsbury would prove to be the biggest challenge to his rule.
Strengths Strong and capable.
Weakness Unable to mobilise as many men as he'd have liked.

DISGUISED KNIGHT
KEY UNIT

One of Henry's strategies was an attempt to focus enemy attention elsewhere, prompting him to disguise two knights as him.
Strengths An effective decoy for the king.
Weakness Only effective as long as they're alive; potential for enemy to see through the ruse quickly.

SWORD
KEY WEAPON

The standard weapon for the royal infantry, it was interchangeable with other pole-type weapons, like bills or daggers.
Strengths Highly versatile.
Weakness Required high amounts of skill to wield effectively.

01 Spies observe Hotspur at Berwick Field

Hotspur based his army on a low hill in a predominantly open area sown with peas. The pea stems were wound together in order to trip up advancing horses and men.

02 The king marches

Henry and his army marched in formation, divided into two battalions: the vanguard (including the archers) were led by the Earl of Stafford, with the king in charge of the main army, and his son Prince Henry joining with another force from the south.

03 Final attempts at negotiations

Henry offered the rebels a chance at safe conduct if they could work things out, but the Earl of Worcester, sent in Hotspur's stead, refused to negotiate.

04 Initial assault

The Stafford-led Royal vanguard led the assault. Despite incurring heavy casualties from the rebel archers, the vanguard managed to engage them in contact after the archers ran out of arrows, thus sapping their strength. Regardless, the king's men were beaten back and retreated, with Stafford being killed in the process.

05 Henry attacks

With much of the vanguard either killed or deserted and the rebel forces pressing the attack, it fell to Henry to lead the assault. On his mark, his trumpeters gave the signal for the main bulk of his army to charge, with Henry leading the assault, meeting the rebel forces at the bottom of the slope. The fighting here was especially fierce, with the king being the main target of the rebels' attacks.

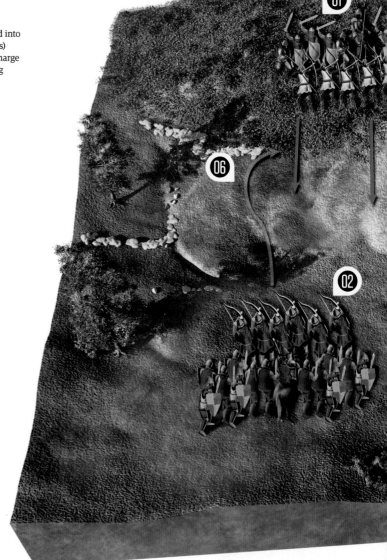

06 Prince attacks on flank

At the same time as the main assault, the king ordered Prince Henry to attack Hotspur's army on the flanks in order to divert the destructive archers from the main force. The attack went well, weakening Henry's forces and decimating the archers. However, the prince was grievously injured when an enemy arrow struck him in the face and penetrated his skull just below his visor, although he would ultimately recover from this wound.

10 Rebels retreat

Leaderless and conscious of the lack of mercy they would receive in a land in which they were now defeated traitors, the rebel forces fled, with the wounded left behind being dispatched by the royalist forces.

09 Hotspur killed

Although they mowed down many men, Hotspur's charge was gradually slowed among the masses, and he was cut down from his horse and killed. The rebels initially thought they'd killed the king after slaying his standard bearer, but Henry revealed himself to proclaim that "Harry Percy is dead."

07 Hotspur charges towards the king

With his forces rapidly diminishing and archers faltering under the two-pronged assault from the royalist forces, Hotspur decided that desperate times called for desperate measures. After gathering 30 of his most trusted men, including the Earl of Douglas and his uncle, the Earl of Worcester, they mounted their horses and charged directly at Henry's men, with the aim of cutting the king himself down.

08 Dunbar orders king to fall back

In the nick of time, Henry's close ally, the Earl of Dunbar, realised what was about to happen. Subsequently, he shouted at the king to fall back, which he did, in the process narrowly avoiding being caught up and killed in the inexorable charge of Hotspur and his men.

Rebels

TROOPS 14,000
INFANTRY 13,000
ARCHERS 1,000

HENRY 'HOTSPUR' PERCY
LEADER

The primary leader of the rebel forces, Hotspur led his forces into battle against the king.
Strengths Well-trained archers.
Weakness Lacking expected support from Glendower and Northumberland.

ARCHERS
KEY UNIT

Large quantities of archers comprised both forces, but it was arguably Hotspur who used his to the most effect.
Strengths Devastating in large numbers.
Weakness Vulnerable once arrows have been used up.

BOW AND ARROW
KEY WEAPON

A weapon that has lived on in folklore, at short range arrows could penetrate armour, and had a killing range of about half a mile.
Strengths Long range and difficult to defend against.
Weakness Requires large supply of arrows.

1413-1422

Henry V

Discover how the Battle of Agincourt proved to be King Henry V's defining moment

While his father, Henry IV, had been preoccupied with consolidating - and in the process effectively legitimising - his rule, his son, King Henry V of England, saw the opportunity to expand England's empire by taking back lands which he believed belonged to him, starting with France.

In 1415, he proposed to marry Catherine, the daughter of the French king Charles VI, in addition to audaciously demanding the handover of the Plantagenet lands of Normandy and Anjou as his dowry. Unsurprisingly, Charles refused this offer from the upstart young king, with one account claiming that he sent the young Henry a case of tennis balls - the upshot being that his time would be better spent playing games than attempting to invade France.

Unperturbed, Henry set sail for France, determined to capture the throne for himself. As well as the prospect of regaining the lost lands of his ancestors, success abroad would have the effect of galvanising support back home, and in the process focus attention away from his cousins' royal ambitions.

His success was almost instant. Upon landing, he captured the port of Harfleur, although while on the way to the port of Calais, he found his path blocked by an army that substantially outnumbered his own. Faced with this much-larger French army, he nonetheless put his tactical acumen to good use, decimating the French forces via the use of vast quantities of longbow archers to devastating effect. Between 7,500 and 10,000 French soldiers are estimated to have been killed according to various accounts, with about 1,500 noblemen taken prisoner, while the English forces' casualties are numbered at around 112, with high-ranking noblemen like the Duke of York and the Earl of Suffolk being counted among the dead. Even more French prisoners were originally taken, but in a show of calculated - but arguably justifiable - ruthlessness, Henry had ordered many of them to be put to death in order to avoid the possibility of them linking up with the remnants of the French forces.

Proving that this was no fluke, Henry followed up this stunning victory with the conquest of Normandy - a campaign that lasted for three years. By June 1419, Henry controlled most of Normandy. Agincourt had not only been a military triumph; it had been a moral victory too, galvanising the English both abroad and at home.

Facing defeat, Charles agreed to the Treaty of Troyes, which formally recognised Henry as the heir to the French throne - at the expense of his own son - and finally allowed Henry to marry Catherine. Flushed with success, in February 1421 he returned to England for the first time in three and a half years as a hero. His successful conquest of much of the his country's hated enemy had made him a hero back home, and the Battle of Agincourt in particular would forever serve as a poignant example of his strength and ingenuity in battle - yet another example of the plucky underdog spirit and ability to triumph against the odds that future British forces would demonstrate again and again.

Front line
The English front line consisted mainly of dismounted knights and men-at-arms. Out of shot, archers were posited either side, hiding in the woods that bordered the battlefield.

King Henry
Unlike the French king, Henry personally led his troops into battle. He was a king first and foremost but never stopped being a warrior - even on his deathbed he insisted on being carried to the next siege.

Crown
Unlike his father, who used decoys at the Battle of Shrewsbury years earlier, Henry's affixing of a crown on top of his helmet made sure he stood out. The crown was damaged in the battle after he took an axe blow to the head.

Prayer
While lined up for battle, Henry led his troops in prayer, asking for God to grant them victory against the French forces.

HENRY V
England, 1386-1422

Brief Bio The hero of the Battle of Agincourt, Henry V believed that France was legitimately his and set out to get it, despite being heavily outnumbered. He achieved a decisive victory, winning lands and the hand of the king's daughter in marriage, but his early death curtailed his vision of an entirely English France.

English

TROOPS 6-9,000
LONGBOWMEN 5,000
KNIGHTS/MEN-AT-ARMS 1,000

KING HENRY V
LEADER

The King was a skilled battle commander, leading his troops into battle and fighting alongside them.
Strengths Brave and experienced military leader.
Weakness His forces were numerically inferior to those of the French aggressors.

LONGBOWMAN
KEY UNIT

The effectiveness of the English longbowmen played a massive part in the success of the battle.
Strengths Long range and difficult to attack.
Weakness Relatively poorly armoured and vulnerable if attacked.

LONGBOW
KEY WEAPON

The longbow's six arrows per minute could wound at 400 yards, kill at 200 and even penetrate armour at 100 yards.
Strengths Accurate and destructive in large numbers.
Weakness Finite number of arrows available to them.

01 Camping for the night
On 24 October, about 30 miles from Calais in the town of Frévent, English scouts reported that an immense French army was blocking the road ahead. Seeing that they could not pass without meeting them in battle, Henry ordered his forces to camp there for the night.

02 Taking their positions
The English positioned themselves across the road to Calais in three groups of knights and men-at-arms: the right side led by Lord Camoys, the left by Sir Thomas Erpingham and the Duke of York in the centre. The French had the Constable of France leading the first line, the Dukes of Bar and d'Alencon the second and the Counts of Merle and Falconberg in charge of the third.

03 Forward banners
Bored of waiting for the French to begin the attack, Henry ordered his troops to advance. Once within range of the French archers, the English troops halted, the divisions closed, and the archers set a series of pointed stakes in the ground, forming a fence. Within the woods surrounding the two armies, Henry directed groups of archers and men-at-arms to move through the trees to get closer to the French.

04 Arrows away
Shortly after, Henry gave the order for his archers to shoot the French, who were massed together in a big, unwieldy group. Taken by surprise, the French forces incurred very heavy casualties.

05 French attempt to move forward
After the shock of this assault, the French forces tried to advance in order to take the battle to the English. However, having already suffered massive casualties, they were impeded by the dead and dying horses and men already shot down in front of them. Reduced to walking pace, they were easily picked off by the English archers concealed in the woodlands on the flanks.

10 French camp ransacked
With the battle over and any local resistance crushed, the English troops ransacked the largely abandoned French camp, having secured a victory that would live on in legend.

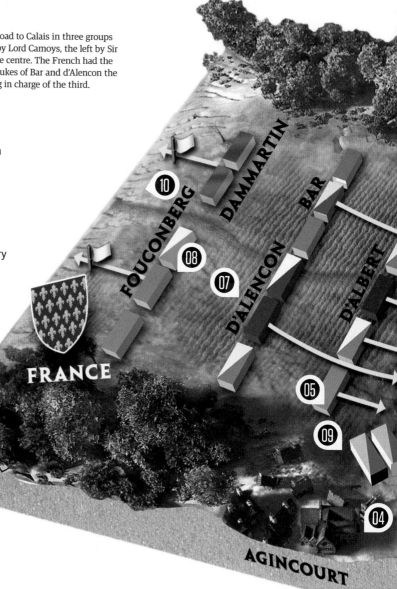

06 Archers join the fray and flanks
With the battle continuing along the fence of stakes, the English archers abandoned their positions and joined the knights in fighting against the French cavalry forces – most of which had been forced to dismount – which were reinforced by soldiers attacking on the flanks.

09 Local French force attacks baggage

Although the main battle was over, it threatened to reignite when a local French force circumvented the forest and attacked the English baggage. Fearing the substantial amount of prisoners would rebel and join this assault, Henry ordered them executed – which many were, until the attack was repelled.

France

TROOPS 12-36,000
CAVALRY 1,200
KNIGHTS 8,800

CHARLES D'ALBRET
LEADER

The former Constable of France co-commanded the French army alongside Jean le Maingre.
Strengths Experienced soldier.
Weakness Low social rank, so orders were ignored by noblemen.

KNIGHTS
KEY UNIT

Much of the French forces consisted of heavy infantry, making them tough adversaries in open combat.
Strengths Heavily armoured and effective at hand-to-hand fighting.
Weakness Slow, cumbersome and easy to pick off by enemy archers.

HORSES
KEY WEAPON

Large numbers of knights on horseback often presented a fearful sight for their opponents.
Strengths Fast and powerful opponents in battle.
Weakness Cramped and boggy location made them useless.

TRAMECOURT

CAMOYS

YORK

HENRY

ERPINGHAM

ENGLAND

MAISCONCEUES

07 French second line moves forward

The French second line, led by D'Alencon, moved forward in earnest to assist the beleaguered first line, but was overwhelmed in a similar fashion. Seeing the futility in continuing, he attempted to surrender to Henry, but was killed before he could reach the king.

08 Third line retreats

Seeing the fate that had met the first and second waves, the third line of the French forces waited on the edge of the field, pondering whether to join. After being greeted by a messenger sent by Henry, who informed them that if they joined the battle, none of them would be spared, they made their decision. Unsurprisingly, considering their options, they left the battlefield.

1422-1461 & 1470-1471

Henry VI

Gentle Henry VI witnessed the end of the house of Lancaster and the rise of the house of York

Some kings were born warriors, others were seasoned in battle, but there have been a few, like Henry VI, who weren't just ill-suited for conflict, they also weren't suited for the crown. As an obsessively pious, honest, quiet and gentle man, Henry VI failed to inspire that all-important conquering spirit that had come so naturally to his predecessors.

Henry VI, born 6 December 1421 in Windsor Castle, was the only child of King Henry V and Catherine of Valois. The infant was handed the mantle of king at just nine months old on 1 September 1422, and once news had spread across the channel that his mother's father King Charles VI had died, he was also proclaimed King of France. After swearing an oath of loyalty in 1423, Henry's nobles established a regency council to govern until he came of age. Henry V's brother John, the respected Duke of Bedford, was appointed as senior regent of the realm and the supervising authority on the ongoing conflict in France. In John's absence Henry V's other surviving younger brother Humphrey, Duke of Gloucester was appointed protector and defender of the realm in England. Just before his eighth birthday, Henry was crowned King of England, in retaliation to the French crowning his rival, Charles VII Valois, in Reims. It wasn't for another two years, however, that Henry was taken to Paris and crowned King of France at Notre-Dame Cathedral.

> Henry was considered shy. He shunned music and sport, preferring to bury his nose in scriptures and ancient chronicles

Henry's appointed council ran England rather effectively for nearly 16 years on his behalf, before he took over the reins in 1437. At the start, as throughout his reign, he was never seen as a natural leader and his shyness and charitable spirit were perceived as weaknesses by his critics. His religious ethics and strong moral compass gave Henry distaste for war, and it was at this time that the Hundred Years' War against the House of Valois in France began to lose momentum on the English side while the French were starting to make a powerful resurgence. In 1445, as a more peaceful step forward, a 23-year-old Henry married 15-year-old French noblewoman Margaret of Anjou, the famously beautiful niece (through marriage) of Charles VII. Although not known by the English Parliament and public at the time, the union had come at the expense of the French territories Maine and Anjou, a very controversial decision that would later spark discontent at court, particularly from Henry's uncle, the Duke of Gloucester and Richard, Duke of York, who were already vocal opponents of Henry's decision not to pursue the war in France. In 1446 the exchange of Maine and Anjou became common knowledge and the earl of Suffolk, who had negotiated the marriage arrangement, bore the brunt of the public's wrath. Possibly due to Henry believing rumours that his uncle (and then heir) was plotting against him, Suffolk had the Duke of Gloucester arrested for treason, but he

Henry failed to show a prolonged interest in government, allowing his wife and closest advisors to make decisions on his behalf

Henry VI's shyness and charitable spirit were observed as weaknesses by his critics, as was his distaste for war

Life in the time of Henry VI

Meanwhile in Scotland

In April 1424 the ransomed James I of Scotland finally returned home to claim his throne after being detained at the English court for 18 years. During his time as hostage he received a solid education, became an accomplished musician and poet, as well as excelling as a skilled sportsman.

French resistance

Joan of Arc cemented her place in history, becoming the heroine of France and a Roman Catholic saint, by taking part in the siege of Orleans after receiving visions of several saints telling her to recover France from the English. Sadly for her, the English captured, tried and burnt her at the stake in 1431, aged around 19.

The end of one war...

From 1337, the house of Plantagenet, rulers of England, fought a series of wars against the house of Valois for control of France. The 116-year conflict, which became known as the Hundred Years' War, finally ended on 19 October 1453 after the French reclaimed Bordeaux, leaving England with only Calais and the Channel Islands.

...and start of another

Just two years after one huge war ended, another began. The War of the Roses was a series of dynastic battles for the throne of England, between two rival branches of the house of Plantagenet – Lancaster and York – ending 32 years later in 1487.

Colours of war

The Yorkists invented their white rose first, as a symbol of light, purity and glory, whereas the Lancashire red rose was adopted later, following the Battle of Bosworth in 1485 where the last Yorkist king, Richard III, was defeated. Henry VII then combined the two symbols to make the Tudor rose.

HENRY VI
England, 1421-1471

Brief Bio
As an obsessively pious, benevolent and peaceful man, Henry VI was not suited for war. Sadly for him, as the last of the Lancastrian rulers, his reign was dominated by conflict. Periods of mental instability consumed the king, requiring his wife Margaret of Anjou to take control, an important factor that contributed to his and his house's downfall.

died suddenly in custody. The Duke of York, seen by many as next in line to the throne, was sent to govern Ireland, thereby removing him from court and disabling his opportunity to conspire. These decisions, plus the breakdown in law and order, widespread corruption, troubled crown finances, the steady loss of territory in France, and a public hate campaign against the royal favourite Suffolk

led to a colossal level of discontentment across England. When Suffolk was charged with treason by Parliament, Henry agreed to have his friend sentenced to five years' banishment. However, Suffolk's ship was intercepted by a privateering ship in the Channel and he was beheaded as a traitor.

By 1449 most of Normandy, which had been arduously won by Henry's father only a few

decades before, was lost, and less than a year later French forces had reclaimed the whole province. An agitated and restless army of men, many of whom hadn't been paid, returned home, causing widespread lawlessness across the south that later ignited a rebellion in Kent, led by John Cade. The rebels successfully duped and ambushed the king's forces in the Battle of Solefields near Sevenoaks, before eventually breaking into London. The fracas only lasted a few days, however, as the city's residents grew weary of disorder and helped the king's army reclaim the city.

By 1453 the struggle of sovereignty was starting to take its toll on Henry, with the dual reign, rebellion, conspiracies, infighting, nationwide discontentment and, to top it all off, the loss of Bordeaux, England's only French territory after Calais. On hearing of the defeat, the king suffered a mental breakdown, leaving him prostrate and unresponsive for over 17 months. Historians claim Henry suffered from hallucinations and religious delusions, possibly symptomatic of schizophrenia or a congenital psychiatric condition he may have inherited from his mother's father, Charles VI of France, who was notoriously also affected by bouts of insanity. Although the queen and her most trusted advisors had done their best to play down the king's condition at the beginning, alarm bells quickly rang throughout court when the king failed to respond to the birth of his son and heir, Prince Edward. This was the opportunity Richard Duke of York, had been waiting for. On being made protector of the realm in 1454, he

Henry VI with Richard the Duke of York, heir apparent to the English crown, and Somerset

> The king was not a man of fashion and preferred plain clothes instead of fancy ornate robes and upturned shoes

Defining moment
Henry's coronation 1429 and 1431

On the 6 November 1429, Henry VI is crowned King of England, a month before his eight birthday. The urgency is due to the rival house of Valois crowning Charles VII in Reims, France shortly before. Two years later Parliament decides it is time for Henry to cross the Channel and be crowned as King of France. The ceremony is carried out in Paris's Notre-Dame on 26 December 1431. Henry is now the sovereign ruler of two countries, a responsibility that will weigh heavy on him and ultimately take a toll in later life.

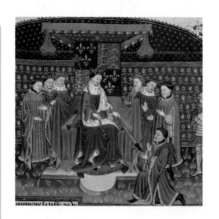

Defining moment
Champion of education 1438-41

Some kings are power-hungry warlords, others are obsessed with improving with the crown's finances, but if Henry VI has an overriding passion it is education. One of his lasting legacies is his achievement in propelling education forward in his kingdom, first founding All Souls College, Oxford in 1438, followed by Eton College in 1440 and King's College Cambridge a year later in 1441. Henry's wife Margaret shares this passion and founds Queens' College, Cambridge in 1448. Each year on the anniversary of his death, the heads of the colleges at Eton and King's lay their respective floral emblems of white lilies and roses on the spot in Wakefield Tower at the Tower of London, where legend has it Henry was murdered as he knelt to pray.

Timeline

1422

● **Becoming king**
War hero King Henry V dies of dysentery while on military campaigns in France, leaving his nine-month-old son and heir Henry to ascend to the English throne.
1422

● **Marriage to Margaret of Anjou**
Enjoying a springtime wedding at Titchfield Abbey near Fareham on 23 April 1445, Henry VI takes the beautiful adolescent Margaret of Anjou – eight years his junior – to be his wife and queen.
1445

● **A power play for the future**
In 1452 Henry makes his half-brothers Edmund and Jasper Tudor earls. When Edmund dies, his 13-year-old widow is pregnant with the future King Henry VII. Jasper is a loyal servant to Henry and Margaret, constantly striving to help their son Edward claim the throne. He later helps to win the crown for his nephew Henry Tudor.
1452

"Civil war broke out between the Yorkist and Lancastrian factions"

allied with Richard Neville, earl of Warwick, later known as 'the Kingmaker', an incredibly rich and powerful man who, due to disagreements with the queen, had previously been excluded from court. Rumours, thought to be created by York's and Warwick's supporters, circulated that Edward wasn't Henry's son. By Christmas of that year Henry had returned to his senses, but it was too late. Many previously disaffected nobles had risen to power in his absence and were now championing a campaign to reinstate the house of York to the throne, claiming the Duke of York was a superior descendant of Edward III.

Civil war, known later as the War of the Roses, broke out between the Yorkist and Lancastrian factions. The Duke of York led his camp, while Queen Margaret took charge of the Lancastrian side. The Yorkists claimed a huge victory in July 1460 when they captured Henry, but the war was far from over and on the last day of that year Richard of York was killed at Battle of Wakefield. Henry was rescued by his troops but later deposed in the spring of 1461 by the Duke of York's eldest son, the charismatic Edward of York, whose forces crushed the Lancastrian army at Towton on 29 March; on 28 June he was crowned Edward IV. The former queen fled into exile with Henry, who after spending time in captivity was now suffering prolonged bouts of insanity. Safe behind the Scottish border, Margaret kept up Lancastrian resistance with many nobles in Northern counties of England and Wales remaining loyal to Henry.

In July 1465, Edward recaptured Henry and swiftly imprisoned him in the Tower of London. But Henry's wife, who was still in exile in Scotland and then later France, refused to give up. Margaret's chance for revenge appeared when Edward quarrelled with his two strongest allies: his younger brother George, Duke of Clarence and the 'Kingmaker' earl of Warwick, over his controversial secret marriage to Elizabeth Grey (née Woodville) in 1464. Clarence and Warwick formed a secret alliance with Margaret under coercion of King Louis XI of France in a deal that would see Henry VI restored as King of England and Margaret's son Edward marry Warwick's daughter Anne.

Warwick returned to England with a powerful army and forced Edward IV into exile. The earl restored an ailing Henry to the throne in 1470 but due to the king's severely deteriorated mental state, served in his stead. Henry's return was short-lived, lasting less than half a year, as Warwick overplayed his hand launching into a war with Burgundy, whose ruler then supported Edward IV. Edward returned from exile and on 14 April 1471 defeated Warwick at the Battle of Barnet. The Yorkists' final blow was to demolish the king's forces at Tewkesbury on 4 May, where Henry and Margaret's only son lay among the dead.

Henry was imprisoned once again in the Tower of London, where he suffered a violent death on the night of 21 May 1471. There is little doubt that it was on Edward IV 's authority, since his younger brother Richard (later Richard III) and other lords were in the building at the time.

Originally buried in Chertsey Abbey, Henry's body was moved in 1485 to St George's Chapel, Windsor Castle

Shakespeare's portrayal

120 years after King Henry VI's macabre death in the Tower of London, famous English playwright William Shakespeare began writing his trilogy of plays about the life of the gentle king. As well as featuring heavily in *Henry VI Part 1*, *2* and *3*, as you would expect, the king makes a cameo appearance as a ghost in *Richard III*. The three plays focus more on Henry's personality, life and the conflicts he faced, but fail to mention his legendary bouts of mental instability. As mental illness was considered a great taboo, it's thought Shakespeare's reason for omitting this fact was to avoid the wrath of the volatile Queen Elizabeth I whose family descended from Henry's Lancastrian line. Shakespeare instead colours the character of Henry VI as a pious, peaceful man, simply not suited to the role of king. Henry is seen to yearn for religion and education, expressing a desire to be any one else but the monarch. As the play develops over the three parts, he is portrayed as progressively weak-willed king who is easily walked over, emasculated by his wife and railroaded by his critics and aggressors.

The English king Henry VI in 1445, with his consort Margaret

An heir is born
Henry VI's son Prince Edward is born on 13 October 1453 at the Palace of Westminster. Henry is said to be largely unaware of or unimpressed by the birth, due to his mental instability.
1453

Imprisonment and freedom
Not a good year for Henry, as he is taken prisoner at Northampton in July and imprisoned until New Year's Eve, when his wife's forces finally overpower the Duke of York, who is killed in battle.
1460

Recapture
Henry is recaptured by King Edward IV and imprisoned in the Tower of London. It is here during his five-year-long stay that Henry's mental state erodes considerably.
1465

Mental breakdown
On hearing the news that Bordeaux has been taken by the French, Henry VI falls into a 17-month-long depressive stupor that some historians argue was the first of many schizophrenic catatonic states.
1453

York gets the upper hand
While the king is suffering from a long period of depression, Richard Duke of York is promoted as protector of the realm. This is his first step of many in taking down the house of Lancaster.
1454

No longer a king
A victory for the Yorkists in March 1461 at the Battle of Towton allows the Duke of York's eldest son Edward to become King Edward IV. Margaret and Henry escape to Scotland.
1461

Return to power
Like a puppet on a string, Henry is reinstated to the throne after Warwick, with Margaret's backing, returns to England and forces Edward IV into exile. Warwick rules in Henry's name.
1470

Death
Edward IV returns to conquer England in 1471. The new king imprisons Henry for the last time. Henry suffers a violent death during the night of 21 May.
1400

1400

© Alamy

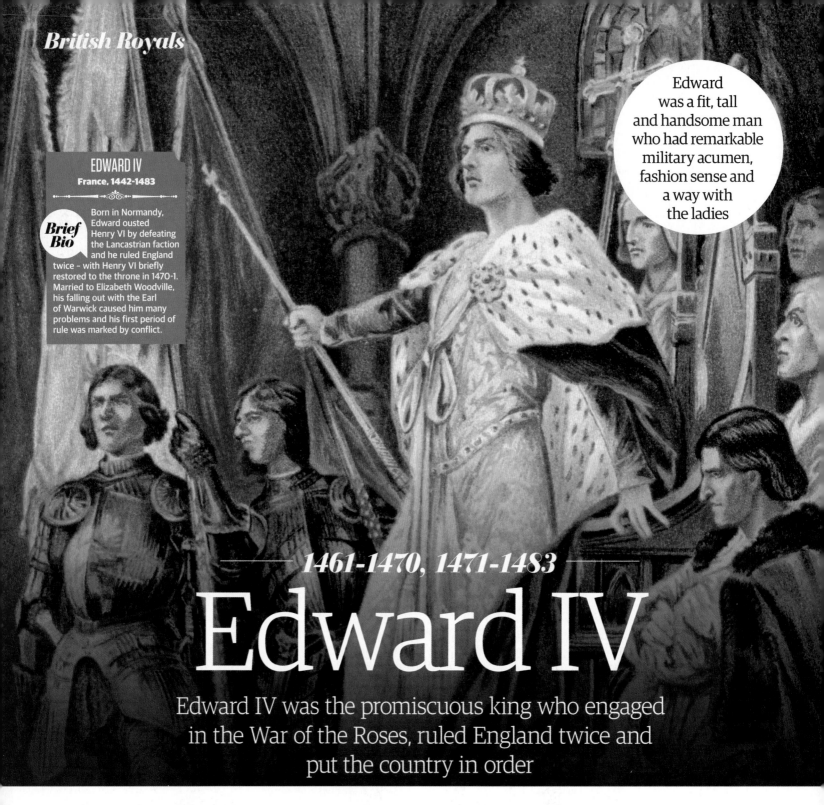

Edward was a fit, tall and handsome man who had remarkable military acumen, fashion sense and a way with the ladies

1461-1470, 1471-1483

Edward IV

Edward IV was the promiscuous king who engaged in the War of the Roses, ruled England twice and put the country in order

Edward's father, the Duke of York Richard Plantagenet, had long asserted his own claim to England's throne. As a consequence, he had battled hard against King Henry VI and it had led to civil war between Richard's Yorkist and Henry's Lancastrian factions in what was to become known as the War of the Roses.

Richard was killed at the Battle of Wakefield in 1460 and Edward, an able commander, took on the conflict aided by the Earl of Warwick, Richard Neville. In 1461, Edward defeated the Lancastrians at the vicious Battle of Towton and this resulted in Henry and his queen, Margaret of Anjou, fleeing to Scotland. With them out of the way, Edward was proclaimed king, aged 18, on 4 March 1461. Edward IV was crowned on 28 June that year at Westminster Abbey.

With the house of York established on the English throne, the Earl of Warwick began to exert his powerful influence over the king. Although Edward was a tall, physically fit man who exhibited great military acumen, it was Warwick who led the Yorkists into successful battle against Lancastrian resistance from 1462 to 1464 and it was he who, thanks to a victory at the Battle of Hexham, had captured Henry VI and saw him imprisoned in the Tower of London.

But Warwick became angry when Edward married widow and commoner Elizabeth Woodville in secret. The discontent grew deeper when Edward began to bestow favours on Elizabeth's family. Warwick fell out with Edward, believing the king's decision to be rash and flying in the face of attempts to create a strong Yorkist nobility. He

also resented the rise of the Woodville family. To make matters worse, Edward was not only ruling well but pulling in the opposite direction to Warwick's wishes. Things came to a head in 1467 when Edward concluded an alliance with France's enemy Burgundy - just as Warwick was trying to tie up relations with France.

With Warwick's power diminished, the earl forged an alliance with Edward's brother George, Duke of Clarence and an army was created to fight against the king. Part of the king's army suffered a swift defeat at the Battle of Edgecote on 26 July 1469 and Edward was subsequently captured. For the next few weeks Warwick tried to rule through the king but it caused unrest, forcing the release of Edward by mid-September. The rebellion having failed, Warwick and Clarence fled to France.

Peace would not last long, though, and Edward would again be troubled when Warwick made peace with Margaret of Anjou and returned to England with an army in September 1470. Edward had little choice but to flee to the Low Countries. Henry VI was then restored to the throne while Edward sought refuge in Flanders.

He bided his time until he was able to gather an army and, with his brother Richard, Duke of Gloucester, he fought a heavy battle in Barnet, defeating and killing Warwick. This was followed by the defeat of Margaret at the Battle

of Tewkesbury in May 1471 and the slaying of Lancastrian heir Prince Edward. Henry VI was killed in the Tower of London.

Edward ruled once more and took on the second part of his reign with relish, bringing greater prosperity to England. He began the rebuilding of St George's Chapel in 1475, the same year in which he declared war yet made peace with France by setting in place a lucrative agreement with Louis XI at Picquigny which earned him £15,000 plus an annual pension of £10,000.

Edward was also taking greater financial control, reducing the crown's debt with astute management of the royal revenues and the building of close ties with the merchant community. Under Edward, the crown did not need to depend on parliamentary subsidies and it was becoming self-sufficient.

England flourished. Edward patronised William Caxton's printing press in Westminster in London and he collected Flemish manuscripts.

What's more, he heralded a peaceful time - although his brother, George Duke of Clarence, with whom he had a falling out, was murdered in the Tower of London in 1478. Since the Lancastrian line had been largely extinguished and there were no further rebellions, law and order was being established.

But in the 1480s, ill-health struck, partly as a result of contentment which had caused this once slender man to put on a lot of weight. In March 1482 he caught a cold while fishing on the Thames in Windsor and it is believed that it developed into pneumonia. Louis XI took advantage of this and revoked Edward's pension. Had Edward not been so poorly, he would have fought against this move but, on 9 April he died aged 40 and his body was buried in the foundations of St George's Chapel.

Edward was survived by eight of his ten children (Margaret of York died aged eight months and George Plantagenet, 1st Duke of Bedford at two years). Edward also had several illegitimate children thanks to his numerous affairs with mistresses. While his young son briefly succeeded him in 1483, as Edward V, all of his children were declared illegitimate by Parliament in 1483. This was at the behest of Richard, Duke of Gloucester, who seized the throne to become Richard III.

> Edward had a cultured outlook. Upon his death, his collection of books formed the basis of the British Library

Edward IV was proclaimed king at age 18, after defeating Henry VI in battle, but later fell out with some of his allies

Life in the time of Edward IV

People were reading
William Caxton's printing press was backed by Edward IV and it was able to churn out a host of books like never before, making them cheaper and more readily available. Poems, grammars and mythical tales were popular and, as a result, the literacy rates of Englanders began to rise.

Trade was booming
Although traders within England were already enjoying a buoyant, more stable economy, especially in the second half of Edward IV's reign, the king reconfirmed an agreement with the Hanseatic League, a sort of medieval Northern European Common Market, and this brought trade concessions.

They liked to play cards
Just not foreign ones. In 1463, a ban was placed on the importation of foreign playing cards because England wanted to protect its own manufacturers. Up until that point they were being brought in from France. As time went on, cards became crucial to Christmas festivities.

Life could be torture
Prisoners were not treated well and to extract confessions from them, torture was routine. The first recorded use of the rack was in 1468; the device stretched the imprisoned as they lay on the rectangular wooden frame, so that their cartilage, ligaments and bones would pop as the torturers pulled hard on the handle.

The English would riot
There was a sense of political injustice in England and riots would break out if there was just cause. When Edward was imprisoned and Warwick tried to control England, an uprising ensured sufficient pressure was put on the earl to let him go. Power to the people!

War of the Roses
Fought between 1455 and 1485, the War of the Roses involved the rival royal houses of Lancaster and York - identified by the colour of their roses, red and white respectively. Both factions were descended from King Edward III but the ruling King Henry VI (a Lancastrian) was unpopular, mainly due to the loss of French lands during his reign. This resulted in a rebellion by supporters of Richard Duke of York; in 1461 his son took the throne as Edward IV. Richard III was the last king from the house of York. Henry Tudor defeated him in 1485, paving the way for the house of Tudor to rule.

Edward's coronation never took place, making him one of only four uncrowned English monarchs since the Norman Conquest

EDWARD V
England, 1470-1483

Brief Bio Remembered as one of the two 'Princes in the Tower', Edward's reign lasted less than three months and was overshadowed by his uncle's desire to claim the crown, culminating in Edward's imprisonment in the Tower of London and, many suspect, the murder of him and his younger brother, Richard.

April 1483 - June 1483

Edward V

How a boy-king's short reign, marred by infamy, treachery and murder, would echo down the centuries

King for just 86 days of a kingdom that never really became his, Edward V could easily have become little more than a forgettable footnote in royal history, were it not for his part in a story that would be remembered as one of the British monarchy's most infamous and enduring mysteries.

The son of King Edward IV and his queen consort Elizabeth Woodville, Edward's early years were shaped by a routine of his father's design. This dictated everything from the hours in which he was educated to the types of stories he was read and the people he might be surrounded by. Under the guidance of his maternal uncle, Anthony Woodville, the king's regime seemed to produce the desired results, with chroniclers of the time reporting the young prince to be polite, charming, educated beyond his years and well versed in literature. With such a positive foundation laid during his childhood, the tragedy of Edward's story is only heightened when considering the type of king he might have grown to become.

Granted the title Prince of Wales as an infant, Edward spent most of his life at Ludlow Castle as

Richard III declared the princes to be illegitimate, leaving him as the rightful heir

titular ruler of Wales and the Welsh Marches, and it was from here that he travelled to London upon the death of his father on 9 April 1483. In his will, Edward IV appointed his brother Richard, Duke of Gloucester as Lord Protector to assist the young king until he was old enough to take on the mantle of ruler. Richard's personal ambitions, however, far exceeded the role of advisor-to-the-king, and as soon as his brother died and Edward began the journey to London, he set plans in motion that would ultimately secure the crown for himself.

Upon reaching Stony Stratford at the end of April, Edward and his entourage were met by Richard, Henry Stafford - Duke of Buckingham and distant cousin of the new king - and an armed escort. The atmosphere was friendly, but the next morning Richard ordered the arrest of Anthony Woodville and several other members of the young king's group and had them taken north, where they were later executed at Richard's command. Edward protested, but was taken into custody by his uncle and continued on to London. Edward's mother, sisters and younger brother Richard, Duke of York, sought sanctuary at Westminster Abbey upon hearing the news of the Duke of Gloucester's actions, fearful that the king's brother had decided to seize the crown for himself and the danger that posed to their safety.

Edward IV had been popular with the people, who were in turn loyal to his son, and acting against the new king could have turned public opinion against Richard had he not managed to calm concern at this apparent and unexpected grab for power by branding the Woodvilles traitors, claiming they had been conspiring against him and the realm's nobility. Arriving at the Tower of London, Edward took up residence in the Garden Tower (later renamed the 'Bloody Tower'), which, given its role as both a royal residence and a prison at the time, was in itself no cause for suspicion. His brother was taken from Westminster Abbey and joined Edward in the Tower, where they would await a coronation that, thanks to their uncle's schemes, would never take place.

With the princes contained within the Tower of London, Richard's plans to claim his late brother's crown proceeded. At a meeting of the Regency Council in June, Richard had William Hastings, a close friend of Edward IV who it is thought might have opposed any attempt to disinherit the princes, arrested and executed without trial. Claims were also made in a sermon outside old St Paul's Cathedral that the princes were not true heirs, owing to the fact that prior to his marriage to Elizabeth Woodville, Edward IV had been contracted to marry Lady Eleanor Butler (née Talbot). His marriage to Elizabeth was therefore invalid, rendering their children illegitimate. With no apparent legitimate heir, and Edward IV's second brother George having been executed for treason in 1478 - and attainted so that his heirs forfeited all rights to the throne - this suggested that Richard, Duke of Gloucester, was in fact the rightful heir to the crown. Having considered these claims, Parliament declared Richard to be the legitimate king and he was crowned Richard III on 6 July.

Throughout this period, the princes were seen little, with only occasional glimpses of them playing in the Tower's gardens and the visits of Edward's physician, John Argentine, to attest that they were still alive at all. But following Richard III's accession, they disappeared from public view completely, presumed by many to have become the victims of their uncle's ambition.

> Edward's uncle, George, was found guilty of treason against Edward IV and executed by being drowned in a barrel of malmesey wine

Edward and his brother Richard lived at the Tower of London until their disappearance

The mysterious disappearance of the princes

What happened to Edward and Richard?

No one knows for sure as their bodies were never found, but over the years a number of possible scenarios have been proposed to explain the fate of the princes...

Richard III killed them

Richard is generally considered the most likely culprit. Despite successfully disinheriting his nephews of any claim to their father's crown, the only way to be sure they could pose no future threat to his rule would have been to have them killed. With a clear motive, access to the princes and the power to silence any that might have objected, the case against Richard is strong, to say the least.

Henry Stafford, Duke of Buckingham, killed them

As an ally who supported Richard III since the arrest of Edward's uncle, Anthony Woodville, it's possible that Stafford killed the boys under Richard's orders. But, as a distant cousin of Edward V, their deaths might also have presented a possible route to succession for Stafford himself. Stafford later rebelled against Richard and was executed in November 1483.

Henry VII killed them

Henry Tudor defeated Richard III at the Battle of Bosworth Field in 1485 and was crowned king, marrying (and legitimising) Edward IV's daughter, Elizabeth. If the princes were still alive, their legitimacy would also have been reinstated, so Henry may have had them killed to prevent any future challenge to his crown.

Sir James Tyrell did it

A trusted subject of Richard III, and the man portrayed by William Shakespeare as the organiser of the princes' murder, James Tyrell confessed in 1502 to killing the boys under Richard's orders, but the confession is now considered unreliable, given that Tyrell was being tortured for treason at the time.

They weren't murdered

Some suggest Edward may have become ill and died, though if this were the case, Richard III would have had nothing to lose by revealing this and absolving himself of suspicion in their disappearance. Other rumours claim one or both princes may have escaped the Tower.

Death in the Tower

Serving as both royal residence and prison over the centuries, the Tower has more than a few bloody tales to its name, with the Garden Tower in particular, where Edward and Richard lived (and presumably died), later becoming known as the Bloody Tower. Built in the early 1220s, the Garden Tower also played host to, among others, King Henry VI's death in 1471 (thought to have been murdered under Edward IV's orders), the alleged suicide of Henry Percy, eighth Earl of Northumberland, in 1585, and the poisoning of courtier and poet Sir Thomas Overbury in 1613.

1483-1485

Richard III

The last Plantagenet king to hold the English throne, Richard III was one of the few individuals who did as much before his reign as during it

Despite a reign that only lasted two years (one of the shortest in British history), Richard Plantagenet had a profound effect on the realm. Raised in the feudal conflict that was later named the War of the Roses, Richard spent most of his life battling to both attain power *and* defend it, an experience that moulded him into a brilliant strategist and someone who always led his military campaigns into battle. Some called him a cruel tyrant, while others saw him as a focused progressive who fought long and hard to strengthen the realm and the House of York's hold on the English crown. He's a monarch surrounded by myth and legend, both in regard to his physical appearance and whether he had a hand in the supposed death of the Princes in the Tower. Little wonder he has fascinated historians for over 700 years.

Born on 2 October 1452, Richard was the son of Richard Plantagenet, third Duke of York and his wife, Cecily Neville. Despite being fathered by a man with a significantly strong claim to Henry VI's throne, Richard was way down the pecking order as the 12th of 13 children. The duke himself was deeply unpopular with the House of York's fiercest rival, the House of Lancaster – this also included Queen Margaret of Anjou, who held sway over the weak-minded king. Richard's father refused to renounce his claim and the dispute eventually culminated with a brutal clash at the Battle of Wakefield. Despite leading a sizeable military force, the Duke of York was killed on 30 December 1460, alongside his second son (and fifth child) Edmund, Earl of Rutland.

With his father dead and disgraced, Richard was packed off with his brother George to the Low Countries (modern-day Belgium and the Netherlands) while his eldest brother Edward (now fourth Duke of York) led a 30,000-strong army into battle with what remained of Henry's forces on 29 March 1461 at Towton. Edward's army destroyed the king's forces and upon hearing the news, the absentee monarch fled to Scotland with his family. Richard returned to England shortly after to see his brother crowned Edward IV. The Yorkists had returned to court and young Richard was about to be thrust into the middle of a new regime.

Edward's ascension to the throne was hardly the end of the conflict. The War of the Roses had really only just begun. After Edward's coronation in 1461, he made Richard Duke of Gloucester as well as a Knight of the Garter and a Knight of the Bath. In order to facilitate Richard's training as a knight and nobleman, Edward sent him to study under his cousin, Richard Neville, the Earl of Warwick. Warwick was one of the most powerful nobles in England and had been instrumental in providing the new king with the military strength he needed to take the throne.

In exchange for providing a place for Richard at his household in Middleham, Warwick organised marriages for both Richard and his brother George to his own daughters. Edward was against the idea and the disagreement drove a wedge between two of the most powerful men in the realm. George would eventually wed Warwick's daughter Isabel in 1469, leading him to side with his new father-in-law, while Richard refused the arrangement and placed his fealty in the king. That show of loyalty would bind Edward and Richard for the next two decades as the war began to escalate.

Warwick would prove to be a chaos factor in the lives of Richard and the new king. He eventually chose to defect and form an alliance with Margaret of Anjou, subsequently organising a number of rebellions to undermine Edward's reign. This discontent, in both civil unrest and propaganda in court, eventually forced Richard and Edward to flee to Flanders in May 1470. Richard accompanied Edward back to England a year later and the king

> Richard III had a great deal of affection for the north of England. He even co-founded the Council of the North

Richard's exhumation in 2012 revealed ten wounds to his body and eight to his head (the back of which had been shorn off)

RICHARD III
England, 1452-1485

Brief Bio His reign on the English throne barely lasted two years, yet King Richard III remains one of Britain's most talked about monarchs. His accession to the throne created a conspiracy that still baffles historians to this day, while his death signified the literal end of the Middle Ages in England. He may have been immortalised by Shakespeare's quill, but Richard's dramatic rule was all too real.

The Battle of Bosworth Field, near Hinckley in Leicestershire, was the last great skirmish of the War of the Roses and effectively brought the conflict to a close

appointed him as his main lieutenant. An already driven and aspiring military leader, the young Plantagenet led Edward's forces in the Battles of Barnet and Tewkesbury, where his use of a small but ruthless force led to the deaths of Warwick and the Lancastrian heir (and the former king's son), Edward, Prince of Wales.

Edward IV was keen to reward his brother's fierce loyalty and with Warwick out of the picture, Richard inherited most of his lands in Yorkshire. He was also appointed constable and warden of the north, positions of power that would slowly consolidate into a power base close to the one Warwick himself wielded before his defection. Richard rarely left the north for the next decade, tired of the politics and intrigue of his brother's court in London. The Lancastrian threat was largely extinguished after Edward's restoration, the only real claimant left being Henry Tudor who was exiled in France.

Edward fell gravely ill and died on 9 April 1483, but not before he named Richard lord protector of the realm and his son and heir, Edward. When Richard was informed of his brother's death and his new position as regent, he marched alongside the Duke of Buckingham in an armed escort bound for London. While on the way, Richard received word that a plot was being formed to assassinate him and remove the threat he potentially posed as the de facto ruler. According to his sources, Anthony Woodville, second Earl Rivers (Elizabeth's brother) was behind the plot, so Richard had him arrested (and later executed) as he made his way out of the north.

In order to protect the young king, Richard escorted him and his brother to the capital. At the beginning of June, Richard and the two young royals arrived in London. Under the guidance of his advisors, Richard placed the two boys in lodgings in the Tower of London to keep them safe. However, all was not what it seemed. In an ironic twist of fate, Richard was now concerned over the same matter that had consumed his former enemy, Warwick: the rise of the Woodvilles. He was certain the once

low-born family had had a hand in the plot to assassinate him and feared that Elizabeth and her allies would find a way to remove him from the equation and assume control over the young king. Something *had* to be done.

On 13 June, Richard called a council meeting at the Tower of London. While there, he accused William Hastings, first Baron Hastings, of plotting to use the princes as a means of usurping Richard's power and summarily had Hastings executed a few days later. Around this time a clergyman (whose name has remained a mystery ever since) informed Richard that Edward IV's marriage to Elizabeth Woodville had been invalid on the grounds Edward had been contracted to marry the noblewoman Lady Eleanor Talbot. If true, this claim would deem Edward and Elizabeth's children illegitimate, making Richard Edward's true heir.

By 22 June, sermons were already being preached that the uncrowned Edward V and his brother Richard were illegitimate. A few days later, the Duke of Gloucester was proclaimed the rightful heir by Parliament and he was crowned King Richard III of England in Westminster Abbey on 6 July. In order to solidify his claim to the throne, in 1484 Richard even had Parliament draw up the

Like many of his forebears, Richard was regarded as a valiant warrior and often led military campaigns from the front

Richard III (second from the left) and the Earl of Warwick (far right) were bitter rivals during Edward IV's conflict-ridden reign

For years historians believed Richard was killed by an arrow through the eye, but exhumation of his remains suggests he was struck multiple times at close range

Five facts from the reign of Richard III

A new tongue

One of the most fascinating changes Richard III made to his court was the introduction of English as its preferred language. The legacy of Roman occupation and William I's Norman invasion had instilled both Latin and French as its base lexicon, but Richard was determined to normalise it to his mother tongue.

Printing popularity

The arrival of printing in England towards the end of the 1400s had a profound effect on its population. Introduced by William Caxton, an English merchant, in 1476, the printing press allowed the mass production of everything from literary works to pamphlets. He was also one of the first to do so in English.

Population problems

Abandoned villages, towns and settlements were far from an uncommon sight in the mid to late 1400s. The Black Death had ravaged England at the beginning of the century, reducing the population by a third. Continued famine from failed crops and harvests also kept the population at a throttled low.

Agricultural changes

Continued bad weather wrecked many a crop in the late 1400s, forcing a significant change in the way Englishmen worked the land. Landowners struggled to find labour to till their land as workers spread to acquire smallholdings of their own. This period also saw the rise of enclosures as many farmers focused on pasturing.

Livery and maintenance

The War of the Roses had a huge effect on England, especially among its nobles. The breakdown of royal authority would lead lords and nobles to offer 'livery and maintenance', whereby a lower class would receive protection for wearing their colours (livery) and bearing arms for them (maintenance).

"In August 1485, news reached the king that Henry Tudor had arrived in West Wales with an army"

Titulus Regius, a legal document that confirmed him as the true successor to his brother's crown. After decades of warring against one king and working with another, Richard was finally the one sat on the throne. However, there would be little time to rest or recuperate. Rebellion was in the air.

Even though living in exile, the presence of Henry Tudor loomed large in Richard's mind. Despite the battles of Barnet and Tewkesbury severely wounding the House of Lancaster's hold in England, it still boasted allies and potential military outlets overseas and Richard knew it was only a matter of time before the Lancastrian upstart would rally enough support to land an invasion and challenge the king for his crown. So it was no surprise when Tudor's name began popping up amid rumours of a rebellion in late 1483. Reports suggest conspirators were in support of Henry taking the throne and marrying Elizabeth of

York (the older sister of the imprisoned, and now possibly deceased, Princes in the Tower), effectively forming a union that would end the costly War of the Roses. When Richard discovered that one of his trusted political allies, the Duke of Buckingham, had sided with the rebels, the king marched to meet them. The uprising had largely fallen apart - due to disintegrating support in the wake of military action and a storm that forced Henry Tudor to return to his exile in France - but it was an ominous glimpse into what was to come.

In August 1485, news reached the king that Henry Tudor had arrived in West Wales with an army of a few hundred men (most of whom were French mercenaries, rather than loyal English soldiers). Richard immediately began mobilising all of his forces, recalling every loyal noble with a standing military force to join his march on the Lancastrian incursion. As Henry moved through

Rebellion of 1483

A few months after Richard's coronation, a conspiracy was beginning to form among some of England's most disaffected nobles. The conspiracy was led by a handful of individuals, most notably Henry Stafford, second Duke of Buckingham. Buckingham had been one of Richard's most influential supporters and had been rewarded handsomely with lands and patronage. He'd played a part in the coup over the stewardship of the young Edward V and his brother, but many historians differ on what it was that led him to conspire against his king. Some argue that Buckingham may have possibly been involved in the princes' supposed deaths, while others believe that rumours of their fates turned him against the Plantagenet monarch. In an ironic twist of fate, Richard actually sent Buckingham to investigate rumours of a plot among his gentry in the south before the duke eventually chose to join it.

Buckingham began planning a coup with two of his main conspirators: John Morton, the Archbishop of Canterbury and Reginald Bray, a fellow disenfranchised noble. Their plan was to invite the exiled Lancastrian claimant Henry Tudor (later Henry VII) to take the throne with their financial and military support. It was an ambitious plan, and the sheer scale needed for its execution would be its undoing.

Richard was livid when he found out about Buckingham's involvement. On 12 October he penned a heated letter to his chancellor, stating: "resist the malice of him that had the best cause to be true, the Duke of Buckingham, the most untrue creature living." Whatever Buckingham's true motives for joining the rebellion were, his contribution would ultimately be for nothing. He was unable to drum up much support from the tenants living on his lands (especially in Wales) and considerable flooding in the south would halt much of the rebellion's progress. Henry had also sailed to meet the rebellion, but his ship hit a storm, forcing him to return to France.

Richard placed a reward of £1,000 on Buckingham's head as the uprising began to fall apart and the duke soon fled. He was eventually caught, tried for treason and beheaded on 2 November.

Propaganda was a key tactic in the War of the Roses. It was vital in undermining Richard's reign and amplifying the significance of his loss at Bosworth Field

Defining moment
Edward IV becomes king
4 March 1461

With the House of York reeling from the loss of the duke, his eldest son and heir Edward, the Earl of March, leads the charge against the Lancastrian forces and the two sides meet at the Battle of Mortimer's Cross in February 1461. Edward is victorious and marches on London, claiming the throne a month later. After driving back another force of Lancaster soldiers later that month, Edward is finally able to establish a Yorkist hold on the most powerful seat in England. With his brother crowned Edward IV in June, Richard is granted the title Duke of Gloucester five months later.

Richard's body was buried at Greyfriars, Leicester, but the friary was destroyed in 1538 during Henry VIII's dissolution

Timeline

1452

Richard is born
Richard of York is born at Fotheringhay Castle, Northamptonshire. He is the 12th of 13 children born to Richard, 3rd Duke of York and Cecily Neville. Richard is born with a pronounced arch in his back.
2 October 1452

The duke falls
When Richard is just eight, his father dies at the Battle of Wakefield, a decisive clash between Yorkist and Lancastrian forces. The death of the 3rd Duke sends a shockwave through the House of York.
30 December 1460

Gaining northern lands
His brother grants him territories across the land to preside over. Edward gives him lordships in Richmond (Yorkshire), Pembroke (Wales) and in East Anglia.
12 August 1462

Governor of the north
The first real position of power that Richard gains is the role of governor of the north. Richard holds a strong affinity for that part of the country and proves popular with its citizens.
2 October 1462

Constable of England
Richard's loyalty to his brother during these formative years of rule pays dividends. He is granted myriad titles during this time, including Constable of England and Lord High Admiral of England.
17 October 1462

Wales and across the border into England, his forces continued to swell with a number of supporters (including influential Welsh landholder, Rhys ap Thomas), adding more soldiers to his army – by the time he arrived in Leicestershire following a 200-mile march, his army was said to have increased to around 5,000 men.

The king and the pretender met on 22 August 1485 at Bosworth Field, just outside of Market Bosworth, Leicester (a city with which Richard III had close ties). The king brought with him 10,000-15,000 men and an arsenal of 140 cannons (one of the largest to ever grace a European battlefield) and the two armies met in a battle of incredible scale. Overlooking the scene was one of Richard's allies, Sir William Stanley, who stood behind the king's forces with a contingent of 6,000 men, watched the two armies clash and waited to see how the conflict would fare.

Despite Richard's superior forces, Henry's army began to turn the tide. With Richard's hold on victory beginning to slip, Stanley made his move. He led his 6,000-strong forces straight into the flank of Richard's army, routing it as Richard attempted to keep the Tudor forces' advance at bay. With his crown hanging in the balance, Richard (who had led his army from the front for the entirety of the battle) spied Henry watching the battle from across the field. In a last-ditch attempt to tip the scales, Richard charged across the war zone to meet his foe but was cut down before he reached him. Tests

> ## "With Richard's hold on victory beginning to slip, Stanley made his move. He led his 6,000-strong forces straight into the flank of Richard's army"

performed on Richard's exhumed remains in 2012 revealed that he received a blow to the head from behind, most likely from a halberd or a long sword. With the king dead, Stanley took the bloody crown from Richard's body and placed it upon the head of Henry Tudor, proclaiming him England's new king. The rule of the Plantagenets was over. The age of the Tudors had begun.

It seems as if Richard's reign was over before it even began, with only two short years on the throne. Nevertheless, in between putting down rebellions and fortifying his kingdom against a Lancastrian invasion, Richard was also responsible for a number of legislative changes that had a profound effect on his subjects. He was the first king of England to take his coronation oath in English, as well as ensuring all laws were published in English so that everyone could read them. He oversaw the enactment of the Land Tenure Act that protected landowners from having their lands stolen or sold by others and even introduced the system of 'bail' – a factor that forms a well-known role in our legal system today.

> Established in 1924, the Richard III Society aims to re-evaluate the historical interpretation of his actions and demeanour

The war with Scotland

One of the most interesting distinctions about Richard was that the amount of power and influence he had *before* he became king. In 1461, Richard's brother Edward became King Edward VI and in turn granted Richard the title of Duke of Gloucester. In the months that followed, Richard acquired a great deal of land in the north and with his brother relying on him more, he was made governor of the north. This effectively made him the most powerful noble in England.

Meanwhile, relations with Scotland were rapidly deteriorating. The Scottish king, James III, had learned that Richard's brother had given his permission for the duke to expand his holdings in the north into the south of Scotland. The threat of such a move and Richard's increasing power on the other side of the border boiled together with Edward's frustration over the failure of the Fotheringhay Treaty (a political arrangement to marry James's son to Cecily of York), leading James to declare war in 1480. Edward made Richard commander of a 20,000-strong army, leading to years of skirmishes, sieges and showdowns. Eventually the Scottish king sent his brother, the Duke of Albany, to agree a treaty with the king in February 1483.

Defining moment
Defeat and flight
13 September 1469
In November 1467, Richard Neville (Earl of Warwick) switches sides and joins the Lancastrian against Edward IV. This defection has catastrophic results for the king and Richard. The king has also become unpopular with large parts of the nation, leading his brother George (Duke of Clarence) to side with Warwick. The two eventually flee to France and orchestrate a series of uprisings against the king with an aim to place Henry VI (a former Lancastrian king) back on the throne. The rebels are successful and Edward and Richard are forced into exile.

Defining moment
Richard assumes control
6 July 1483
When Edward IV dies in 1483, he names Richard as Lord Protector of his 12-year-old son and heir, Edward V. Under advisement, Richard moves the princes to the Tower of London to keep them safe. In the meantime, some of Richard's allies propose the claim that Edward's marriage was not valid and that the Princes in the Tower are in fact illegitimate. It's not known if this is a plot engineered by Richard himself to undermine his brother's legacy, but key supporters in government help to add weight to Richard's rightful claim to the throne. With overwhelming support he is crowned king in 1483.

1485

● **Edward and Richard return from exile**
Edward and Richard land in England and reclaim York. From this northern base, and with Richard as his main military commander, Edward defeats the Lancastrians at the Battle of Barnet.
11 March 1471

● **Richard's power grows**
Following the disgrace of the Earl of Warwick, Richard takes control of most of his assets. He also marries Anne Neville which, collectively, makes him the second most powerful man in England.
May-July 1472

● **Buckingham's Rebellion**
In the first months of his reign, Richard confronts a rebellion led by former ally the Duke of Buckingham. Ultimately it fails and Buckingham is executed.
October 1483

● **Tudor propaganda**
While Richard would always find support in the North of England, his Lancastrian enemies continue to undermine his regime with skirmishes and incessant propaganda that undermine his rule.
April 1485

● **Battle of Bosworth Field**
The conflict with the House of Tudor culminates in a huge battle between the two sides. Richard leads the charge and is cut down. Henry Tudor becomes king.
22 August 1485

1485-1509

Henry VII

The king who won his crown through battle and had to fight throughout his reign to keep it, and so establishing the mighty Tudor dynasty

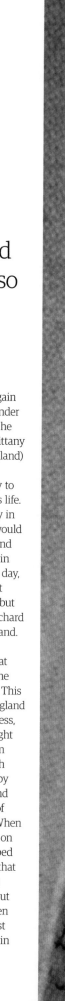

An invasion force set off from France and landed in Wales before heading into the heart of England itself. The year was 1485 and at the head of this ragtag army was a man who, for most of his 28 years on Earth had been on the run, had been constantly looking over his shoulder and unable to find peace. This man was called Henry Tudor and when he first set foot on the wet sand of Wales, he is said to have fallen to his knees and uttered, "Judge me O Lord and favour my cause." It was unsurprising that he was praying, for the odds seemed stacked against him; his claim to the throne was weak and the army of the king of England, Richard III, was much stronger than his own.

There were two reasons why the force landed in Wales - Henry wanted to remain undetected for as long as possible to give him time to build up support and it was also the land where he had been born in 1457, at Pembroke Castle. The man who would go on to found the Tudor dynasty was born to an earl and a countess and had a minor claim to the throne through his mother, Lady Margaret of Beaufort, a descendant of Edward III. Despite this tenuous royal lineage, by the early 1470s he was the main Lancastrian claimant remaining, as the War of the Roses - a battle for the crown between the houses of Lancaster and York that began in 1455 and saw the fortunes of the two rival houses ebb and flow - had resulted in the deaths of the rest.

When the course of the War of Roses changed again in 1471 with the reclaiming of the throne by the Yorkist king Edward IV, Henry fled to Brittany for safety. He would not set foot in England again for 14 years and this life of constantly being under threat, of never feeling safe, would affect how he ruled when he became king of England. In Brittany (a duchy independent of both France and England) Henry was under the protection of Francis II, who resisted Edward's attempts to send Henry to England and in the process probably saved his life. It was Edward himself who died unexpectedly in 1483 and Richard of Gloucester, who would become Richard III, took control and imprisoned Edward's two sons in the Tower of London. To this day, debate still rages about what exactly happened to them, but there was no doubt that Richard was now in control of England.

Richard was now king, but many were unhappy that Edward's sons wouldn't get the chance to succeed their father. This increasing political division in England meant that, after years in the wilderness, Henry was thrust back into the political spotlight with many believing he should assert his claim to the throne. This situation was managed with what would become typical political cunning by Henry, who announced that if he did return and become king then he would marry Elizabeth of York and thus unite the two warring houses. When he learned that Richard was exerting pressure on Francis to release his rival to him, Henry escaped to France dressed as a servant. It was in Paris that his supporters gathered around him and made their plans for an invasion of England and to put to an end to the Yorkist king who had only been sitting on the throne for two years. On 7 August 1485 Henry landed at Milton Haven Waterway in

> Henry and Elizabeth had eight children, but only four survived through to adulthood

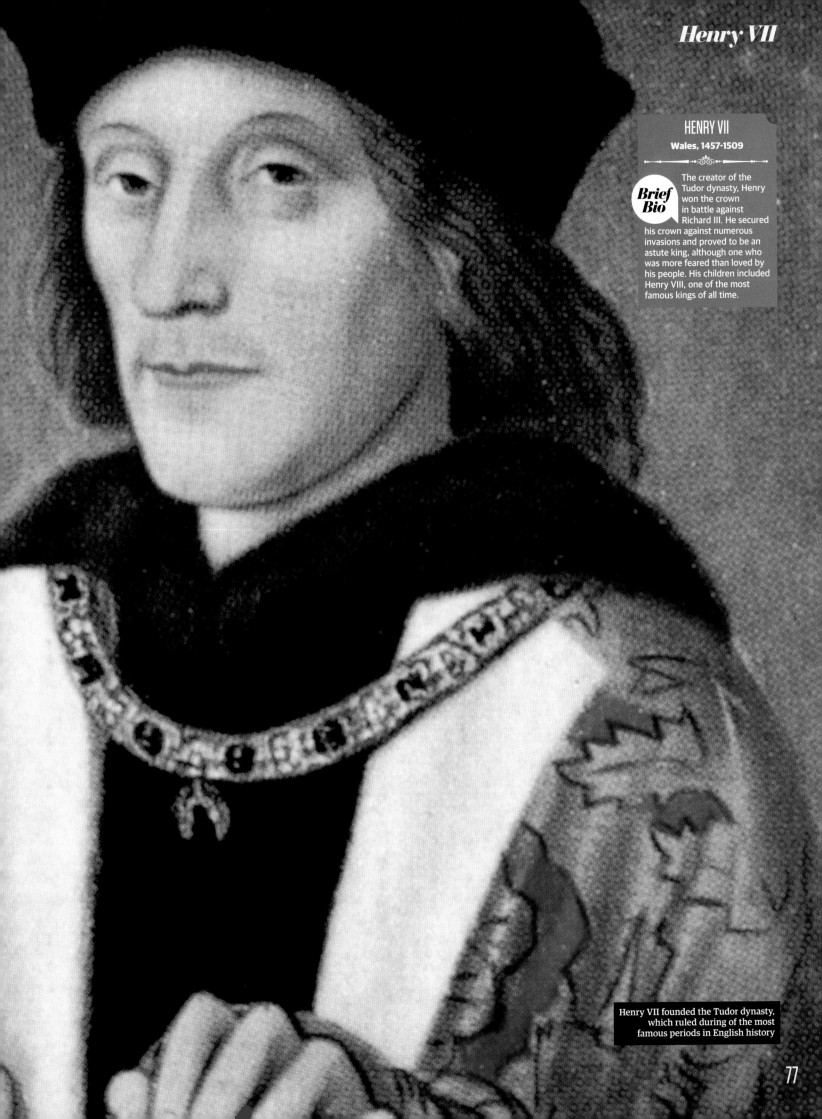

HENRY VII

Wales, 1457-1509

Brief Bio The creator of the Tudor dynasty, Henry won the crown in battle against Richard III. He secured his crown against numerous invasions and proved to be an astute king, although one who was more feared than loved by his people. His children included Henry VIII, one of the most famous kings of all time.

Henry VII founded the Tudor dynasty, which ruled during of the most famous periods in English history

Henry's father, Edmund Tudor, died three months before Henry was born

Henry was crowned king after defeating Richard III at the Battle of Bosworth

"Henry's forces were in danger of being overwhelmed when William Stanley threw his men into battle and instructed them to attack Richard"

Wales and said his prayer to God while kneeling on the wet sand of the beach.

Henry's invasion force didn't stay secret for long and soon Richard's larger army was in pursuit and eventually intercepted Henry's forces south of Market Bosworth in Leicestershire. On 22 August what would turn out to be the last confrontation of the War of the Roses took place as the two rivals met each other on the battlefield. Henry's forces were in danger of being overwhelmed when William Stanley, who had been watching from the sidelines, threw his men into battle and instructed them to attack Richard. This action by one of the most powerful men in the land was the decisive moment in the battle and the king of England was cut down, murdered by common men, battered to death and then stripped naked and taken to Leicester, where his dead body was exposed to

the public glare. Against all odds, the man who had been living in exile for most of his life had won. The crown was his, but Henry knew that if he had won it in battle then he could also lose it in battle. The struggle to keep hold of his crown and establish a legacy had only just begun.

All the years that Henry had spent in exile had robbed him of an intimate knowledge of the workings of a royal court, but had made him a sharp observer and his keen mind immediately grasped how important appearances were; it was not enough to just be king – he had to look, act and sound like a king. It is often said that history is written by the victors and following his coronation on 30 October, that is exactly what Henry did. He used his first parliament to change the date that he became king to a day before the Battle of Bosworth, thereby making Richard the attempted

usurper and ensuring that everyone who had opposed Henry could in the future be tried with treason. His marriage to Elizabeth of York, daughter of Edward IV, united the warring houses of the white rose of York and the red of Lancaster and led to the creation of a powerful symbol: the Tudor rose, which incorporated the two colours. He also commissioned the first ever pound coin, a gold sovereign with an image of Henry sitting on a throne in all his splendour on the obverse and a Tudor double rose on the reverse.

While these symbols were powerful propaganda tools, important in trying to legitimise the new Tudor rule, they were nothing compared to the importance of producing a male heir. So when, in 1486, Prince Arthur was born to Henry and Elizabeth, the new king could breathe a little easier. While the nation rejoiced at the birth of the prince, who had been named after the mythical king of Camelot, there were still those who weren't buying into Henry's image of the legitimacy of the Tudors. In 1487 a rebellion began in Ireland around a boy called Lambert Simnel who claimed to be the Yorkist Earl of Warwick, son of Edward IV's brother George, Duke of Clarence. The force invaded England but was no match for Henry's battle-

Bosworth remains as one of the most well-known battles in English history

Columbus's 'discovery' of the New World would change the face of European politics

Life in the time of Henry VII

Old enemies
France and England had a long history of conflict before Henry became king, such as the Hundred Years' War of 1337-1453. As Henry was first and foremost interested in securing his throne, he mostly pursued a strategy of peace with France but did launch a small invasion in 1492 which led to the Treaty of Étaples, the terms of which helped to swell Henry's coffers.

Power of the nobles
In England many noble families were very powerful and possessed land and armies that could potentially challenge the king. Henry used two main tools to limit their power: taxation and the Court of the Star Chamber. The court operated unusually quickly for the time and would act against those so powerful that ordinary courts wouldn't convict them. However, as its actions were carried out in secret, it could be used tyrannically by rulers.

The New World
In 1492 Genoan explorer Christopher Columbus (backed by Spanish money) landed in the New World, an action that would change the world forever. The discovery of a path from Europe to this new area would lead to many of the major European nations trying to colonise it and saw a raft of gold and exotic goods flood into the continent.

Money, money, money
Years of war with France had led to England being in severe debt and Henry worked hard to build up his own personal finances and that of the nation. He was personally involved in this aspect of government and his trade agreements and policies were designed to boost finances. By the end of his reign, tax revenues were significantly higher and Henry VIII inherited a far richer monarchy than many who had gone before him.

A new world power
The marriage of Ferdinand of Aragon and Isabella of Castile in 1469 began the process of uniting Spain as one country (although Aragon and Castile remained independent from each other in some ways) and increased its power. Spain would emerge as a powerful player on the world and international stage and a country that England had to be increasingly wary of.

---

hardened troops, who decimated the rival army at the Battle of Stoke. Simnel, who was merely a puppet in the plan, was pardoned by Henry. However, the fact that Henry had been forced into battle to keep his crown was a further indication that his place on the throne was not secure.

Just four years later, history repeated itself and Henry had to deal with another rebellion; this time a young man called Perkin Warbeck claimed to be one of the Princes in the Tower whom it was thought Richard had killed. This was a serious problem for Henry as he knew that much of his support had only come because of the disappearance of the two princes - while Warbeck's claim was widely discredited, it would provide a good excuse for people to rise up against him. Henry responded by setting up an extensive surveillance network, with spies across the country and the continent keeping a close eye on anyone who seemed likely to cause trouble.

Henry had always been a suspicious, even paranoid king, and with Warbeck's claim this only increased. The spying network was increasingly well funded and Henry's Privy Chamber, his personal space where he worked and slept, became harder to gain admittance to as the number of people whom he trusted decreased. The king became obsessed with two things: money and security. His style of government became increasingly personal, with his signature required for all substantial financial transactions. For Henry, money meant control.

When in 1497, Warbeck - who had been a constant thorn in Henry's side - was captured, and executed two years later, it was a vindication of the king's refusal to loosen his grip on government. However, with Warbeck killed and the king having been on the throne for more than a decade, he could begin to focus more attention on matters outside of the island nation and look to further legitimise his dynasty. Marriage alliances were a formidable diplomatic tool and Henry had given customary care and attention to whom Arthur would marry.

> By his death he had amassed a fortune that in today's money would be worth approximately £950 million

The Tudor spy network

John Morton was someone whose political support was fluid, to say the least; originally a Lancastrian supporter, he changed sides to the Yorkists before allying himself with Henry after his victory at the Battle of Bosworth. While Morton's loyalty could be called into question, his skills and talent could not. Henry needed capable men and appointed him to the prestigious position of Archbishop of Canterbury. Morton was then effectively given carte blanche to set up a spy and surveillance network which would report directly to the king and the king alone.

Henry had spies throughout Europe and also at home and these agents of the king were instructed to keep a close eye on those who might pose a threat. This spy network was especially helpful to the first Tudor king in the case of Perkin Warbeck, as it meant that Henry knew of the pretender's whereabouts and who his supporters were, and so could act accordingly. Indeed, it was through this network that he learned that William Stanley – whose army had effectively won him the crown at Bosworth – was plotting with traitors and so he was executed and his vast estates went to the king. Henry's spy network played a key role in enabling him to stay on the throne.

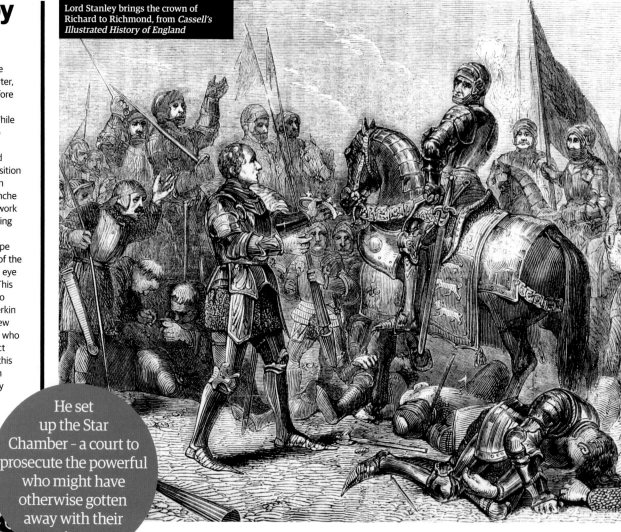

Lord Stanley brings the crown of Richard to Richmond, from *Cassell's Illustrated History of England*

> He set up the Star Chamber – a court to prosecute the powerful who might have otherwise gotten away with their crimes

A coin produced during Henry's reign - the king had a well-known love of money

Defining moment
Invasion of England
1485

Henry and a small invasion force, made up mostly of foreign mercenaries and exiled Englishmen, land in Wales and try to muster support. Henry's army eventually numbers around 5,000, but Richard III soon learns of its presence and Henry is forced to fight at Bosworth Field on 22 August. Richard's army gradually begins to grind down the opposition. However, when nobleman William Stanley instructs his forces to attack Richard, the tide of the battle turns. Henry is crowned king on the bloody battlefield and makes his way from Bosworth to the capital and his new throne.

The battle saw Henry's 5,000 troops take on an army that was almost double in size

Timeline

1457

- **Henry is born**
  The future king is born in Pembroke Castle to Edmund Tudor and Margaret Beaufort. The only drops of royal blood in his veins are through his mother's side.
  1457

- **Edward IV becomes king**
  When the Yorkist Edward regains the throne, Henry flees to Brittany, where he will stay for the best part of 14 years.
  1471

- **Princes in the Tower**
  When Edward dies, Richard places his two sons in the Tower – they are never seen again. Richard is crowned king but his actions mean that many don't support him.
  1483

- **Uniting two houses**
  Henry marries Elizabeth of York on 18 January 1486. This action unites the two warring houses of York and Lancaster.
  1486

- **Revolt**
  A group of Yorkists crown Lambert Simnel as Edward VI and land in England. Henry's army defeats them in battle in Stoke and so he keeps his crown.
  1487

"Henry, who normally had a strong poker-face, could not contain his grief and shut himself away for six weeks. He was mentally and physically exhausted"

He favoured a union with a Spanish princess, thereby uniting two enemies of France, and as far back as 1489 (when Arthur was just three) the treaty of Medina del Campo had betrothed him to Catherine, the daughter of Ferdinand and Isabella of Spain. By the time of Warbeck's death, Arthur was nearing the age when he could marry and so preparations for the lavish wedding could begin.

On 14 November 1501 the two were married by the Archbishop of Canterbury in St Paul's Cathedral. This was a momentous occasion for Henry; the wedding legitimised his rule, as it meant a foreign power such as Spain saw him as the true king and ensured that his dynasty would continue long after his death. The lavish two-week wedding celebrations turned London into a party city and all commented on how beautiful Catherine looked. Henry's joy would be short-lived, though, as mere months later Arthur contracted an illness and died, something that caused an immense political impact. Worse would come for Henry when in 1503 Elizabeth died nine days after childbirth, with the baby also not surviving. Many had supported Henry out of loyalty to Elizabeth and with her joining Arthur in the grave it seemed that the king's crown, which he had worked tirelessly to secure, was slipping through his fingers like grains of sand.

Henry, who normally had a strong poker-face, could not contain his grief and shut himself away for six weeks. He was mentally and physically exhausted, but when he returned to normal government life he was even more ruthless than before. He saw conspiracy theories everywhere and decided that if his subjects would not love him then they would fear him. He used a series of large financial bonds on leading citizens and merchants to ensure their good behaviour - for many the cost of betraying the king became financially impossible - as well as the Council Learned in the Law, possibly the most notorious expression of his rule. This council had unprecedented powers and was answerable only to the king. It could overrule normal legal proceedings to look at any cases it wished and was not above extorting money, either as a punishment or simply to swell the king's coffers. From 1503 the council was run efficiently and ruthlessly by Edmund Dudley, who later wrote that the king wanted, "Many persons in danger at his pleasure... bound to his grace for great sums of money."

Genuine fear and unease swept the country at this repressive regime, but Henry's dynasty was further secured thanks to a stroke of outrageous good fortune: in 1506 a ship carrying Philip the Fair of Burgundy was shipwrecked in England.

> The marriage of his daughter Margaret to James IV of Scotland meant their descendants would have a claim to both thrones

Henry ensured Philip had everything he wanted at the royal court, but through this thin veneer it was clear that Philip was effectively a prisoner until he agreed to release to Henry's care the Duke of Suffolk, who had been agitating on the continent for a rebellion in England. Philip agreed and when the boat containing Suffolk arrived, he was promptly escorted to the Tower of London.

In his last few years, Henry became increasingly ill and withdrew from public life. All eyes turned to his prince and heir Henry, who seemed to be very different from his father - where the king was cold and calculating, the young prince was a fine physical specimen interested in honour and chivalry. After the paranoid regime of his father, the people were looking forward to a more traditional king, but if it hadn't been for Henry VII's shrewd actions, there would have been no crown to pass down. When in 1509 the light in Henry was fading fast, he could reflect on a job well done: a man who had spent much of his early life on the run had won the English crown and been able to hold onto it. His people may have celebrated the passing of the penny-pinching king, but the fact that there was no opposition towards his son becoming monarch was probably his greatest achievement and one that was won through cunning, hard work, greed, ruthlessness and ambition.

Defining moment
Defeat of Warbeck
1497

Perkin Warbeck is a pretender to the English throne who claims to be Richard Duke of York, one of the Princes in the Tower. He first stakes his claim in 1490 in Burgundy and gains support from those who oppose Henry's rule. In 1491 he and a small force land in Ireland but receive little support and return to Europe. In 1495 he lands in Kent, but is soon forced to flee to Scotland. He is welcomed by James IV, but their attempted English invasion of 1496 soon fails. Captured after landing in Cornwall in 1497, Warbeck is eventually executed in 1499.

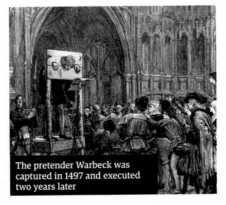

The pretender Warbeck was captured in 1497 and executed two years later

Defining moment
The king is dead, long live the king
1509

On 21 April, Henry, who has been suffering from an unidentified illness (now thought to be tuberculosis), dies at Richmond Palace and is buried in Westminster Abbey next to his wife Elizabeth. Henry leaves behind a prosperous country with money in the coffers and a number of successful peace and trade agreements. It is believed that on one of the last nights of his life he calls his son Henry to him and instructs him to keep the alliance with Spain strong by marrying Catherine of Aragon, the widow of Arthur. The mere fact that his son Henry enjoys such a peaceful accession to the throne, with no hint or rebellion or other candidates, illustrates what a good job his father has done to establish the Tudors as kings and queens of England.

1509

Namesake born
Elizabeth gives birth to their second son on 28 June. He will go on to become Henry VIII, one of the most famous British monarchs of all time.
1491

Intercursus Magnus
This trade treaty with the Netherlands, a key market for the export of British wool, is seen as one of Henry's most important achievements.
1496

Death of a prince
Arthur, Henry's first-born, dies just six months after his marriage to Catherine of Aragon. He is just 16 years old.
1502

Scottish union
Henry marries his daughter Margaret off to the Scottish king James IV. This is an attempt to end the fighting between the two nations and the marriage is part of an agreement called 'The treaty of Perpetual Peace.'
1503

1509-1547

Henry VIII

In pursuing dreams of victory in France, Henry threw England into decades of war and the chaos of a Europe in conflict

Henry VIII was born dreaming of war. When he took the throne in April 1509, with his bride Catherine of Aragon at his side, Henry knew exactly what kind of king he wanted to be. His would be a glorious reign that would restore England to the magnificence it deserved. His father, Henry VII, had become unpopular by levying punishing taxes to restore the country's finances, but the new king had no intention of focusing on matters as petty as the treasury. He would be a conqueror.

By the end of his life, Henry was a bloated and frustrated mockery of the athletic youth that he had once been. He had grown up jousting, riding and hunting, and would often participate in chivalry tournaments in disguise. He had grown up hearing the stories of the great Henry V – the hero of Agincourt – and had dreamed of the battles that years of peace had deprived him of. He was determined that he would repeat his ancestor's triumphs in France and expand England's territory beyond Calais – perhaps even as far as Paris. He wholly believed that France belonged to him and

"He had grown up with stories of the great Henry V – the hero of Agincourt – and dreamed of such battles"

- fortunately for the English monarch - he did not have to wait long to stake his claim.

Henry had grown up in years of stultifying peace thanks to his father's treaties with France and Aragon in Spain. Meanwhile, just across the Channel, the continent was in the throes of war. The powers of Europe clashed over the possession of Naples, essentially turning Italy into one big battleground. A quarrel over the region of Romagna had set Venice against the Vatican, and so Pope Julius II rallied France, the Holy Roman Empire and Spain (under Ferdinand II) in the final weeks of 1508, planning to split the Venetian territories among them.

Venice fell, but Julius feared French occupation of Italy. He mounted an impulsive attack on his allies which backfired as French forces stormed south in retaliation. A terrified Julius formed the Holy League, and Spain and the Holy Roman Empire sided with the papacy in 1511.

Henry VIII had now been on the throne for two years with his queen Catherine of Aragon (Ferdinand's daughter) at his side. A strong royal family was vital to his dream of a glorious England and he announced that he would marry her shortly after his father died. Catherine was fiercely loyal and determined to meet her king's expectations. She became pregnant almost immediately but their child was stillborn. It was a matter of weeks until Catherine was with child again, and she gave birth to a son, Henry, on New Year's Day, 1511. Sadly, Henry would survive for just seven weeks.

At this point, Henry was a young king just beginning his reign. He was the head of a proud royal family and he had shown his subjects that he

"Wolsey was the perfect right-hand man, able to counterbalance the king's violent rages with his own skilled diplomacy"

was not the penny-pinching tyrant that his father was. The Holy League would enable him to serve his God and show France the power of England's might. The full force of that might would be delivered by Henry's expanding Royal Navy, which would boast the world's largest and most advanced warships. It is important not to underestimate the importance of the pope's blessing. He was still a devout Catholic and would go on to condemn the Protestant Martin Luther so harshly that the pope would give him the title 'Defender of the Faith'. His religion also included the concept of Divine Right; France was his God-given property. The Holy League should have been undefeatable.

However, the first attack ended in disaster. An English force sailed to Gascony in June 1512, due to meet up with Ferdinand's army and claim the region of Aquitaine for Henry. Unfortunately, Ferdinand decided that he was more interested in claiming Navarre for

himself and directed his troops in that direction. Ill-equipped and ravaged by dysentery, the English troops were forced to retreat. Henry was furious but resolute.

Less than a year later, a second invasion plan was underway, with much of the organisation left in the hands of the invaluable Cardinal Thomas Wolsey. Wolsey was the perfect right-hand man for a king like Henry, able to counterbalance the king's violent rages with his own skilled diplomacy while sharing a similarly rabid ambition. Wolsey was a fixer; he made sure that whatever Henry wanted, Henry got. What Henry wanted was France, and so, in April 1513, an army was raised and an attack was made on Brest.

This incursion proved even more disastrous than the attempt on Aquitaine, but Henry would not be dissuaded and personally accompanied the English landing at Calais in June. With his feet on French soil and standing at the

THOMAS WOLSEY
English, circa 1475-1530

Brief Bio Cardinal Wolsey rose to power due to his ability to ensure that Henry got what he wanted. He was deeply ambitious and a skilled political operator. He became archbishop of York, and was made a cardinal and lord chancellor in 1515. He was instrumental in the peace process following Henry's first war in France, and often took public blame for Henry's mistakes. Wolsey's ambitions of becoming pope would be scuppered when Henry's determination to split from Catherine of Aragon destroyed England's relationship with Rome. Scrabbling to reconcile his position in Rome with his duty to his king, Wolsey's failure to deliver papal approval would prove to be his downfall.

Debacle at Gascony
June 1512

Henry's only concern prior to the expedition to Gascony was that he couldn't be there. It was the first attack on France during his reign and it should have been the first step in a glorious campaign. Henry was all too eager to ally himself with his father-in-law, Ferdinand II, who had similar ambitions to claim French territory. Both kings had joined the Holy League, which had been created in response to France's military activity in Italy. The League had decided that Ferdinand and Henry should attack together and it should have been an impressive display of force.

The Marquis of Dorset was given control of the English forces and the invaders were due to march with Ferdinand on Aquitaine. However, once the Marquis set foot on dry land, he discovered that the Spanish king had not kept his word. Instead, Ferdinand was occupied with his own attack on Navarre, which better served

the Spanish king's own interests. The Marquis's troops quarrelled with the few Spanish forces that they had been given and many of his men succumbed to dysentery. As a result of all this, he had no choice but to retreat.

Although Henry can't be blamed for the failure of this attack, it shows the Holy League for what it really was. The kings were fighting with the pope's blessing and the glory of God, but they were all out for themselves. Once the fighting started, each monarch was really only interested in what land they could claim – their allies only functioned as a bank and backup.

Verdict

The forced retreat enraged Henry, pushing him towards leading his own attack, and also sowed the seeds of distrust that would come more prominently to the fore throughout his further campaigns

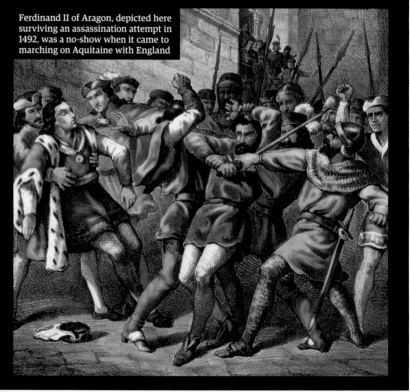

Ferdinand II of Aragon, depicted here surviving an assassination attempt in 1492, was a no-show when it came to marching on Aquitaine with England

Victory at Flodden Field

9 September 1513

With the king's attention focused on France, the timing was ripe for an attack from the north. King Louis XII reached out to his ally in Scotland and James IV was very agreeable. He wrote to Henry instructing him to abandon his war on the French – an instruction that Henry roundly ignored. The Scottish troops rallied and marched south to the border, sending word that they intended to invade. Having appeased their sense of honour, they waited for the English troops at Flodden.

Catherine of Aragon was acting as regent while her husband was at war in France. Catherine was a woman who believed fiercely in duty, honour and loyalty, and the prospect of losing a battle in her husband's absence was too awful to even consider.

Together with the Earl of Surrey, Catherine raised an army from the Midlands to meet the Scottish invaders. Surrey met the Scottish army at Flodden Field and subjected them to a crushing defeat. The number of Scottish dead numbered in the thousands, and King James IV himself was among the fatalities.

While Henry's refusal to leave France may have been the final straw that prompted the attack, he had very little to do with the result of the battle – it was the Earl of Surrey who won the day. The Scottish king fell on the battlefield, and his cloak was sent to France as a trophy for Henry. A decisive victory, but not one which can be attributed to any military excellence on Henry's part.

Verdict

While the victory would assure Henry of England's military might, it was the start of a long and costly struggle with the Scots that would distract him from his goals in France.

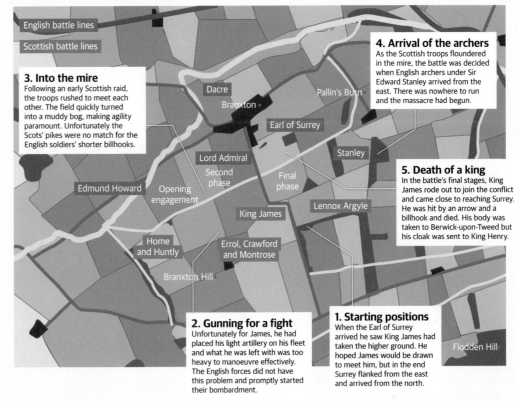

English battle lines
Scottish battle lines

3. Into the mire
Following an early Scottish raid, the troops rushed to meet each other. The field quickly turned into a muddy bog, making agility paramount. Unfortunately the Scots' pikes were no match for the English soldiers' shorter billhooks.

4. Arrival of the archers
As the Scottish troops floundered in the mire, the battle was decided when English archers under Sir Edward Stanley arrived from the east. There was nowhere to run and the massacre had begun.

Dacre
Branxton
Pallin's Burn
Earl of Surrey
Stanley
Lord Admiral
Second phase
Final phase
Edmund Howard
Opening engagement
King James
Lennox Argyle
Home and Huntly
Errol, Crawford and Montrose
Branxton Hill
Flodden Hill

5. Death of a king
In the battle's final stages, King James rode out to join the conflict and came close to reaching Surrey. He was hit by an arrow and a billhook and died. His body was taken to Berwick-upon-Tweed but his cloak was sent to King Henry.

2. Gunning for a fight
Unfortunately for James, he had placed his light artillery on his fleet and what he was left with was too heavy to manoeuvre effectively. The English forces did not have this problem and promptly started their bombardment.

1. Starting positions
When the Earl of Surrey arrived he saw King James had taken the higher ground. He hoped James would be drawn to meet him, but in the end Surrey flanked from the east and arrived from the north.

"The Scottish king fell on the battlefield, and his cloak was sent to France as a trophy for Henry"

The Scottish army outnumbered the English by about 15,000 at Flodden, but some clever tactics won out

Father of the Royal Navy

Henry might be known as the founder of the Royal Navy but its creation had begun during the reign of Henry VII. Five royal warships had been built by the time Henry VIII took the throne, but the young king wanted more from his military might.

Henry knew that Scotland had invested in their own navy and that he was potentially facing a two-pronged attack by sea. Henry ordered the construction of two great warships: the infamous Mary Rose (which embarrassingly and mysteriously sank while leading the defence against the French at the Solent) and the Peter Pomegranate. Henry's ambition knew no limits and the English Navy would be the biggest, the most advanced and the most fearsome. He equipped his ships with the latest guns and the heaviest cannons, while employing new innovations like hinged gun ports. By the end of Henry's reign, his fleet numbered 58.

Enormous gunships aside, perhaps the most important innovations Henry made to the navy were on land. He created the first naval dock in Portsmouth, he gave the Grant of the Royal Charter to Trinity House (which developed beacons, buoys and lighthouses), and he created the Navy Board and the Office of Admiralty. Henry is known as the father of the Royal Navy because he didn't just bulk up its muscle, he created its backbone.

Inside the Mary Rose

Castle
The Mary Rose looked like a traditional warship, with a low middle between high 'castles' on either end, but it was significantly bigger. The design added a further tier of broadside guns, and the hull grew narrower as it went up in what was known as a tumblehome structure.

Hold
The hold was where food was stored and prepared, and the ballast was kept to ensure the Mary Rose stayed on an even keel. There would also have been a bilge pump to expel water, although it obviously wasn't enough to keep the Mary Rose from sinking.

---

head of an English army, Henry was exhilarated. He made straight for the town of Thérouanne and promptly laid siege to it. The Holy Roman Emperor and fellow Holy League leader, Maximilian, joined him soon afterwards, helping to assure Henry that he was on the side of the angels. Finally, Henry tasted glory on 16 August 1513 when the French attacked in the Battle of the Spurs. The light French cavalry were unable to withstand the combined forces of the invaders and fled. Henry claimed the day as a great victory, which was consolidated when Thérouanne surrendered on 22 August. The subsequent capture of Tournai was just as important to Henry, and he kept that town as an English stronghold while giving Thérouanne to Maximilian as a gesture of their allegiance.

What had Henry actually achieved? He'd taken two towns from the French, but Paris was a long way away. Nothing he'd done would tip the scales in either direction, but this was just the beginning. Henry was in his element. He was re-enacting the glories of Henry V and who knew how far he could go? Even as Henry celebrated his victories in France, trouble at home soon threatened to bring everything to a halt. All too aware of the English forces currently on their soil, the French reached out to King James IV of Scotland and suggested

that this might be the perfect opportunity to mount an attack of their own. James marched south to Flodden Ridge with his armies to await the English.

While England may have seemed weak, Queen Catherine, acting as regent, had no intention of allowing such a challenge to go unanswered. An army was raised and met the Scots on 9 September. The English victory was brutally decisive and King James was killed. The gleeful queen sent the fallen monarch's bloody cloak to her husband in France, with the message: "In this your Grace shall see how I keep my promise, sending you for your banners a king's coat." Henry was conquering his enemies abroad, while his queen was seeing off attackers at home.

Sadly for the warrior king, peace was just around the corner, whether Henry wanted it or not. He had been acting as a war chest to his allies and England's

coffers were so depleted that there was simply no way that he could carry on alone. He would have to make peace. The next few years presented Henry with a new potential ally, and a new enemy.

The ambitious Francis I took the French crown, while the Austrian King Charles V was elected Holy Roman Emperor (adding Spain and a huge portion of Italy to his kingdom). Wolsey, aware of the financial sinkhole that the wars had been, worked hard to keep the peace. He managed to put quills to paper with the Treaty of London in 1518, while friendship would be forged at the Field of the Cloth of Gold on 7 June 1520. The plan was that Henry and Francis would spend a week enjoying the festivities and settling their differences, while Wolsey met with Charles V. It did not go according to plan.

For all Wolsey's good intentions, this attempt at friendship was doomed from the start. Henry had never wanted peace to start with,

THOMAS MORE
English, 1478-1535

Brief Bio Thomas More trained as a lawyer and nearly became a monk before entering Henry's employ in 1517, taking on a variety of roles from interpreter to writer and chief diplomat. The two quickly became close confidants and More was knighted four years later, before becoming the speaker of the House of Commons in 1523. It was his strong Catholic faith that would prove his downfall. Although he was made lord chancellor in 1529, he rejected the formation of the Church of England with Henry at its head, so resigned soon after. His refusal to accept the new denomination would lead to his arrest and eventual execution on 6 July 1535.

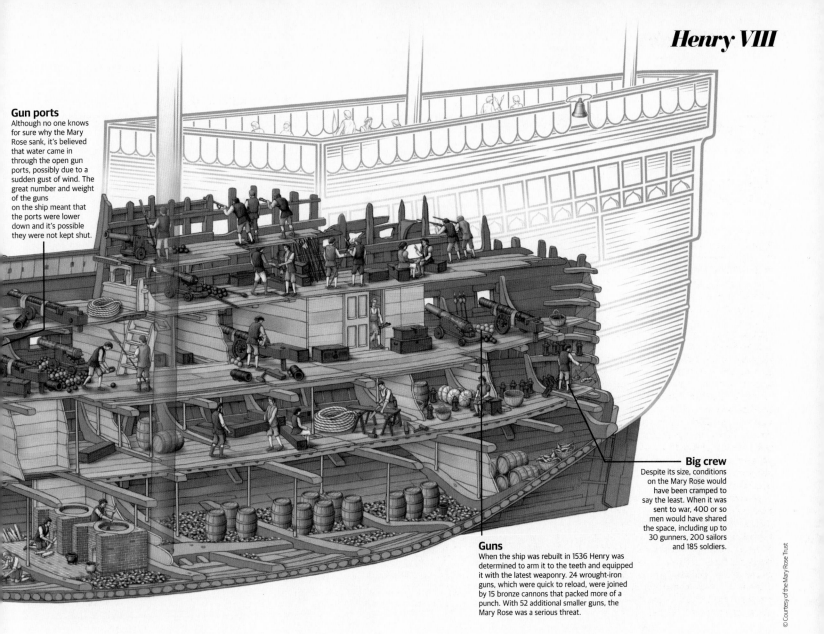

Gun ports
Although no one knows for sure why the Mary Rose sank, it's believed that water came in through the open gun ports, possibly due to a sudden gust of wind. The great number and weight of the guns on the ship meant that the ports were lower down and it's possible they were not kept shut.

Big crew
Despite its size, conditions on the Mary Rose would have been cramped to say the least. When it was sent to war, 400 or so men would have shared the space, including up to 30 gunners, 200 sailors and 185 soldiers.

Guns
When the ship was rebuilt in 1536 Henry was determined to arm it to the teeth and equipped it with the latest weaponry. 24 wrought-iron guns, which were quick to reload, were joined by 15 bronze cannons that packed more of a punch. With 52 additional smaller guns, the Mary Rose was a serious threat.

"Henry's ambition to conquer France was hamstrung by the fact that he couldn't afford it"

and Francis had no intention of bowing down to his English counterpart. Ambitious, stubborn and proud, the two men were too similar for any attempts at friendship to work. After the first meeting was concluded, the two kings engaged in a week of oneupmanship and competition. It was a week dedicated to flaunting power and status; the 'cloth of gold' referred to the ludicrously lavish tents. Henry was determined to prove his athleticism and joined the competitions, but Francis had a similar idea. Henry had to suffer the humiliation of losing to the French king in a wrestling match, and it is hardly surprising that the only result of the meeting was a greater sense of hatred. Instead, Henry turned his diplomatic attentions to Charles V.

Henry's alliance with the Habsburgs had continued throughout the years of peace, despite one or two hiccups involving marriage arrangements. Crucially, Charles and Henry shared a mutual loathing of Martin Luther and King Francis. His hatred of the French king meant that war was inevitable and Henry eagerly awaited the perfect opportunity to mount another attack. When hostilities resumed in 1521, Henry declared that England was now allied with the Holy Roman Emperor and signed the Treaty of Windsor in 1522 to make 'The Great Enterprise' official. At

this point in his plans, Henry could not afford a full-scale invasion and an attack on Picardy failed due to a lack of communication and, perhaps more importantly, trust.

Henry's ambition to conquer France and claim the throne for himself was hamstrung by the fact that he couldn't afford it. He had previously helped to bankroll Ferdinand and Maximilian and he had seen them make peace without him. Henry was scared that Charles might repeat his father's trick and, for his part, Charles had no particular interest in seeing Henry on the French throne. Their mutual distrust would only grow.

Trust wasn't the only problem. In an echo of 1513, Henry was distracted by the constant threat from the north. Whenever he began a campaign in France, the Scottish forces would threaten attack, forcing him to wage a war on two fronts. Henry was enraged and infuriated but he would not give up. He mounted another attack in 1523 to support

the rebelling Duke of Bourbon, but Charles sent no help and the English troops were forced to retreat.

The line was finally crossed when Charles captured Francis at the Battle of Pavia in 1525 and showed no interest in sharing his spoils with the English king. Henry decided that the time had come for a full-scale invasion. With nowhere near enough money, Henry and Cardinal Wolsey tried to create the 'Amicable Grant' tax to pay for the attack, but opposition proved so fierce that Henry was forced to scrap his plans and publicly blame Wolsey. The humiliation of backpedalling helped Henry to realise that he was not going to get what he wanted. He signed the Treaty of the More with Francis's mother, Louise of Savoy, and turned his attention towards his family.

Not surprisingly, Charles's rejection rankled Henry. The Holy Roman Emperor's increased presence in Italy once again caused the panicking Pope Clement VII to create the League of Cognac,

Battle of the Spurs
16 August 1513

The Battle of the Spurs was so named for the speed with which the French cavalry fled

Henry and his English forces had been laying siege to the town of Thérouanne since July 1513. Following the embarrassment at Gascony, he had finally arrived in France to lead his army to great conquest. He camped close, but not too close to the city, and laid siege. A stalemate ensued until French action on 16 August tipped the scales.

The French forces had seen Maximilian's Holy Roman Army join Henry's and decided that the time had come to attempt a counterattack. On the morning of 16 August, French light cavalry, a few thousand strong,

attacked the invaders' positions. However, word had reached the Holy League's camp of the planned attack and a trap had been prepared, leading to a brutal skirmish. It was an attack that was ultimately doomed to fail, with Henry and Maximilian's combined forces coming to roughly 30,000 men. The speed with which the surviving French rode away led to the name of the battle.

It was not a significant military victory in any other term than morale. Henry had been looking for a victory to claim in France, and this encounter was the first real

battle of his campaign. He celebrated it but the actual gains from the Battle of the Spurs and the subsequent fall of Thérouanne would impress nothing but his ego. At great financial expense, Henry's dreams of Agincourt came a little closer.

Verdict
The victory at the Battle of the Spurs did more for Henry's ego than it did for the outcome of his campaign, essentially proving to be an incredibly expensive display.

---

which united Venice, Florence and France against Charles. Henry was not a member, but offered to help bankroll the group. His treaty with Francis in the Treaty of Westminster on 30 April 1527 was a sign that his mind was elsewhere.

Henry was desperate to be separated from Catherine and marry Anne Boleyn. He had no interest in a divorce and instead wanted to prove that it had been illegal to marry his brother's widow. This would soothe the good Catholic in him, but it set him against Charles V, who was appalled by what the accusation said about his aunt, Catherine. However, circumstances were not in Henry's favour; Charles had attacked Rome in retaliation for the League's advances. Pope Clement VII was now his prisoner and Catherine's nephew made his influence felt. Clement gained his freedom in December, but the emperor had no interest in peace talks with the League. Once again, Charles had frustrated Henry's plans and he declared war with the Holy Roman Emperor in January. However, England lacked the finances to do any more than declare itself at war; it's unlikely that this worried Charles too much. The situation

"Overjoyed at having the queen he lusted after, Henry realised that a Europe united against him was dangerous"

in Europe finally resolved itself in 1529 with the Treaty of Cambrai. However, Henry's determination to end his marriage had made enemies out of his old allies. Francis offered to plead his case to the new Pope Clement, but he was more concerned with cementing his own alliance with the Holy See. Anne Boleyn's pregnancy pushed Henry into taking decisive action and his marriage to Catherine was annulled by Thomas Cranmer in 1533. In the eyes of the English court, his secret marriage to Anne was now completely legal. Finally, Henry was recognised as Head of the Church and abolished the right of Appeal to Rome. England was no longer Catholic and the pope had no more influence over the king.

Although he was overjoyed at finally having the queen he lusted after, Henry realised that a Europe

united against him was a dangerous prospect indeed. He tried to take advantage of the frequent arguments between Charles and Francis, but in 1538 the excommunication order for Henry was finally delivered and the pope declared that the Vatican would support anyone who deposed the English king; his death was something God would turn a blind eye to. Luckily for Henry, Charles was busy with the Ottoman Empire and, if Francis planned to attack England, he had no intention of doing so alone. Henry knew that the differences between Francis and Charles would prevent them from ever remaining allies for long. He just had to be patient. Finally, in 1542, they declared war and Henry could return to the battlefield.

By this point Henry was obese, sickly and prone to violent rages. The war gave him a sense of

The Siege of Boulogne

19 July – 18 September 1544

The Siege of Boulogne would be the closest thing to an unqualified victory that Henry would get in all his years of war with France. However, the conquest of a single city at tremendous expense tells us that unqualified is not really the most accurate adjective to use. Henry had been waiting for an excuse to resume hostilities with France and he eagerly joined his old ally (and old enemy) Charles V when war broke out in 1544. He raised a huge invasion force to set sail across the Channel.

The English force was split into two;=, attacking Montreuil and Boulogne, with Henry himself joining the latter. While the attack on Montreuil failed, the Siege of Boulogne, though lengthy, would result in success. The siege began on 19 July and the English forces quickly took the lower part of the city. However, they were unable to breach the castle walls and the siege stretched from weeks into months. Henry wrote to his wife (number six, Catherine Parr) praising the strength of his opponents, but it was only a matter of time before the French were forced to surrender, which they did after Henry's forces tunnelled beneath the walls.

However, Henry's triumph would be short-lived. He learned that Charles, fearful of the Ottoman threat and caring little about Henry's personal ambition, had made his own peace treaty with France without England. Henry returned home to attend to Scotland, leaving Boulogne occupied, and Francis began preparations for a counterattack.

Verdict

Henry may have taken the city, but the financial cost was enormous. Although Charles's treaty led to threats of a French invasion, Francis's attempts ultimately failed.

Charles Brandon, First Duke of Suffolk, was left to defend Boulogne after Henry returned to England

---

purpose and Charles was finally back on his side. For all their past differences, now there were no personal reasons why Henry and Charles could not resume their alliance. Catherine of Aragon had passed away and, by executing Anne Boleyn, Henry had removed the insult to Charles' honour. Across the Channel, Francis wasn't sitting idly by and he knew how to keep Henry distracted.

Scotland had proved to be a continual thorn in Henry's paw during his attempts to invade France, attacking every time his attention was focused across the Channel. Having hoped that James V would be a more amenable ally than his predecessor, Henry was livid when Scotland refused to follow him in separating from Rome. When James did not appear at the diplomatic talks at York in 1541, outright conflict followed. Following a minor Scottish victory at the Battle of Haddon Rig in 1542, the two armies met at Solway Moss. In a brutal echo of Flodden Field, the Scottish army suffered a humiliating defeat. James V died of fever about two weeks later and Henry, once again buoyed by such a decisive victory, turned his attention to France.

Henry was taking no half measures and invaded France on two fronts. Stretching his finances as far as they would go, he sent troops to Montreuil under the Duke of Norfolk, while another force attacked Boulogne under the Duke of Suffolk. While Norfolk failed, Suffolk succeeded. Henry himself arrived to take charge of the siege which lasted from July until September when the city fell. He basked in the glory of a French city claimed, but his elation was short-lived. Henry was forced to turn his attention back to Scotland, where a rebellion had sprung up. His retaliation was so brutal that it became known as the 'Rough Wooing'.

The Rough Wooing

December 1543 – March 1550

The Rough Wooing was the result of Henry's failed attempt to subdue Scotland while he turned his attention to France. Although he might have won a huge victory at the Battle of Solway Moss, Henry's hopes that the Scottish would be amenable to peace proved to be ill-founded. He had given them his terms, but Henry may as well have given them a blank piece of paper, as Scotland declared its renewed allegiance to France.

At the time, Henry was planning his invasion with Charles V and could not afford to be distracted by yet another full-blown conflict with his neighbours in the north. Deciding against open battle, Henry commanded that a force should sail north and show the Scots how furious he was. It was led by Edward Seymour, Earl of Hertford, who was told to "Burn Edinburgh town, so razed and defaced when you have sacked and gotten what you can of it, as there may remain forever a perpetual memory of the vengeance of God."

Towns and villages were to be burned down and destroyed, and the king's strict instructions as to what to do with anyone who opposed Hertford were clear; he was commanded to continue "putting man, woman and child to fire and sword, without exception, where any resistance shall be made against you." Hertford obeyed his liege's orders with relish, sending frequent reports of his conquests back to his king, and capturing Edinburgh and the nearby port at Leith. However, France did not sit idly by, but instead sent forces to help Scottish counterattacks. This dual campaign of aggression between England and Scotland would only be (temporarily) halted by the Treaty of Camp in 1546.

Verdict

Although it had the immediate effect that Henry wanted, which was to give a show of force and wrath, the Rough Wooing only served to deeper entrench hatred and distrust of the English.

The invasion of France fell apart when Charles signed another continental peace treaty that excluded England. Francis had no intention of making peace with Henry and mounted an invasion in the summer of 1545. It was a very real threat but, fortunately for Henry, the attack was a dismal failure and Francis was forced to retreat. The Treaty of Camp brought an end to the years of war in Henry's reign, as England, France, Scotland and the Holy Roman Empire agreed to peace in 1546.

He died a year later, sickly, angry and defeated. So what does Henry VIII's history as a military commander show us? It shows him to be a man unable or unwilling to grow out of the romantic, heroic dreams of his youth. He was constantly fighting for the glory that he saw for himself and for England. In his mind, France was English property that no one before him had been able to claim. He saw himself as the king who would bring it under English rule, and it was a childhood dream that became an adult delusion. By joining with allies who had no interest in his dream, and reacting rashly to insults, real and imagined, Henry spent many years at war with little to show for it.

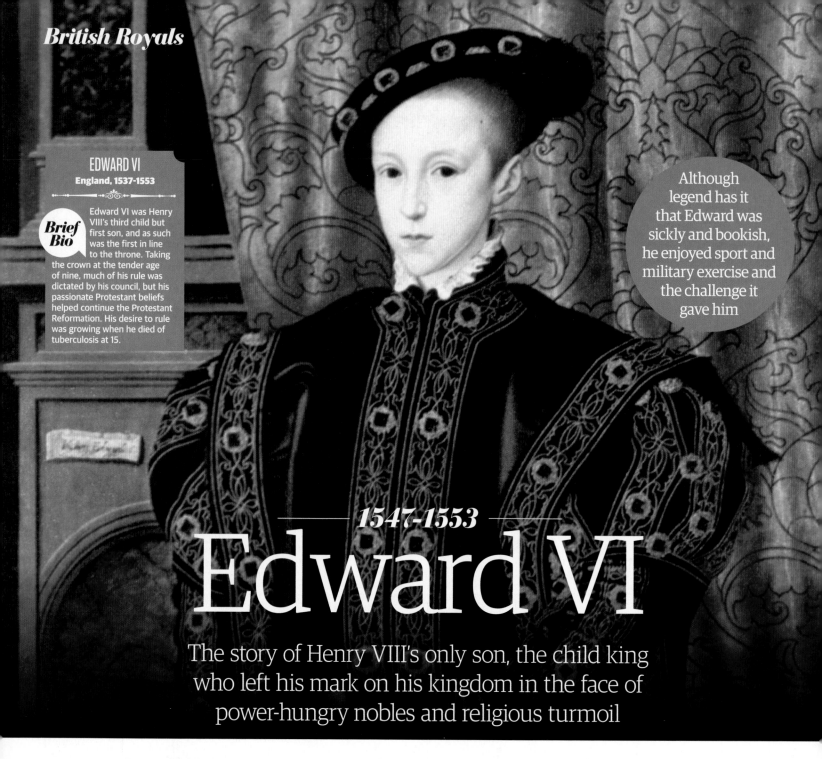

Brief Bio

Edward VI was Henry VIII's third child but first son, and as such was the first in line to the throne. Taking the crown at the tender age of nine, much of his rule was dictated by his council, but his passionate Protestant beliefs helped continue the Protestant Reformation. His desire to rule was growing when he died of tuberculosis at 15.

Although legend has it that Edward was sickly and bookish, he enjoyed sport and military exercise and the challenge it gave him

1547-1553

Edward VI

The story of Henry VIII's only son, the child king who left his mark on his kingdom in the face of power-hungry nobles and religious turmoil

E dward VI's birth was a blessing. For years, Henry VIII had been desperate for a son to carry on his legacy. Catherine of Aragon had not been able to give him this; nor, despite her many charms, had Anne Boleyn. It would be Jane Seymour who gave Henry his male successor, but this triumph was tempered with tragedy. Two days after giving birth, the queen fell ill and she passed away two weeks later.

Despite his pride in his Edward, Henry would be absent for much of his son's childhood, who would remember being brought up "among the women." Much of the familial affection that Edward enjoyed came from his devoted half-sister Mary, daughter of Catherine of Aragon. Security around the boy was incredibly strict (no one ranked lower than a knight was allowed near him) while an attack of quartan fever in 1541 created a terrible panic. However, Edward recovered, and by the age of six had begun to spend more time with his father.

In 1544, Henry went to fight in France and Edward began his education at court. A prodigious student, Edward's abilities were impressive and he was encouraged by his stepmother Katherine Parr (whom Henry had left in charge of his household), but more serious duties loomed. As Henry's death approached, he created a council to assist his young son. It was led by a power-hungry Edward Seymour, Duke of Somerset, whose role as protector was approved by the council led by the canny Sir William Paget, ignoring the late king's will.

Acting more as ruler than advisor, Somerset's lust for power led to unrest at court and his own brother Thomas schemed against him by marrying Katherine Parr, attempting to seduce Elizabeth, and literally bribing Edward to win his affection. Thomas's efforts to gain power grew desperate when Katherine died after giving birth and he was caught trying to break into Edward's rooms. He was executed for treason 20 March 1549, another strike

"Edward was committed to removing any last trace of Catholicism from England"

against his brother that the already unpopular Somerset did not need.

The Protestant Reformation had not died with Henry, continuing apace under archbishop of Canterbury Thomas Cranmer in the face of strong opposition. Cranmer's introduction of an English Book of Common Prayer and the First Act Of Uniformity, banning Catholic mass, in 1549 led to rebellion in Devon and Cornwall. Revolt broke out in Norfolk over social injustices, and the blame was laid at the feet of Somerset. Into this chaos stepped the Earl of Warwick John Dudley, who had been responsible for putting the Norfolk rebels to the sword. The council rallied to him and threw Somerset into the Tower while Dudley stepped in to guide the young king.

He already had the support of Edward as they shared a commitment to the continued Reformation. He took the title of lord president of the council and made an effort to restore stability. For his part, Edward showed himself to be committed to removing any last trace of Catholicism from England, including mass tables, idols and Latin services. After a brief but serious bout of illness in September 1550, his religious reform continued, creating conflict with his Catholic sister Mary. Despite their mutual affection, their differences were a serious problem, both personally and politically. He sent a letter scolding her for hearing mass and for flagrantly ignoring his instructions; this shocked Mary, who believed that many of his actions had been dictated by his advisors.

Mary arrived at court to plead her case and Edward realised that action needed to be taken. When Emperor Charles V threatened war if she was not given her rights as a Catholic, Edward refused to back down despite disagreement from his council. Edward understood the sorry state his

country was in and studied hard to gain a better understanding of its needs.

In the summer of 1551 a terrible outbreak of 'sweating sickness' occurred in London, leading to more concerns over the king's health. Arrangements began for Edward to marry the French King Henry II's daughter Elizabeth but got nowhere, while Somerset schemed for his daughter Jane to take her place. After years of bickering with Dudley, Somerset was finally arrested on conspiracy charges and executed on 22 January 1552. Although Edward held Dudley (now Duke of Northumberland) in high esteem, he took a more active interest in ruling after seeing his previous guardian so violently dispatched. In 1552 the second Book of Common Prayer was introduced.

However, Edward's reign was about to come to an abrupt end. In April 1552 he fell ill with what he described as measles and smallpox. The first signs of tuberculosis appeared at Christmas 1552 and by March 1553 it became clear that his condition would not improve. Lacking an heir, Edward began to work on his plan of succession, intending to disinherit his sisters Mary and Elizabeth. Northumberland arranged a series of marriages that would see his own son marry Lady Jane Grey, who had been decided upon as the best possible candidate to succeed Edward.

Edward's condition was incredibly painful and his sickness was protracted, but when it looked as though the judges of the king's bench would not approve his succession plan, he summoned them and warned them of the trouble that Mary accession could cause. After a final public appearance, he died on 6 July 1553. Despite the efforts of his chief advisor and himself, the work Edward had put into securing England's Protestant legacy would soon be undone.

> Seymour was able to buy Edward's affections as he had little money and wanted to give gifts expected at a Tudor court

Life in the time of Edward VI

The Reformation continues
Following the death of Henry VIII, the nobility were split between the religious conservatives and those who wanted to advance the Protestant Reformation. Fortunately for the Protestants led by Thomas Cranmer, Edward soon showed a keen interest in ridding the country of any last trace of Catholicism, leading to massive unrest as the new laws were brutally enforced.

The rough wooing
It wasn't long before Henry had marital plans for his son. In 1543 he had decided that Edward would wed Mary, Queen Of Scots, and a treaty was signed on 1 July. By December, the Scots had broken the treaty and made an alliance with the French, leading to Henry's furious retaliation, the 'Rough Wooing'.

Kett's rebellion
When robber barons took the common land relied upon by the peasants of Wymondham, a group led by Robert Kett marched on Norwich in the summer of 1549. They gained plenty of attention and were soon numbered at 15,000 rebels. While Somerset dithered, it was finally the Earl of Warwick who led an attack with 13,000 men, killing hundreds and arresting Kett, who would later be executed.

Saving Britain's economy
When Northumberland took over as Edward's protector, he realised the terrifying shape the British economy was in. His first step was to debase the coinage, which bought him time, but his masterstroke was in employing William Cecil and Thomas Gresham, who convinced wealthy trading companies in London to help support the national debt, before travelling to the Netherlands to work the stock market. By 1552, the economy had been restored.

Sweating sickness ravages Europe
The sickness that swept across England and Europe caused widespread panic. It was first seen in 1485 before recurring several times before the end of the 15th Century. 1528 saw the most serious outbreak in years and Henry VIII was evacuated from London as a result. Its causes were unknown and it wasted no time destroying its host body. Even if you survived it, there was no guarantee that you would not suffer from it again.

The king's sisters
Princesses Mary and Elizabeth doted on their young half-brother and their love for him was always clear. It was a difficult time for both sisters. Mary's position was perhaps most obviously dangerous, as she refused to relinquish her Catholic faith and was frequently used as the centrepiece of conspiracies, both real and imaginary. Elizabeth's life appeared quieter, but the amorous attentions of Thomas Seymour put her in very real danger when he was tried and executed for treason. However, despite their obvious differences, Edward never believed either sister to be capable of betraying him.

LADY JANE GREY
England, 1537-1554

Brief Bio

The daughter of Henry Grey, marquess of Dorset, and Lady Frances Brandon, Jane was the great-granddaughter of Henry VII and spent a great deal of time in the court of Katherine Parr. She was described as beautiful, intelligent and pious, and her unwavering Protestant beliefs made her the perfect candidate to take the throne.

—— *10-19 July 1553* ——

Lady Jane Grey

An unfortunate case of right place, wrong time befell this short-lived queen, who served just nine brief days on the throne

Jane Grey's tumultuous encounter with the throne began when she was just nine years old. Jane had always inhabited a place at the edges of the court, but it was not until she was nine that she entered the court of Katherine Parr, Henry VIII's surviving wife, in spring 1547. Her father became Duke of Suffolk and the influence of the Protestant, academic court moulded the already intelligent Jane (who at such a young age, could already speak and write Latin and Greek) into a devoted religious scholar.

This intense intelligence and fierce religious fervour made Jane seem mature beyond her years, but it did not mean she was not vulnerable to the Machiavellian figures who prowled the court pursuing their own agendas. Katherine's new husband Thomas Seymour, one of Edward VI's maternal uncles, planned to marry her to the young king himself. However, when Seymour was beheaded for 33 counts of treason after an alleged

plot to kidnap Edward VI, the plan was foiled. Jane returned to her true love, her studies, at Bradgate house, her childhood home.

An advantageous marriage was still inevitable for Jane and, soon enough, another suitor appeared in the strapping form of young Lord Guildford Dudley. The son of Edward VI's lord president the Duke of Northumberland (who would consolidate his power by arranging a successful marriage), Guildford's high birth and position of influence weren't enough to sway Jane. She was adamant that she didn't want to marry him, until her parents forcefully persuaded her. According to them, this was an opportunity too good to miss: despite Guildford's young, petulant and spoilt attitude, how could she spurn the chance to consolidate her claim to the throne, continuing the Protestant line that the dying Edward VI was so keen to preserve?

On 25 May 1553 Jane and Guildford were married at Durham House, London. Guildford was pleased that his attempt at the crown was in motion, and Jane went back to her parents' London home. The duchess of Northumberland was impatient, though, and convinced Jane that she should prepare herself to be crowned.

When Edward VI died on 6 July, Jane was recovering at the royal manor in Chelsea from an illness that she was convinced was a result of poisoning. It was a paranoid start to what would be a fateful fortnight for the prospective queen. One of Northumberland's daughters informed Jane that she had been chosen by Edward VI as his successor, and she was reportedly so shocked by the news that she fell to the ground weeping, declaring her own "insufficiency", but praying that if the position was "rightfully and lawfully" hers, that she would be granted "grace to govern the realm to his [God's] glory and service."

Far from a distressed and fragile girl, Jane pressed on with resolve. She recovered from her illness and the very next day processed in state down the river Thames to the Tower, with Guildford eagerly by her side. No matter how much he insisted, Jane was adamant that she would not proclaim him king, reputedly quipping that "the crown is not a plaything for boys and girls."

Jane later wrote that this was the moment when she realised the extent to which her marriage had been a fraud. The persuasion from Northumberland, bullying from her mother and father - it had all been in pursuit of the crown for Northumberland and son. She held her position steadfastly in the face of the family argument that ensued and she refused to concede the crown to her husband.

Jane was proclaimed queen at the Cross in Cheapside, while Bishop Ridley of London supported her rightful claim to the throne in a sermon at St Paul's Cross. It should have been a jovial time, but the mood was unusually subdued. The accession was recorded and proclaimed across the kingdom, but there was no rejoicing. It was clear that trouble was brewing.

Residing at the Tower of London to prepare for her coronation, Jane was unaware that it would soon become her prison. By 12 July news arrived that Princess Mary was prepared to put up a fight for the throne. She had gathered support in East Anglia and the country's Catholics were readying themselves to stand with her. Jane's father, Duke of Suffolk, planned to suppress the rebellion in East Anglia, but Jane wouldn't let him leave her side and so Northumberland was sent in his stead.

Northumberland was at his lowest ebb, lacking supporters and being out of general favour. He failed in his mission and was brought back to the Tower as a prisoner. The tide had turned on Jane and the crown was now Mary's for the taking. Three days later, Mary was proclaimed queen throughout the country.

At first, Mary would not allow Jane to be executed, driven by her conscience to keep the girl alive. Jane spent a month in comfortable residence with the Tower's gentleman jailer, Partridge, who afforded her dignity and treated her with respect. All seemed well considering the tumultuous events before, and Jane was grateful to Mary for sparing her life. When Jane and Guildford were tried for treason on 19 November, they were condemned, but both their lives spared.

In early 1554, however, came Thomas Wyatt's rebellion. Jane's father foolishly joined the rebel ranks against the marriage of Mary and Philip of Spain and, in the process, gave Mary and her supporters a reason to suspect his motives and fear once again the threat of his daughter as the 'past queen'.

With this act of rebellion, Suffolk sealed his daughter's fate. On 12 February 1554, Jane waited until she had seen the disembodied head of her husband pass in a cart to face her own execution. She was led to the yard on the arm of the Tower's lieutenant, steely-faced and composed. Upon the erected scaffold, she spoke to the gathered crowd, imploring them to recognise her as a good Christian woman, and to pray for her while she was still alive. She was given a handkerchief to cover her eyes, and she fumbled to find the block in her panic. With one swift blow to the neck, Jane and her dalliance with the throne were finished.

> She was named after Jane Seymour, wife of her great-uncle Henry VIII and mother of Edward VI

Blindfolded at her execution, Jane struggled to find the block on which to lay her head

Life in the time of Jane Grey

16th Century education
Education was not compulsory in the 16th Century, but was an integral part of life for royalty and privileged members of society. Jane's education was particularly thorough, covering Latin, French, Greek and Italian, as well as needlework, music and philosophy. She was known to be studious and particularly pious, which was part of what made her an attractive claimant to the throne.

A legitimate claim
Confusion was placed over the next in line to the throne, as both Mary and Elizabeth had been declared illegitimate by Parliament in 1536. When Mary did take the throne, she passed an act overturning the declaration, and so legitimised herself. Elizabeth, however, never did so.

Wyatt's rebellion
Jane was considerately treated in the tower until her father sealed her fate by joining Wyatt's rebellion. The rebellion was led by nobles, including Wyatt, who was from Kent. The rebellion was in response to the marriage of Mary I to Philip of Spain, as the nobles feared that the Spanish influence would seep into Mary's rule, but without the support of the people, the rebellion failed.

An obsession with time
Jane Grey reportedly had a fondness for clocks and watches, as shown by the number of timepieces delivered to her while she was in the Tower. Many of these were incredibly ornate, including one described as being of "sable skin with a head of gold, containing in it a clock, with a collar of gold, enamelled black, set with four diamonds, and four rubies." Watches had been in use since around the 1520s, worn at the belt by wealthy women.

The first queen?
There are three women in contention for the title of 'first female ruler of Britain', and Jane is one. Some argue that the 12th Century's Empress Matilda, daughter of Henry I, was the first, though she was never crowned. Others give the title to Mary I, perhaps due to the brevity of Jane's reign. Indeed, Mary was first to reign in her own right, but the fact remains that Jane was the first queen crowned.

The nine days queen
Less than 24 hours into her nine-day reign, Jane was visited by the lord treasurer, bringing her a selection of jewels. When she was presented with the crown for resizing, she hesitated: there would be no turning back once it was on her head. Jane herself sent for 20 yards of velvet, 25 ells (a contemporary unit of measurement) of fine Holland linen and 33 ells of lining material. What she did not do, however, was make herself known to the people. When Mary became queen, Jane did not protest or rebel - proof, perhaps, that she never wanted the burden of the role that had been forced upon her.

———— *1553-1558* ————

Mary I

The first legitimate queen regnant of England, Mary was a devout Catholic whose love for her nation became lost in a bloody legacy

MARY I

England, 1516-1558

Brief Bio

Few monarchs are quite as notorious as Henry VIII's eldest daughter. Raised as a devout Roman Catholic, her faith burned hot during the religious upheaval of the Reformation, leading to a purge of beheadings and burnings when she finally took the crown. Yet despite the 'Bloody' moniker, Mary was a complicated woman.

O f all the dynasties to rule over England and its territories, few were as varied and impactful as the house of Tudor. Mary I, the first English queen to reign in her own right, was no exception. The eldest daughter of Henry VIII, she was defined by the turbulent religious metamorphosis England experienced in the early 1500s. In a time when religion and politics were inextricably intertwined, Mary would become a monarch so driven by her beliefs that she would murder hundreds of her own subjects in order to restore the sanctity of her own realm. But who was the woman behind the name 'Bloody Mary'? Was she really a bloodthirsty tyrant? Or was she a product of a country divided by the distinctions of its faith?

The answers find their roots in her early years. Born on 18 February 1516, Mary was the daughter of Henry VIII and his first wife Catherine of Aragon. Henry, a man not to be denied any desire, desperately wanted a son and heir to secure the house of Tudor's hold on the English throne - however, a series of miscarriages and the birth of a daughter only served to push the king further away from his Spanish queen. His pursuit of Catherine's maid of honour, Anne Boleyn, when Mary was around ten years old, would push Catherine further out of favour with Henry's court - and the young princess along with her.

In early 1533, something happened that few could have predicted. Having already secretly married Anne Boleyn in January, and enraged at the pope's refusal to annul his first marriage to Catherine on the grounds it was unlawful in the eyes of God, Henry defied Rome and ended papal authority over the English crown. Henry then appointed himself supreme head of the English church and deemed his union to Catherine void. As a result, she was stripped of her title as queen and demoted to dowager princess of Wales, while Mary lost her princess status and instead gained the title 'The Lady Mary'. With her mother's marriage to the king in ruins, Mary was deemed illegitimate and no longer the heir apparent to the throne.

The year 1536 was another eventful one for Mary. Her mother Catherine passed away on 7 January. A few months later, tired of his second wife's inability to provide him with a son, Henry had Anne disgraced and eventually executed for a multitude of crimes. That year also saw the Pilgrimage of Grace, a political movement in the North of England that demanded the Act of Supremacy be repealed and Mary be reinstated as heir apparent - the rebellion came to nothing thanks to the king's merciless reaction, but it proved that Mary would always serve as a figurehead for loyal papist plotters.

Mary attempted to create some distance between herself and the marital affairs of her father in the years that followed, but she remained the trump card of many a Catholic plot, including a supposed attempted marriage to Reginald Pole (an English cardinal who would eventually serve as archbishop of Canterbury under Mary's own reign). Mary enjoyed something of a better relationship with her father's sixth and final wife, Katharine Parr. Parr did her best to repair Mary's relationship with the king, with Henry eventually signing a revised Act of Succession in 1544, which restored both Mary and Elizabeth as his heirs.

> Mary loved music as a child and even entertained a group of French delegates by playing the virginal (harpsichord) at the age of four

Throughout her life, Mary was an avid gambler. Records of her personal accounts show she regularly bet money on card games

Mary's husband Philip of Spain cared little for her and spent little time in England

War with France

In January 1556, Mary's husband, Prince Philip of Spain, became King Philip II following his father's abdication. The Spanish monarch rarely visited Mary in England, but when he landed on English soil in March 1557 he came seeking her support for Spain's war with France. Mary, keen to preserve ties with such a powerful Catholic nation, was in favour of joining the conflict, but her closest allies persuaded her to hold off due to a wave of bad harvests and a tattered economy inherited from Edward VI's reign.

When Thomas Stafford, a noble who had already incited a rebellion against Mary in 1554, invaded England in June with the blessing and financial backing of the French king, Henry II, everything changed. The rebellion was put down fairly easily, but it was enough to convince Mary to commit to Philip's campaign. The decision was a disaster for England, both financially and politically. Not only did it place strain on the relationship between England and Rome (since Pope Paul IV was allied with the French monarch), it also led to the loss of Calais, the last territory England had control of on the mainland of Europe. It was a terrible blow for the country – so much so that Mary was quoted as saying, "When I am dead and opened, you shall find Calais lying in my heart."

As Mary grew older, her dedication to her faith was always strong. Like many, she was forced to openly accept the king as her supreme ruler, but in secret her Catholic faith never wavered. When Henry died in 1547 and his only son Edward VI became king, England was launched into even stricter Protestant reform. As much a puppet for his guardians as he was a devout Anglican, Henry's young successor clashed regularly with Mary. The two rarely spent time together but when they did, the 15-year-old king was exasperated with his sister's barely veiled Roman Catholicism. When Edward passed away from what was most likely tuberculosis on 6 July 1553, Mary's right as heir apparent was struck another body blow when Edward defied the Act of Succession and named Lady Jane Grey, the daughter-in-law of one of his guardians, as his rightful heir.

Edward had invited Mary to visit him at his bedside, but Mary's advisors warned her that it was most likely a trap to imprison her, so she fled to the pro-Catholic county of East Anglia. With public support slipping following Grey's ascension, Mary and her allies amassed a sizable military force at Framlingham Castle in Suffolk and eventually marched on London and deposed Grey and her supporters. On 1 October, Mary was crowned Queen Mary I of England and, with the natural authority that gave her, she was finally ready to right the wrongs of her half-brother and father.

Now that she was queen, there was the important matter of finding a husband who provided the right political stability for England. Keen to return the country to its former Catholic self, Mary became engaged to Prince Philip of

> When Jane Seymour was pregnant with Edward, Mary sent her cucumbers to help with her cravings

Spain (the son of Holy Roman Emperor Charles V and heir to the Spanish throne). The union was controversial and far from a love match, but it was the first move that tied England to the Roman Catholic territories in Europe. As England's first queen regnant (a queen made monarch by inheritance, not by marriage), the terms of the marriage were also amended to ensure that Mary's authority as queen could never be usurped by her husband. Mary and Philip were married on 25 July 1554, a mere two days after meeting for the first time in person.

Yet organising a political alliance with a powerful Catholic nation was no mean feat considering Mary had inherited a Protestant kingdom. Charles V and Prince Philip needed reassurance that England was indeed committed to restoring the old ways. Mary's English Counter-Reformation began almost

This 1848 print depicts Mary as she signs the death warrant of her Protestant cousin, Lady Jane Grey

Defining moment
Act of Supremacy
November 1534

Mary's father, Henry VIII, has grown tired of bowing to the will of papal authority in Rome. When Pope Clement VII refuses to grant him an annulment for his marriage to Mary's mother, the king has Cardinal Wolsey and Parliament draw up a new act that proclaims the monarch to be, "the only supreme head on earth of the Church of England." By breaking away from Rome, Henry begins a systematic Reformation that drains monasteries and funds and lands and secures Anglicanism as the one true faith in the kingdom.

Act of Succession
After the aging king marries Catherine Parr, his sixth and final wife, he finally relents to the idea of restoring his two daughters to the line of succession behind his son Edward. The Act of Succession 1544 effectively revokes Mary's illegitimacy.
14 July 1543

Mary proclaimed queen
Following the death of her half-brother Edward VI, Mary has his named successor, Lady Jane Grey, imprisoned in the Tower of London. Citing the Act of Succession, Mary is proclaimed the new monarch.
19 July 1553

Timeline

1516

A princess is born
Daughter of King Henry VIII and his first wife, Catherine of Aragon, Princess Mary is born at the Palace of Placentia in Greenwich, London. She is the first of many pregnancies not to end in miscarriage for the queen.
18 February 1516

Mary is betrothed
In order to establish stable ties with France, Henry betroths the two-year-old princess to the Dauphin of France, the infant son of the French king, Francis I. Despite the potential strength of the arrangement, it falls apart three years later.
1518

Another engagement ensues
With the potential marriage to the French king's young son in tatters, Henry is still determined to use his daughter as a pawn in another political alliance. Now six years old, Mary is betrothed to marry her second cousin, Holy Roman Emperor Charles V. This too falls apart a few years later.
1522

Princess of Wales
Mary is sent to Ludlow to preside over the Council of Wales and the Marches. She is only really there to represent the king while his courtiers preside for her. She is referred to as the Princess of Wales at this time, but is never officially granted the title by the king.
1525

"Mary demonstrated that a woman could rule in her own right"

immediately with her first parliament in October deeming the marriage of her late parents valid while passing the First Statute of Repeal (which essentially negated all the religious legislation enacted during Edward VI's reign). Her father's Act of Supremacy was also rejected, with religious authority removed from the crown and returned to Rome.

These changes were largely a popular move since England had only been a Protestant nation for six years, but such legislative restoration also came with a sting in the tail: the revival of the Heresy Acts. These acts deemed anyone practising any faith other than Roman Catholicism a heretic by proxy, leading to the voluntary exile of over 800 nobles who refused to renounce their new faith. The Heresy Acts decreed that heretics should be put to death by beheading or by being hanged, drawn and quartered; however the use of burning was also adopted. During Mary's reign, around 290 Protestants were executed – many of them burnt at the stake – for heresy, creating an air of aggressive persecution.

So was Mary really the bloodiest monarch of the Tudor line? Despite her dramatic nickname, Mary's brief Protestant purge was a single drop compared to the oceans of blood spilled by her predecessors. Edward VI had 5,500 rebels murdered in the Prayer Book Rebellion in 1549, while Henry VIII executed a staggering 72,000

> The annual cost of the Great Wardrobe shot through the roof in the early part of her reign due to her taste for lavish materials and dresses

people (including two of his own wives) during his reign, according to Holinshed's *Chronicles*. It was more the stark violence of Mary's executions during a time when Reformist and Counter-Reformist propaganda was flying around Europe that gave her actions such a lasting infamy.

Mary's reign only lasted five years and while it was marred by the mass burnings of Protestants and the largely disastrous alliance with Spain (which even led to the loss of Calais to France in one of the Tudor dynasty's most embarrassing military debacles), Mary did attempt to make some changes that ultimately benefited the kingdom. Financial reforms included changing the way the government collected taxes, including the normalisation of import tax. She even used Philip's reluctance to include England in Spain's grip on the lucrative trade with the New World to create new trade opportunities with the east coast of Africa.

By the time of her death on 17 November 1558, Mary's attempts to restore England to its Catholic roots had left the country in religious and political turmoil. However, for all her violent acts of religious reform, and her poor choice of a marital alliance with Spain, Mary appears to have loved her country deeply. She also demonstrated that a woman could rule in her own right, setting a precedent upon which her half-sister and successor Elizabeth I would build.

Mary I often indulged herself by buying expensive dresses from the continent

Life in the time of Mary I

Irish settlement
During her reign, Mary continued the Tudor conquest of Ireland by establishing a number of English settlements. These were placed in the Irish Midlands, effectively creating the King and Queen's counties. The two main towns were named Maryborough and Philipstown.

Rainy season
The five years of Mary's rule were uncharacteristically rainy. Persistent rain for months on end led to oversaturated soil, which in turn ruined entire crops. This, and damage from flooding, plunged the country into famine.

A strained economy
Poor weather conditions and harvests contributed to an already strained economic climate. Despite the alliance between England and Spain, trade between them was brittle at best. Spain refused to include England in its lucrative hold on the New World.

Mary and money
Mary made attempts to implement changes to the state of English currency and taxation. Prior to her reign, sheriffs had failed to adequately enforce and collect import taxes, so the queen had new legislation drawn up that clearly defined new rules for efficiently taking incoming resources.

Monastic restoration
While the lands confiscated in Henry VIII's Reformation were not relinquished by the crown, Mary was determined to help rebuild the monasteries that were torn apart decades before. She even used her own finances to restore a number of sites across the nation.

● **Marriage to Prince Philip**
Less than a week after dealing with the conspiracy to place Lady Jane Grey on the English throne, Mary marries Prince Philip, the son of Holy Roman Emperor Charles V. Such a marriage blocks her Protestant half-sister's position as heir.
25 July 1554

Defining moment
England drawn into war
March 1557
In January 1556, Prince Philip's father Charles V abdicates from the throne, effectively making Philip the new king. Often absent from Mary's side for great periods, the new Spanish monarch finally returns to England in March 1557. Philip has reignited the war with France (following a very brittle peace treaty between the two nations) and is keen to use his alliance with England to bolster his forces. War is officially declared in June, but the conflict causes strain with the papacy as Rome has political ties to the French king. The war is a political and economic disaster for England and even leads to the loss of Calais in January 1558.

1702

● **Mary is crowned**
After riding into London in August with her half-sister Elizabeth and 800 supporting nobles, Mary releases the imprisoned Stephen Gardiner, bishop of Winchester, whom she makes lord chancellor. She is crowned by Gardiner at Westminster Abbey.
1 October 1553

● **The false pregnancy**
Around September 1554 Mary's menstruation cycle stops – she then begins gaining weight as well as dealing with bouts of nausea. Mary takes this as a sign of pregnancy, but her belly recedes more than a year later. It was a phantom pregnancy.
Sep 1554 – Oct 1555

● **Burning Protestants**
At the beginning of 1555, the restoration of Roman Catholicism in England leads to the return of the Heresy Acts. With religious doctrine on her side, Mary starts executing Protestant nobles. Burning at the stake is the most prevalent method and around 290 are executed in the purge.
February 1555

Defining moment
The queen is dead
17 November 1558
As 1557 draws to a close, Mary appears to fall pregnant yet again. Sadly it proves to be another phantom term and the queen is forced to make the defining decision of her reign. In 1558 she names Elizabeth as her lawful successor. Mary falls ill during an influenza pandemic that is gripping London. It's not known whether it was the influenza that took her life or ongoing complications with ovarian cysts and uterine cancer.

ELIZABETH I
British, 1533 – 1603

Brief Bio

Elizabeth assumed the throne after the death of her Catholic sister Mary, upon which she faced an unstable nation torn apart by religious conflict. Over the course of her reign she fought enemies at home and abroad, uniting England under one church and oversaw the exploration of new lands.

—— *1558-1603* ——

Elizabeth I

She fought off foreign invasions and domestic rebellions but did she really preside over a golden age?

I n 1588, against the advice of her most trusted aides, Elizabeth I rode out on her grey gelding to address her troops gathered at Tilbury in Essex in preparation of repelling the expected invasion force of the Spanish Armada. Looking out at the assembled faces before her, she delivered a speech that would go down in history and for many would forever define her: "I know I have the body of a weak, feeble woman; but I have the heart and stomach of a king - and of a king of England too."

The speech would have to be transcribed and redistributed for the soldiers who were unable to hear the queen but they had all seen their monarch, armoured and on her steed, ready to stand by them to repel the Catholic invasion. This image of Elizabeth has been the key to our popular perception of her for centuries, but there's much more to her. Elizabeth was cunning and capricious, but she could be blinded by affection, if only temporarily. She was tremendously clever, with an almost unfailing sense of what her people wanted or needed from her, but had to see off foreign invasion attempts and homegrown rebellions. While she was sitting on the throne of England the country became acquainted with some of its greatest triumphs and darkest hours.

When Elizabeth came to the throne in November 1558, the whole of Europe was on tenterhooks. How would the new Protestant queen follow the reign of her Catholic sister Mary? With an unstable nation and conspiracies at home and abroad, the situation required diplomacy, intelligence and bravery; three qualities which Elizabeth had always had in ample supply. In fact, the unstable situation was nothing new to her; Elizabeth's position had been precarious from the moment she was born. The daughter of Henry VIII's second wife, Anne Boleyn, she was immediately deemed as illegitimate by any Catholic nations, who regarded the king's divorce of Catherine of Aragon as illegal. In their eyes, Catherine's daughter Mary was the only rightful heir to the throne.

Although both parents had been desperate for a boy, Anne would be a doting mother to her infant child, but she was sent to the executioner's block

in 1536 after failing to produce a male heir for her king. Although Henry's third wife Jane Seymour was kind to Elizabeth and Mary, she had her own child to attend to with the birth of her son and Henry's heir, Edward. Henry himself would not see much of Elizabeth until 1542, when he decided the time had come to reacquaint himself with his young daughter. He found her to be intelligent and charming, and decided that he would reinstate both Mary and Elizabeth back into his lineage.

In 1543, Henry married Catherine Parr, his last wife, and relations within the royal family warmed, as Mary took a maternal interest in young Edward, while Elizabeth enjoyed a sisterly relationship with both. However, when Edward took the throne upon their father's death, cracks started to form. First, Elizabeth had to contend with the amorous attentions of Catherine's new husband Thomas Seymour, which caused a scandal at court in 1548. Seymour's intentions were seen as treasonous, and Elizabeth was reported to be pregnant. The young princess denied these rumours, confounding her interrogator. "She hath a very good wit and nothing is gotten of her but by great policy," he wrote. This

"She was tremendously clever, with an almost unfailing sense of what her people wanted, or needed from her"

How good was Elizabeth at balancing the books?

While the popular image is that Mary left England in a sorry state, Leanda de Lisle explains that Elizabeth's fiscal behaviour was far from immaculate. Mary left England £227,000 in debt, while her sister produced debts of £350,000. "Mary's reign was not a 'disaster'. The popular image of Mary – always 'Bloody Mary', rarely Mary I – has been greatly influenced by a combination of sexual and religious prejudice," explains De Lisle. "Mary I had named Elizabeth as her heir, despite her personal feelings towards her sister, and so allowed the crown to be inherited peacefully. Elizabeth continued to refuse to name anyone. In 1562, believing she was dying, she asked for Robert Dudley to be made Lord Protector with an income of £20,000." Elizabeth was notoriously reluctant to engage in warfare because of its costs and risk, but the Spanish conflict dragged on for years, while she awarded monopolies to her favourites at court and crops failed. "While we remember Elizabeth's success in repelling the Armada in 1588," says De Lisle, "We forget that the war continued and impoverished the country and the crown, a situation made worse by the corruption of court officials including notorious high-ranking figures such as Robert Cecil. People starved in the 1590s and the elite even began to fear possible revolution."

Verdict

Elizabeth was forced to deal with circumstances beyond her control, such as poor harvests and an ongoing conflict with Spain, but the fact is that she was not the financial marvel many believe her to be.

Borrowing money in the 16th century

Before the English merchant Thomas Gresham came to prominence, the Tudors had borrowed money from the great European banks such as the Antwerp Exchange. However, these banks charged a high interest rate and it was generally acknowledged that going around Europe borrowing money did nothing to improve England's image as a serious power. Money could also be borrowed from independent merchants, such as Horatio Palavicino, from whom Elizabeth was forced to borrow money late in her reign. Gresham had previously helped Edward VI rid himself of most of his debts and founded the Royal Exchange in 1571 to challenge the power of Antwerp.

Now that Elizabeth could seek loans from within her realm, she was able to exert greater pressure to get what she wanted, while Parliament could grant her more funds if they chose. Royal revenues were supposed to cover the basic expenses of governance, while Parliament could add to the war chest. Later in her reign, she began to use increasingly severe taxation, which contributed to her decreasing popularity.

Queen Elizabeth I opening the Royal Exchange

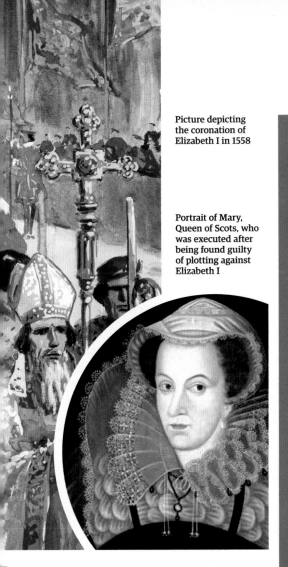

Picture depicting the coronation of Elizabeth I in 1558

Portrait of Mary, Queen of Scots, who was executed after being found guilty of plotting against Elizabeth I

Was a religious compromise met?

The Church of England was one of compromise and middle ground. While Elizabeth was a Protestant, she didn't hold the puritanical beliefs of some of her council members. She introduced the Act of Supremacy in 1558, which reaffirmed England's separation from Rome and established her as the head of the Church. Elizabeth understood the dangers of trying to impose religion and allowed Catholicism to continue, provided it took place in secret.

However, Leanda de Lisle reminds us that we should not forget Elizabeth's willingness to crack down when necessary. "Elizabeth's conservatism and pragmatism has seen her described as a religious moderate, in contrast to the 'fanatical' Mary," she explains. "But as the new Protestant Queen of a largely Catholic country Elizabeth was necessarily moderate, and as her reign grew longer, she proved that, like Mary, she could be utterly ruthless when faced by a threat. The hundreds of executions of villagers following the Northern Rebellion far exceeded anything her predecessors had done in similar circumstances; her later persecution of Catholics was also relentless and cruel. It is a little-known fact that she also burned heretics – namely Anabaptists - these were far fewer in number than Mary's victims, but then there weren't that many Anabaptists!" She executed both Protestants and Catholics for publicly disobeying the laws of the Church of England. However, events in Europe show the English Queen in a much more favourable light. Comparatively, Elizabeth was extremely tolerant. The St. Bartholomew's Day Massacre in Paris showed the fervour with which Catholic Europeans detested Protestants. She was also much more tolerant than many of her advisors.

Verdict

Elizabeth successfully found a moderate middle ground in a very turbulent time during her reign, but would crack down mercilessly if the rules she had laid down were broken.

VS

Catholic

1 The services were held in Latin, countermanding the reformation's ideal that everyone should be able to understand. The English prayer book was banned.

2 Church furnishings were restored to their former lavish state and the buildings were now decorated completely with Catholic artwork.

3 Catholic Mass was reintroduced, and Holy Communion was now banned by law.

4 The clergy were not allowed to marry. Priests who had married before the new law came into effect were given a choice of two options: leave their families or lose their job.

C of E

1 The image of the minister became much simpler. They were not allowed to wear Roman Catholic vestments, such as the surplice.

2 All rood lofts, a screen portraying the crucifixion, a common feature in Catholic churches, were removed. The Pope was not the head of the church.

3 The Bishop's Bible, which was in English rather than Latin, was restored, opening it up to a wider readership.

4 There was a general removal of 'superstition', such as making the sign of the cross during communion. Simplicity was what the Puritans strived for.

---

practice would serve her well once Mary took the throne but not all players were as skilled in the game of thrones; Seymour was executed the following year.

When the staunchly Catholic Mary refused to convert, Edward began proceedings to remove both his sisters from the line to the throne, fixing his hopes on his cousin, Lady Jane Grey, instead. However, the prince was seldom in good health during his short life, so it was no surprise that he died before the contract could be finalised and Mary became the new Queen of England. Just as Edward had asked Mary to change her faith, the new queen was determined that her sister should convert. She acquiesced without enthusiasm, but it was clear to both Protestants and Catholics that her true allegiance still lay with her father's Church of England rather than the Pope's Catholic Church. Over the course of Mary's reign, many conspiracy plots were designed to get Elizabeth onto the throne. None of them succeeded, but they did almost manage to get her killed.

In 1554, Thomas Wyatt attempted a rebellion following the announcement that Mary would marry the Spanish king Philip. The queen's reprisal was brutal and swift, executing not only the ringleaders, but Jane Grey as well. Elizabeth claimed ignorance, a trick she managed to successfully repeat a year later after another attempted rebellion in 1555, but her sister's patience was wearing thin and Elizabeth was placed in the Tower of London, with some Catholic supporters clamouring for her execution.

"The queen's reprisal was brutal and swift, executing not only the ringleaders, but also Jane Grey"

Elizabeth's future prospects were looking anything but golden, and the next few months saw her walking a political tightrope. Mary, desperate to provide her husband and her country with a Catholic heir to end the uncertainty surrounding the throne, announced that she was pregnant, but by 1558, it became clear that Mary's condition was not pregnancy, but a devastating illness. Her health broke quickly, and she died on 17 November of that year after begging Elizabeth to keep England Catholic once she took the throne. Her wishes would not be fulfilled.

Elizabeth's coronation was a stunning balancing act. With countless eyes waiting for any hint of an overtly Protestant or Catholic gestures, Elizabeth managed to confound them all. Instead, the emphasis was elsewhere: Elizabeth's intention to restore England to a state of prosperity. The new queen knew that if she was to have any chance of surviving her early years she would need trusted and astute advisors, and chose William Cecil and Robert Dudley. Cecil had worked for Edward, survived the reign of Mary and was fiercely loyal to Elizabeth. In contrast, Dudley's appointment and favour with the queen had nothing to do with his abilities as a politician. He had known Elizabeth since childhood and her affection for him had only grown stronger, and rumours abounded that she spent the nights as well as the days with him.

Cecil disapproved of Dudley and agreed with the majority of Parliament that Elizabeth should marry as soon as possible. The eyes of France and Spain were fixed on England and it made sense for the queen to create a marriage alliance with one of these major powers for her and the country's

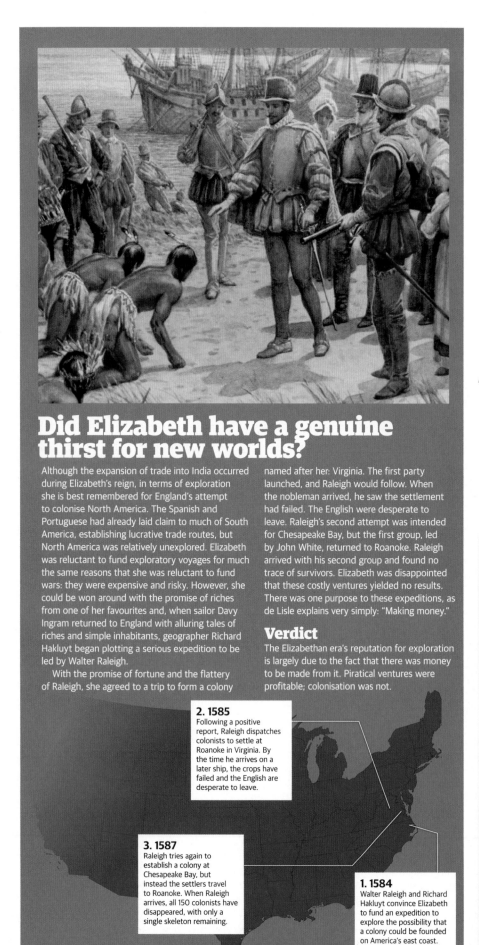

Did Elizabeth have a genuine thirst for new worlds?

Although the expansion of trade into India occurred during Elizabeth's reign, in terms of exploration she is best remembered for England's attempt to colonise North America. The Spanish and Portuguese had already laid claim to much of South America, establishing lucrative trade routes, but North America was relatively unexplored. Elizabeth was reluctant to fund exploratory voyages for much the same reasons that she was reluctant to fund wars: they were expensive and risky. However, she could be won around with the promise of riches from one of her favourites and, when sailor Davy Ingram returned to England with alluring tales of riches and simple inhabitants, geographer Richard Hakluyt began plotting a serious expedition to be led by Walter Raleigh.

With the promise of fortune and the flattery of Raleigh, she agreed to a trip to form a colony named after her: Virginia. The first party launched, and Raleigh would follow. When the nobleman arrived, he saw the settlement had failed. The English were desperate to leave. Raleigh's second attempt was intended for Chesapeake Bay, but the first group, led by John White, returned to Roanoke. Raleigh arrived with his second group and found no trace of survivors. Elizabeth was disappointed that these costly ventures yielded no results. There was one purpose to these expeditions, as de Lisle explains very simply: "Making money."

Verdict

The Elizabethan era's reputation for exploration is largely due to the fact that there was money to be made from it. Piratical ventures were profitable; colonisation was not.

2. 1585
Following a positive report, Raleigh dispatches colonists to settle at Roanoke in Virginia. By the time he arrives on a later ship, the crops have failed and the English are desperate to leave.

3. 1587
Raleigh tries again to establish a colony at Chesapeake Bay, but instead the settlers travel to Roanoke. When Raleigh arrives, all 150 colonists have disappeared, with only a single skeleton remaining.

1. 1584
Walter Raleigh and Richard Hakluyt convince Elizabeth to fund an expedition to explore the possibility that a colony could be founded on America's east coast.

safety. King Philip II made no secret of his desire to marry Elizabeth, but she had no interest in marrying Mary's former husband. Henry of Anjou was suggested as a match, but he was still a child. Elizabeth spoke instead of being married to her nation, but scandal struck when Dudley's wife Amy died suddenly after apparently falling down the stairs in 1560. It was rumoured that Dudley had committed the deed for his queen, and Elizabeth was forced to expel him from her court.

In 1561, Elizabeth's cousin, Mary, Queen of Scots, returned to Scotland from France. For many Catholics, Mary was the true successor and she did little to downplay those clamouring for a Catholic monarch. Her arrival was perfectly timed, as Elizabeth was on the verge of death due to smallpox. However, she recovered and, with the scandal over Dudley dissipating, Elizabeth chose him to be Lord Protector, bringing him back into her court, before shocking everyone by suggesting a marriage between him and Mary. This was Elizabeth showing her political astuteness; she knew well that Scotland with a Catholic heir would

"The Queen rallied troops by declaring that she would fight by their side to repel anyone who dare set foot on their land"

have too much power, but an heir produced by her favourite and Mary, Queen of Scots could potentially unite the two countries. However, Dudley refused and Mary had no interest in marrying her cousin's paramour.

Instead, Mary married for love, choosing Lord Henry Darnley. Seeing this may have prompted Elizabeth to renew her interest in Dudley, which greatly upset the council, in particular the ambitious Lord Norfolk. When the tension between Norfolk and Dudley grew too great, Elizabeth understood that she needed to assert her authority. "I will have here but one mistress and no master," she told Dudley. It was both a political statement and a personal one. The lack of a husband and heir was only made worse in 1566 when Mary gave birth to a son, James, but she was desperately unhappy. Darnley was a violent, drunken husband: many believed he brutally murdered her secret lover, David Rizzio. Darnley would meet his own nasty end a year later, when he was found strangled in the garden of a house. Mary quickly married the Earl of Bothwell, the man who had allegedly murdered Darnley, and Scottish forces rose against her. Imprisoned and forced to abdicate, she eventually fled to England. Elizabeth agreed to give Mary shelter, but her arrival in the north had given Catholics a figurehead and rebellion brewed.

The northern Earls suggested that Norfolk should marry Mary: soon, the Northern Rebellion had begun. As the rebel forces marched south, Elizabeth moved Mary to Coventry and mustered troops of her own. The southern Earls rallied to her cause, which stunned the rebel forces, who

The return of Mary, Queen of Scots to Edinburgh

began to retreat. Elizabeth's victory was quick and decisive, with 700 men being executed in a brutal display of power. Norfolk was placed under arrest, but a lack of concrete evidence postponed his execution, until he was implicated in the Ridolfi plot, which aimed to make Spain's Philip II king. Elizabeth ordered and rescinded Norfolk's execution three times - a prime example of how indecisive she could be at times - before finally deciding that he simply had to die.

If Elizabeth's position at home appeared shaky it was positively stable compared to how she was viewed abroad. The Pope decreed that anyone who murdered the heretical English queen would

be forgiven, a statement King Philip took to heart. Not wanting to risk open war, Elizabeth found other ways to aggravate her enemies. She quietly patronised the piratical exploits of John Hawkins and later his cousin Francis Drake. In 1577, when he planned to travel to South America to raid Spanish gold, Elizabeth met Drake with Francis Walsingham, one of her ambassadors to France.

The cautious Cecil had to be kept in the dark, but she told Drake explicitly that she supported him: "I would gladly be revenged on the King of Spain for diverse injuries I have received." Having sailed through the Straits of Magellan and captured a Spanish ship carrying up to £200,000 in gold,

Queen Elizabeth I knighting Francis Drake in 1581

Drake decided to sail across the Pacific, becoming the first Englishman to circumnavigate the globe. Elizabeth gloried in his achievement, and when she met the Spanish ambassador in 1581, she pointedly wore a crucifix Drake had given to her from the loot. She dined with Drake on the Golden Hind and knighted him. He had done her proud.

These piratical exploits stood in sharp contrast to the events of 1572. The St. Bartholomew's Day Massacre in Paris - the assassination of a number of French Calvinist Protestants - shocked England and the ambassador Sir Francis Walsingham was forced to take refuge. Elizabeth brought him back to London to become her spymaster, where he advised that Mary, Queen of Scots was a real danger. The uprising was not only a shocking scene for English Protestants; it was also a sign that the Protestant Netherlands and their booming wool trade would soon be in danger.

When William the Silent asked Elizabeth for military assistance, she did not want to be seen to intervene and give Philip of Spain an excuse to attack. Walsingham counselled war, while Cecil continued to preach marriage. So Elizabeth entertained the idea of marrying the Duke of Anjou, roughly ten years after it had first been suggested. Then, he had been an ugly youth and she had been a beautiful queen. Now, she was visibly older and the flattery of the French ambassador and Anjou's letters began to win her over. When they finally met, it appeared that Elizabeth really was in love, but there were genuine concerns over how the English people would react.

"The anxieties Elizabeth expressed to the emissary of Mary, Queen of Scots in 1561, that she too could not marry anyone without triggering unrest in one group or another, only deepened following Mary, Queen of Scots's disastrous marriages to Darnley and then Bothwell - which ended in her overthrow," explains Leanda de Lisle, author of *Tudor: The Family Story*. "Elizabeth continued to look publicly for a husband to fulfil national expectations that she would provide them with an undisputed heir, and surely she hoped it was not impossible. She was married to her kingdom - a phrase she had learned from Mary Tudor. But while Mary had married, Elizabeth did not because she feared revolt by those who disapproved of her choice."

Although she clearly wanted to marry the man that she had nicknamed her "frog," the English people found the idea of their Virgin Queen marrying a French Catholic absolutely repulsive. When a pamphlet appeared that condemned the union, Elizabeth decreed that both the author and his printer should have their right hands cut off. Her Privy Council was split in half, with the jealous Robert Dudley vehemently opposed. Elizabeth was heartbroken, but she agreed to abstain. She gave Anjou £10,000 to continue his war against Philip in the Netherlands, but did not see him again. He tried to take power for himself but failed and died a year later. When William the Silent was assassinated in his own house in 1584

Main players of

Council and Government

William Cecil
1520-98

A canny political operator who understood the difficulties that were ahead, Cecil was Elizabeth's first appointment and was fiercely loyal, dedicating his life to helping her. Although he believed she should marry, Elizabeth knew Cecil was invaluable and pressured him into staying on, even when he was sickly and deaf.

Robert Dudley
1532-88

Dudley had known Elizabeth since childhood, and was her first love. His appointment to court had more to do with her affection for him than any outstanding abilities as a politician, however, and his presence at court proved to be a continual source of rumour and scandal. Their relationship was rocky and driven by passion.

Francis Walsingham
1532-90

The Protestant Walsingham was allowed to return to England after Mary's death, and quickly became one of Elizabeth's most invaluable assets. A brilliant spymaster and politician, he understood the threat that Mary, Queen of Scots posed, and engineered her downfall. He also supported Drake and Raleigh's explorations.

Family

Henry VIII
1491-1547

Henry was desperate for a boy to carry on his family name, and was disappointed when Anne Boleyn gave him Elizabeth. He was absent for much of her childhood, but was kept informed of her progress nonetheless. When he finally met his daughter he was very impressed, so much so that he reinstated her and Mary into his legacy.

Mary Tudor
1516-58

Despite their differences, Mary, Elizabeth and their brother Edward had a relatively close relationship as children. When she became Queen, Mary was desperate for Elizabeth to convert and unable to understand why she wouldn't. She came close to executing her sister, but abstained, finally requesting that she keep England Catholic.

Catherine Parr
1512-48

Catherine and Elizabeth became close during her marriage to Henry, and Elizabeth lived with Catherine for some time after his death. However, Catherine's husband Thomas Seymour was more interested in their young charge than his wife, and she assisted in his attempts at seduction, dying soon after they failed.

the golden age

Explorers

John Hawkins
1532-95

Hawkins may have possessed a coat of arms, but he first managed to find favour with the Queen as a pirate. With Elizabeth's implicit permission, he planned and executed a series of daring raids on Spanish ports in the West Indies, but after a disastrous third voyage he returned to England, where he began working for the Queen in a more direct capacity.

Francis Drake
1540-96

Having sailed on his cousin John Hawkins' expeditions, Francis Drake had no love for the Spanish. He was willing to circumnavigate the globe in order to rob them of their riches and deliver them to Elizabeth, who was delighted with his exploits, and continued to commission him to undertake raids on Spanish ports.

Walter Raleigh
1554-1618

Raleigh gained Elizabeth's favour at court and quickly set his sights on expanding her empire. He decided he would establish Britain's first colony in North America, and told the Queen it would be named after her: Virginia. To his great dismay, the colony at Roanoke failed. He is often falsely credited with bringing potatoes and tobacco to England.

Enemies

King Philip II
1527-1598

The main religious threat to Elizabeth for the majority of her realm came from the King of Spain. The Pope might have given the bull that deposed Elizabeth but the fiercely Catholic Philip was the man with the army that could enforce it. He had attempted to woo the princess while still married to her sister but, once rebuffed, relentlessly opposed her.

John Whitgift
1530-1604

As the issue of religious tolerance became increasingly difficult to manage, Elizabeth hand-picked her old chaplain for the role of Archbishop of Canterbury. He was a stubborn man, as evidenced by his refusal to leave England during Queen Mary's reign. Like Elizabeth, he was a Conformist and ruthlessly punished those who publicly strayed from the 'right' path.

Pope Pius V
1504-72

As the head of the Roman Catholic Church, Pope Pius V saw Elizabeth's status of Queen of England and head of its church not only as an affront to his religion, but as an act of heresy. He went as far as to issue a Papal Bull on 27 April 1570, which declared that her subjects no longer owed her any kind of allegiance.

"She bitterly resented the circumstances of Mary's execution"

by a Catholic fanatic, it was clear that military intervention could not be put off any longer and so in 1585, to the relief of her impatient councillors, she agreed to send a small force of men. Dudley took command in the Netherlands but proved to be incompetent, losing territory to Philip's general, the Duke of Parma. Mary was now more dangerous than ever. Elizabeth ordered her imprisonment at the urging of Francis Walsingham, who had no intention of allowing her to live much longer. He arranged for a servant, one of his own spies, to suggest that Mary smuggle letters in beer barrels, allowing Walsingham to read everything. When Thomas Babingdon wrote to Mary with a plan to assassinate Elizabeth and give her the crown Mary wrote back with her approval; the spymaster's trap had worked perfectly, and he had ensnared his unwitting prey.

Walsingham leapt into action and ordered the conspirators' execution. Elizabeth had always been reluctant to execute her cousin, but she agreed she would have to stand trial. It was no surprise when the court decided that Mary should be put to death. Elizabeth grieved for Mary, or at least lamented her death. The man who had delivered the warrant was imprisoned and stripped of his title.

Elizabeth was always reluctant to sign a death warrant - or at least she was reluctant to be seen to sign it. We can't know how much of Elizabeth's grief was genuine, but she bitterly resented the circumstances of Mary's execution.

"Elizabeth was reluctant to be seen to execute first the senior nobleman in England, in Norfolk, and then a fellow queen, in Mary," says de Lisle: "That is not

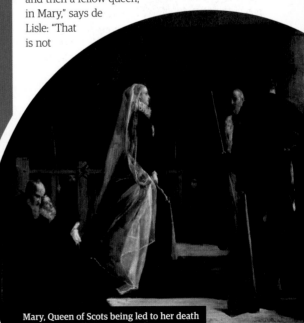
Mary, Queen of Scots being led to her death

The Spanish Armada is put into disarray by English fireships on 8 August 1588

The gun-crew on an Elizabethan ship - she funded the journeys of numerous privateers

to say she regretted their deaths. She would have preferred to have Mary murdered, for example, as she made very clear.

It is also notable that she was quite ruthless in ordering the deaths of traitors of humble birth - the 900 or so executed after the Northern Rebellion testifies to that. This was three times the numbers Henry VIII had executed after the far more serious Pilgrimage of Grace, and ten times the numbers Mary executed after Wyatt's revolt."

Mary's execution provided Philip II with the reason he needed to declare war and his Spanish Armada co-ordinated with the Duke of Parma's forces in the Netherlands, with the two forces meeting before sailing on England.

They launched on 12 July 1588, their forces possessing more than twice the number of English ships, but the English ships did have some advantages; they were smaller, faster, and designed to carry guns rather than men. The English ships could outmanoeuvre the Spanish fleet in open water and began to engage them in small skirmishes. It was at this point that Elizabeth rode out to meet her troops. With the threat of a Catholic force at their doorstep, the queen rallied the spirit

"The queen rallied the spirit of the English troops by declaring that she would fight by their side"

Did England become a nation to be feared?

Elizabeth's foreign policy was decidedly more cautious than expansive. She was desperate to avoid conflict because it was expensive and the outcome always uncertain. However, she had a spirit that could easily be won over by the idea of adventure. She delighted in the expeditions of John Hawkins and Francis Drake, which could be seen to be aggravating the King of Spain without actually declaring open conflict. In 1562, she agreed to a military expedition in Calais, which was crushed by Catherine de' Medici's forces, and this failure would influence her military decisions for the rest of her reign.

"There was no glory in it for Elizabeth as there was for a male monarch," Leanda de Lisle reveals. "She understood the truth of the adage of Mary of Hungary: that war made it impossible for a woman to rule effectively, 'all she can do is shoulder responsibility for mistakes committed by others.'"

Her ally and enemy lines were drawn by religion. France and Spain were clearly opposed to England on these grounds, which is why her courtiers were so anxious that Elizabeth marry an eligible man from either country. Even after the St Bartholomew's Day Massacre in 1572, Elizabeth was reluctant to be drawn into open war. The piecemeal way in which she gave the Dutch her assistance shows her reluctance to engage in open conflict of any kind, first offering financial support to the Dutch troops, then the Duke of Anjou, before finally agreeing to send an English force when there was no other option. Her cautious attitude towards foreign policy doubtless saved the kingdom a lot of money. However, it was taken out of her hands when the Spanish Armada sailed on England."

Verdict

The victory against the Armada was a shining moment but for the most part Elizabeth kept out of foreign conflict. When she didn't, she regularly suffered defeats.

Why did the Armada fail?

King Philip amassed his Armada and sent them to the Netherlands to join up with his ground troops, led by the Duke of Parma. The English outposts saw the ships coming and alerted the admiralty. The weather was against the Spanish, as they were blown off course. While they outnumbered the British fleet by two to one, the Spanish ships were enormous, built to carry troops that could board enemy vessels. Their crescent formation was famous, but it did little against the smaller English ships. When the English sent fireships into the Spanish fleet, the enemy panicked and scattered. They managed to regroup for one confrontation, and lost. The Spanish retreated, with many ships crashing on the rocks of the English and Irish coastline.

6. Bad weather
Bad weather prevents the Spanish fleet from organising and the English pursue them. Their ships are faster and much more effective.

3. Early warning
The Armada is sighted west of the English Channel. The English fleet is put to sea as the south coast warning beacons are lit. Legend says that Sir Francis Drake finishes his game of bowls first.

7. Ships wrecked
The weather blows the Spanish fleet into the North Sea and they are forced to retreat up England's east coast, beyond Scotland and down past Ireland. Many ships are wrecked.

4. Rendezvous
The Armada sails to Calais to meet Philip's most revered general, the Duke of Parma. However, he is delayed and they are forced to wait.

2. Delays
Severe weather forces Philip to dock in Coruna to make repairs to his fleet. He is delayed by more than a month.

5. Fireships
Spanish commanders panic when the English navy sends fireships in among their vessels. They scatter into the English line of fire but the losses are not too heavy.

1. Armada sets sail
On 28 May 1588, Philip is ready to begin his invasion of England. He gathers his Armada and they sail from Lisbon.

---

of the English troops by declaring that she would fight by their side to repel anyone who dared to set foot on their land.

This grandstanding was impressive and may have gone down in history's annals but was ultimately unnecessary. The Spanish Armada failed and Elizabeth's victory was the seal on her status. 'The Golden Age' had begun, where art and literature flowered. With England a visibly powerful state, the aristocracy began to patronise the arts with great abandon.

The famous playwrights of the age enjoyed patronage, albeit with some caveats. When Shakespeare wrote Richard II he was encouraged to remove a scene suggesting the ageing monarch should step aside. "Elizabeth did not care for plays," confirms de Lisle: "All too often they were used to lecture her on this or that."

Her crown may have been safe for now, but she received devastating blows with the deaths of two of her most trusted advisors, Dudley and Walsingham. Dudley was replaced at court by his handsome stepson, the Earl of Essex, and the young flatterer quickly became her favourite.

"Robert Dudley's death in 1588 signalled the passing of the old order, but Elizabeth still hoped she could continue ruling according to her motto, 'Semper Eadem' ('Always the same')" explains de Lisle. "As the years began to pass and her servants died she either did not replace them or find a near-equivalent to the servant she had lost." It's a sign of how much she leaned on her old guard that she continued to place her trust in William

Cecil, even though he was almost entirely deaf and increasingly ill. It was only when he died in 1598 that Elizabeth finally agreed to appoint Robert Cecil to his father's old post. When it became known that the Spanish were attempting to rebuild their fleet, Essex led a fleet on Cadiz and decimated their forces in port. The success gave Essex fame, something Elizabeth was taken aback by. She tried to curb him, aware that her standing among the people was her greatest asset, but Essex continued to promote his own celebrity. She became more and more frustrated with his outrageous behaviour at court, which came to a dramatic head when he half-drew his sword on her in a fit of pique.

The arts and literature may have been flourishing, but those who subscribe to this being a golden age in England's history often forget that even after the defeat of the Spanish Armada, other uprisings, such as the 1598 Irish rebellion, occurred. The country had long been a problem for Tudor England, which had attempted to impose English values and had seen the Irish as tenants on English territory. Now, with a Spanish-backed uprising, Elizabeth needed to take decisive action.

She sent her army at the start of 1599, led by Essex, who was looking to prove himself once more. He was a disaster. Rather than confronting Tyrone on the battlefield, he met him in secret and returned to England having made a treaty without the queen's authority.

When Essex thought Cecil was plotting against him, he rushed to plead his case. Assuming he was still the queen's favourite, he burst into her bedchamber while she was preparing for the day. He had seen Elizabeth without her make-up and regal dressing; not as a queen but as an old woman. She could not afford to be seen like this. The queen dismissed him before summoning him later to confront him with his failures and strip him of power. Rather than accepting his fate, Essex attempted rebellion. He assumed Londoners would back the popular war hero, but Elizabeth proclaimed him a traitor and sent her troops to meet him. The rebellion was a failure and Essex was executed as a traitor.

Although the later years of Elizabeth's reign were far from golden, she could still rally her people when needed. The war in Ireland was expensive and unsuccessful, while overcrowding and failed harvests caused agitation. When Parliament publicly condemned her for granting monopolies to her favourite courtiers, which had led to price-fixing, Elizabeth was forced to address them in 1601. She agreed to put a stop to the monopolies and she reaffirmed her love for England. She won over Parliament, there was a good harvest, and a truce was reached in Ireland and Spain. "Elizabeth, old and ill, did lose some of her former grip, but never entirely," states de Lisle. "She had followed Mary I's example in wooing the common people from the beginning of her reign, and they continued to support her."

Having seen off another uprising, the 50-year-old monarch's health was failing and after an all-too-rare period of good health, Elizabeth grew sickly. She was desperately frustrated by Cecil's growing

> ## "She wooed her people with smiles, words of love and great showmanship, and so won their hearts"

Did peace reign in England?

The early years of Elizabeth's reign were extremely unstable. The Catholics regarded her as a heretical bastard without a just claim to the throne, and she had to prove to her people that she was capable of ruling alone. Conspiracies at home and abroad plotted to remove her from the throne, and when Mary, Queen of Scots took refuge in England, her Catholic enemies finally had someone to rally around. 1569 saw her face the first real uprising with the Northern Rebellion. The Earls of Westmorland and Northumberland rallied the rebel aristocracy around them, but they were not prepared for the force of her reprisal.

In her later years she saw rebellion rear its head again as Essex overstepped his bounds. With famine and overcrowded of cities, Elizabeth's position became unstable once again. "Imagine if Elizabeth had died in October 1562 when she had smallpox," asks de Lisle: "Elizabeth had been on the throne almost four years: only a year short of her sister's reign. If she died, as many feared she would, how would her reign have been remembered? Elizabeth's religious settlement was not viewed as settled by anyone save the Queen. One of her own bishops called it 'a leaden mediocrity'. In military matters, while Mary I's loss of Calais is still remembered, Elizabeth's failed efforts to recover Calais by taking Le Havre and using it as a bargaining tool are completely forgotten. The campaign had ended that August 1562, with the huge loss of 2,000 men."

Verdict

Elizabeth's reign featured numerous rebellions and uprisings, but this was not unusual for a Tudor monarch, and given the religious uncertainty in the country at the time, she handled the uprisings quickly and decisively.

Rebellions against Elizabeth

When Elizabeth ascended to the throne she immediately faced the threat of rebellion from the Catholic nobility, who resented the fact that she was turning away from the changes made by her sister Mary. The first great uprising came in 1569, when the northern noblemen took advantage of the return of Mary, Queen of Scots to England, and attempted to overthrow her. The Duke of Norfolk, unhappy with being sidelined by the Earl of Dudley, entertained a marriage plot with Mary, while the northern Earls mounted rebellion. It was summarily crushed and hundreds were executed.

The Earl of Essex, Elizabeth's great favourite, attempted a rebellion in 1601 after he was stripped of his powers in an attempt to gain power. In line with his apparently oversized ego, he overestimated his personal popularity, the people's dissatisfaction with their monarch and his Queen's capacity for forgiveness for one of her former favourites. When Elizabeth was confronted with open defiance she rarely hesitated to crush it. She understood when to be brutal and when to charm. With the rebellions against her she was unforgiving and generally unsparing, meting out punishments swiftly and unsparingly to rebels and traitors.

Elizabeth's golden moments

2. 1566
Elizabeth announces to a Parliament desperate to see her choose a husband that she is married to England.

5. 1587
Elizabeth is forced to execute Mary, Queen of Scots, which is the final straw for Catholic Spain.

7. 1601
Following famine and controversy over her granting monopolies to her favourites, Elizabeth gives her 'Golden Speech' to a furious Parliament and wins them over.

1550	1555	1560	1565	1570	1575	1580	1585	1590	1595	1600	1605

1. 1559
Elizabeth is crowned Queen of England. Everyone watches to see if she displays a Protestant leaning but the ceremony is ambiguous.

3. 1569
The Northern Rebellion is crushed. Elizabeth brutally punishes those responsible and sends a shocking reminder to anyone who would challenge her.

4. 1577
Francis Drake circumnavigates the globe and returns with boats filled with riches stolen from the King of Spain.

6. 1588
The Spanish Armada sails for England, but is decisively defeated. Elizabeth delivers her famous Tilbury speech from horseback, which becomes legend.

The deathbed
of Queen Elizabeth
in 1603

power over her and refused to go to bed as she realised that the end was coming soon. Elizabeth finally died on 23 March 1603. Although she had struggled to change with the times in the face of younger, ambitious advisors, she had been a formidable political operator. She had still shown the cunning and cleverness to understand her situation, and had never lost the image of a queen loved by her people.

"That image was not created for her," explains de Lisle. "Elizabeth never forgot the events of 1553 when the ordinary people had backed the Tudor sisters, while the political elite had supported Jane Grey. Nor did she forget how in 1554, Mary had made a speech at the Guildhall that roused London in her defence against the Wyatt rebellion. Mary had spoken of her marriage to her kingdom, describing her coronation ring as a wedding band, and her love of her subjects as that of a mother for her children. These were the phrases and motifs Elizabeth would use repeatedly and would become absolutely central to her reign.

In addition, Elizabeth also had an instinct for the crowd's demands. Even her enemies would admit she had 'the power of enchantment'. She wooed her people with smiles, words of love and great showmanship, and so won their hearts. Elizabeth's people would never forget her. When she died and James I become king, people hugely missed the Tudor theatre of reciprocal love, of which Elizabeth had been the last and brightest star."

Elizabeth's reign was not the golden age that legend so often depicts; she faced serious uprisings, both internal and external, during her reign. She was capable of heartlessness and ruthlessness, and could be indecisive and impetuous. During the course of her rule, England saw famine, rebellion and war. However, there's no mistaking her dedication to her country and her determination to listen to what the people wanted from her - and then give it to them. She walked a political tightrope for most of her life, and the fact that she died peacefully in her bed as queen was a major triumph in itself. The English people loved her, and she, in turn, loved them. In the hearts and minds of many of her subjects, she was - and will always be - Britain's golden monarch.

1603-1625
James I

James I, King of England and Scotland, struggled throughout his reign to create a united and prosperous realm of Great Britain under a Stuart dynasty

I t was widely hoped by English courtiers that King James VI of Scotland represented a safe pair of hands for the English monarchy in 1603. Elizabeth I had died after nearly 45 years on the throne and had left no clues as to who should succeed her. As far as the English court was concerned James was the natural choice even if he was the son of that notorious Catholic, Mary Queen of Scots. Unlike his mother, he was a Protestant. He had also reigned in Scotland successfully for 36 years. Secret meetings between James and members of Elizabeth's inner circle had been conducted to see if he would be interested in the job; as far as the English were concerned, his credentials were excellent.

James' disruptive and unstable childhood had forced him to become adaptable in dangerous situations, something that served him well when he became King of England. His mother had been forced to abdicate the Scottish throne in 1567 by a Protestant uprising, after which he was placed in the charge of her enemies to be raised as a Protestant. Not long into his adult reign as King of Scotland, he was kidnapped by a group of nobles and was compelled to rule through their influence for a year. These were dangerous times for James; he had been little more than a child and at the mercy of men who wanted nothing more than to claim the power behind the throne for themselves.

It was an unforgiving and impoverished life, his strict Protestant teachings made for a bland existence that consisted of rules and punishments. The sober education James received in his early years along with the impoverishment of the Scottish crown meant that when he journeyed south in 1603 he was astonished at the comparative abundance of the English realm. He quickly took to enjoying his new-found wealth by lavishing English gifts on his Scottish courtiers controversially from the English treasury.

His court became one of the most extravagant and audacious institutions in England, James did not care for studying documents or enacting laws. He'd rather go hunting, hawking or hosting his infamously drunken banquets. He was a man enjoying his new-found freedom away from the cold monotony of ruling Scotland and he did not want to make a new prison for himself by trying too hard to rule England. He left it up to his courtiers to do the day-to-day business, namely an old trusted advisor, Robert Cecil, who died nine years later from exhaustion. While James' new-found extravagance irritated those who paid the bills, it was instead his religious beliefs that caused the most controversy.

> After the events of the Gunpowder Plot, James became paranoid, and would, in public, wear a padded doublet as a type of armour

> James believed in the divine right of kings, that he was placed on the throne by God and it was his heavenly duty to rule

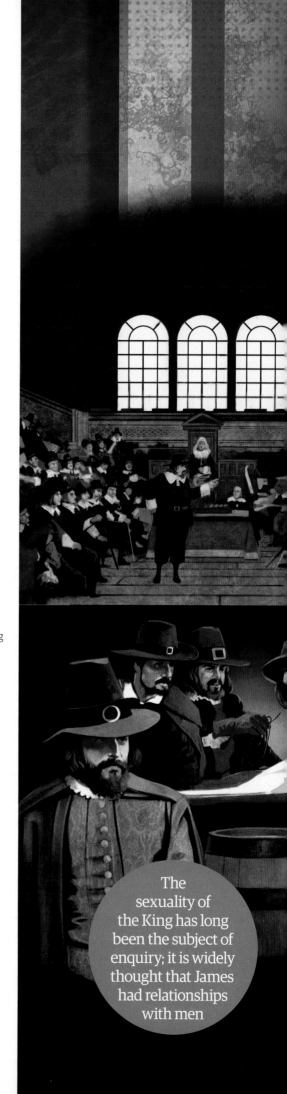

> The sexuality of the King has long been the subject of enquiry; it is widely thought that James had relationships with men

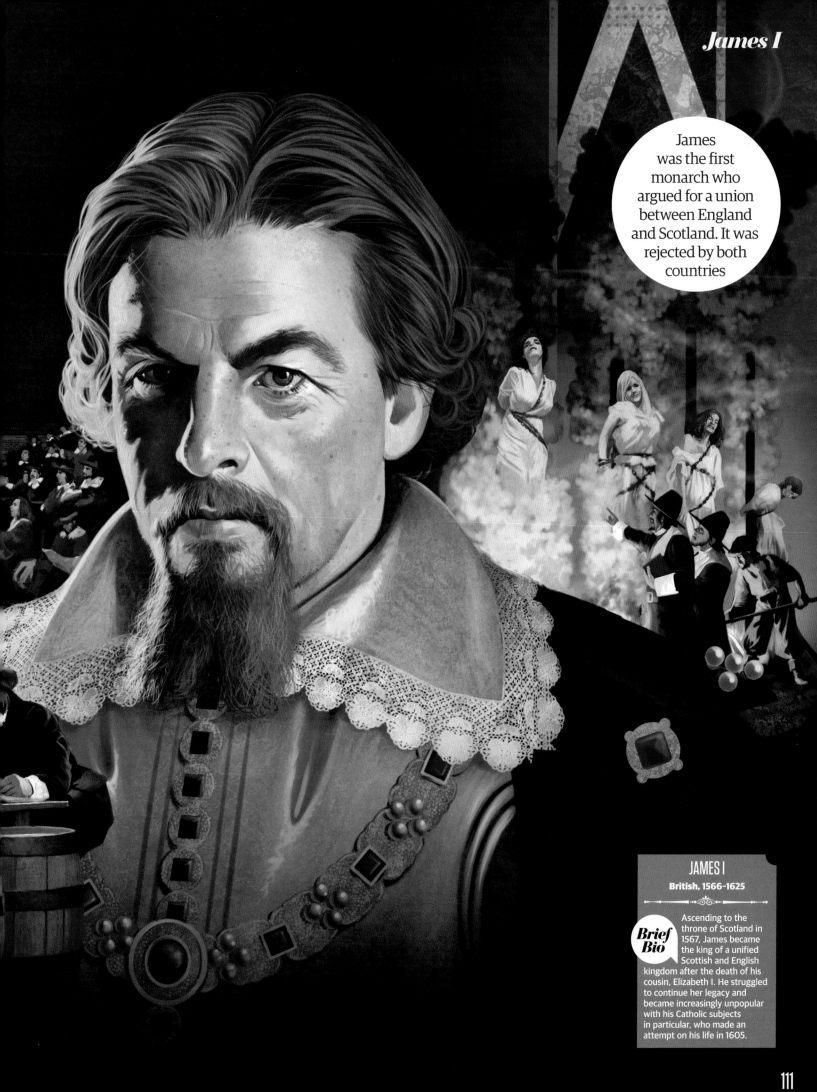

James was the first monarch who argued for a union between England and Scotland. It was rejected by both countries

JAMES I
British, 1566-1625

Brief Bio

Ascending to the throne of Scotland in 1567, James became the king of a unified Scottish and English kingdom after the death of his cousin, Elizabeth I. He struggled to continue her legacy and became increasingly unpopular with his Catholic subjects in particular, who made an attempt on his life in 1605.

The last King of Scotland

James was the last Scottish monarch to rule a fully independent Scotland without governing by proxy from other kingdoms. A Scottish King needed to be strong-willed and able to adapt quickly especially when dealing with the touchy and volatile clan system. James proved himself to be an able negotiator and a strong leader in this regard; he stopped the country tearing itself apart with religious violence and gained universal respect from the numerous clan-based factions within the Scottish court. Perhaps his greatest achievement was the book he authored called *The True Law of Free Monarchies*. In it he outlined a theory of absolute monarchy by which the King, granted his prerogative powers from God, could create laws and enact commands without consulting privy counsellors or Parliaments. This was a radical and explosive idea in the British Isles, where the power of Parliament governing in partnership with the monarchy was a long-respected institution. In Scotland the Parliamentary system was easier to manage because it was smaller and relied on business being conducted personally with the King. When James journeyed south to claim his English throne he quickly found that the English Parliament was not only far larger but also more vocal in its criticism of the monarch.

On 5 November 1605, a group of conspirators connected to the Catholic Jesuit community in England acted on a plot to assassinate James by attempting to blow up Parliament. The conspirators were appalled at James' overtly Protestant beliefs, so they decided to kill him in order to install his nine-year-old daughter Elizabeth as Queen in the hopes that she would become a pro-Catholic monarch. The plan on the face of it made sense: rather than just kill James they planned to kill his entire Protestant party at the opening of Parliament and thus create enough chaos for a pro-Catholic monarch to be installed in its wake. James was not in the Parliament building when a suspicious attendant discovered Guy Fawkes guarding barrels of gunpowder in the cellars.

When news of the conspiracy reached James, he acted decisively. He was no stranger to intrigue of this kind and knew what had to be done. He ordered Fawkes to be interrogated using the 'gentler tortures' which included racking, where Fawkes was tied to a device and stretched until his bones were forced out of their sockets. In keeping with his style of dealing with matters on a personal level, he journeyed down to the tower and interrogated Fawkes himself, asking him how he could conspire 'such a hideous a treason'. Fawkes replied: 'A dangerous disease required a desperate remedy.' James was appalled but he admired Fawkes' spirit, noting later that he put on a 'Roman resolution.' Eventually the King's torturers broke Fawkes: he gave up his fellow conspirators and they all suffered a traitor's death. While James had not

been physically harmed during the whole affair, mentally it affected him greatly. He had always known that he'd had English enemies and now some of them had tried to kill him. From then on he didn't travel without guards, he wore an extra-thick doublet and carried a knife at all times for additional protection.

Four days after the Gunpowder Plot on 9 November, James addressed the first session of Parliament with the following preamble, "it may well be called a roaring, nay a firing sin from fire and brimstone, from the which God hath so miraculously delivered us all." The sitting MPs heartily agreed. Unfortunately for James it would be about the only thing him and his Parliament would agree on for the next 20 years. They argued incessantly over money, religion and taxation. James was furious. It was his view that a monarch be unquestioned by their subjects, that ruling was his business and not theirs. After a particularly difficult session, he commented, "I will not thank where I feel no thanks due... I am not of such a stock as to praise fools... I wish you would make use of your liberty with more modesty in times to come."

Parliament held on to its liberty and refused James' proposal for a standard lump sum of money to be given to him to run the country, known as the 'Great Contract' of 1610. The MPs felt James simply couldn't be trusted with such a lucrative proposition. James blamed the insolence of the members of the house and listened to his favourites in court who sneered at what they saw as common

> James suffered from weak knees and later developed crippling arthritis in his knee joints; he was seen hobbling in later years

Defining moment
Crowned King of England
25 July 1603

James had ruled Scotland as the sixth king of his name for 36 years when his cousin Elizabeth I died. Despite the family tension between the houses of Tudor and Stuart, he was the closest living relative of the unmarried, childless queen and became, by default, her heir. Ascending to the Scottish throne as a child, he becomes somewhat of a puppet prince for the Protestant nobles who support his rule. They ensure that he too adopts the Protestant faith, and this is a factor in his claim to the throne of England when Elizabeth dies. He becomes England's first King James at the age of 37.

Timeline

● **Flight of Mary Queen of Scots**
After facing a Protestant uprising from her nobles, Mary is forced to abdicate and flees south into England leaving the young James at the mercy of her enemies.
24 July 1567

1566

● **Birth of James**
James is born to Mary Queen of Scots on 19 June 1566. James is Mary's only son and while this secures the line of succession, his mother is deeply unpopular in Scotland.
19 June 1566

● **Crowned King of Scotland**
The nobles ensure that James is crowned King of Scotland while he is still in his minority so they can influence his upbringing and stop him from becoming a Catholic like his mother.
29 July 1567

● **Marriage to Anne of Denmark**
James marries Anne of Denmark by proxy to strengthen the ties of Protestant monarchies within Europe. The couple would go on to have seven children.
August 1589

● **Journey south**
After the death of Elizabeth I it is decided that James has the strongest claim to the throne of England and is invited south. He takes his household and courtiers with him.
5 April 1603

upstarts impoverishing the crown. In the end he refused to call another Parliament for four years, only trying again in 1614 but ending with the same unhappy results. With no Parliament, there was no money, and James could not champion the Protestant cause abroad nor could he put his mind to building his kingdom at home. Deeply resentful, he retired to his court, allowed his ministers to run the country and became increasingly distracted with his own personal life.

James' sexuality had always been a subject of court gossip, but by 1620 it was actively destroying the trust between him and his courtiers. It was widely believed by the men closest to James that patronage and influence could only be obtained if you were male and the King took an interest in you. The situation was inflamed by men like George Villiers, the Earl of Buckingham, who was rumoured to be in a sexual relationship with the King. A handsome man from minor gentry, Villiers had risen from a knight of a small county to the second most powerful man in the Kingdom thanks to James, who once commented, '[I] confess to loving those dear to me... I love the Earl of Buckingham more than anyone else... Christ had his John and I have my George.' Whether sexual in nature or not, their relationship grew over the years; James called himself George's 'sweet husband' and George was James' 'wife', among other pet names. As James' marriage to Anne of Denmark resulted in seven children, the question of whether James was openly attracted to men as well as/instead of women is still a matter of debate.

The problem by 1620, at the age of 53, was that he had allowed the men he associated with to cloud his judgement. The astute negotiating skills he possessed in Scotland had abandoned him and he was now surrounded by less competent men like Villiers who gave poor advice to the aging King. It was this poor advice that made James continue to hope for a Spanish match in the closing years of his reign. A marriage between his son, Charles, and the Spanish Infanta Maria Anna would be a prestigious prize for James, so in 1623 Charles and Villiers boarded a ship bound for the Spanish mainland with James' blessing so Charles could attempt to woo the Infanta in person.

As soon as they stepped off the boat and introduced themselves to the Spanish court, they were arrested and held as 'guests'. James waited in England in anxious anticipation; a Spanish match would solve all of his financial troubles through the Infanta's dowry. When he received news that his favourite and his only son had been arrested by the Spanish court, he was furious. After some tentative negotiations, Charles and Villiers were released and returned to England with their tails between their legs. The Spanish had caused great offence in arresting Charles and now he was demanding war.

Neither James nor the country was in any state to wage a war with Spain to save Charles' honour, and with deteriorating health after a bad case of dysentery James died 27 March 1625. He passed away deeply unhappy; his dream of a united and prosperous Britain with strong foreign allies and a humble Parliament hadn't been fulfilled. He would later be known as the 'wisest fool in all of Christendom', extremely able but counselled badly. He left behind an England that had become deeply suspicious of the monarchy and its role in governing the country.

> James had an overly large tongue, which was commented on negatively at the time by certain members of the English court

Religious intolerance

England at the time of James' reign was deeply intolerant of the Catholic minority that existed within the Kingdom. Catholicism or 'Popery' as it was more commonly referred to was seen to be in league with the devil and many of James' subjects feared a clandestine Catholic conspiracy to take over the country.

The rights of Parliament

After the end of the Tudor dynasty, Parliament had become more powerful through its ability to grant money to an increasingly impoverished monarchy. Often Parliaments granting the crown money was dependent on Parliament being bought off with new laws favourable to representatives in the chamber.

The King's court

The King's court was made up of the nobility of the realm and it acted as another organ of state that the King could use to govern the country. During James' reign the court became even more important because he used the presence of both English and Scottish courtiers to rule both his Kingdoms.

Troubles abroad

The prejudice the Protestant population had for Catholics in England was inflamed by the outright hostility experienced by Protestants from Catholic countries in Europe. England remained largely untouched by the fighting, however the influence of events abroad had a dramatic effect on religious prejudices and mental attitudes.

The New World

The first permanent settlements in America were established during James' reign starting with Jamestown, Virginia, founded in 1607. The allure of making a fortune in a new world free from religious persecution was an attractive prospect to many of James' subjects.

Defining moment
The Gunpowder Plot
5 November 1604

A plot to kill James while he attends the opening of Parliament is thwarted when guards search the cellars of the Parliament building and find Guy Fawkes guarding barrels of gunpowder. The plan was to ignite the gunpowder when James entered Parliament and destroy the English government. Fawkes and his fellow conspirators are all arrested, tortured and sentenced to a traitor's death. As a result of the plot, anti-Catholic violence increases throughout the country. James continues to call for religious moderation but has to allow a certain amount of anti-Catholic behaviour to stay popular with his subjects.

Defining moment
The Spanish match
March 1623

James had always dreamt of an alliance between England and the most powerful country in Europe - Spain. While the difference in religion was seen to be insurmountable, England being Protestant while Spain was Catholic, James insisted on pursing a match with his son Charles and the Spanish Infanta, Maria Anna. Charles travelled to Spain but was arrested and held temporarily in custody, with his travelling companion George Villiers.

1625

Jamestown established
The first permanent English settlement in America is established on the coast of Virginia, the settlers name it Jamestown after the King of England and battle to keep the settlement alive.
24 May 1607

The Great Contract
A plan to get the crown out of debt through Parliament giving James an annual subsidy is overturned by the members of the house because they don't trust James with the money.
February 1610

Dissolved Parliament
After wrestling with Parliament for more money to prop up his out-of-control spending, James dissolves the house and does not call another session for four years.
31 December 1610

King James Bible
The King James Bible is published by James and his bishops to bring a universal Protestant faith to the British Isles. It is still used as the basis for global Protestantism today.
January 1611

Investigation of monopolies
In an effort to break up the monopoly of businesses that are strangling commerce in London, James calls Parliament to take action but his sour relationship with the house prevents any progress.
December 1620

Death of a Stuart
James dies aged 58 after his health deteriorates. He leaves behind an uneasy and reformist England that his son Charles struggles to control.
27 March 1625

1625-1649

Charles I

How Charles I lost his head - the King of England became the first British monarch in history to be tried and convicted of treason

On 20 January 1649, Charles I stood where no English monarch had been before him. He faced charges levelled by his own subjects, who accused him of treason against the country he claimed to rule. If Charles was found guilty, the penalty was death. He faced a rigged court made up of hand-picked enemies of the crown who demanded that he answer for the crime of being a "tyrant, traitor and murderer; and a public and implacable enemy to the Commonwealth of England."

However, Charles had never made a habit of listening to Parliament. Even as he faced the men who were waiting to pass their verdict, in his mind they had no power to do so. He was the king, after all, and the king answered to no one. "I am no less confident," he told the court, "that no learned lawyer will affirm that an impeachment can lie against the king, they all going in his name: and one of their maxims is, that the king can do no wrong." The assembled men before him saw things differently.

Charles's refusal to acknowledge the authority of Parliament wasn't just a final gesture of defiance; it was a hallmark of his reign which he had inherited from his father and one of the principal causes of the English Civil War. Frustrated by the fact that the House of Commons constantly attempted to put a stop to his lavish spending, criticised his favourites at court and continued to raise questions about his increasingly Catholic leaning, Charles decided to take them out of the equation. Parliament was called by the king and Charles saw a simple solution to his problem. In 1629, beginning what would come to be known as the 11 Years' Tyranny, the king refused to call Parliament to session. During this time he levied increasingly extreme taxes and introduced unpopular measures to the Church of England that moved it away from Calvinism, such as appointing the despised Anglican William Laud as Archbishop of Canterbury. His opponents, who were already disgusted by his marriage to the catholic Henrietta Maria of France, believed that he was reintroducing Papal traditions to England. But as long as Charles didn't need Parliament there was nothing that they could do to stop him.

Everything changed when Charles attempted to introduce his new English prayer book to Scotland in 1637. Discord spread and Charles refused to negotiate as rebellion brewed until The Bishops' War finally began in 1639. Still the king was reluctant to call Parliament and attempted to put down the uprising himself, only to suffer a humiliating defeat. He was faced with the grim reality that, if he wanted to raise enough

> Charles I was a great lover of the arts and spent large sums of money on paintings, which plunged England further into debt

> He married Henrietta Maria of France, who was a Catholic, by proxy. His choice of bride greatly angered Parliament

CHARLES I

British, 1600-1649

Brief Bio

The art-loving Charles presided over a decadent Baroque court and was married to a French Catholic. This caused a schism with the increasingly Puritan Protestant majority, eventually leading to the political uprising and Civil War that tore the country apart and saw Charles put to death for treason against Parliament.

From 1647 onwards Charles refused to allow anyone to shave his face, possibly out of fear of assassination

"The final line was crossed when Charles was refused entry to the garrison at Kingston upon Hull"

The Divine Right of Kings

Charles I was unwilling to even consider negotiating with Parliament because he believed absolutely in the divine right of monarchs. The concept that Kings and Queens had been chosen by God Almighty to rule their kingdoms had been around for some time in various guises, but it was brought to the forefront during the reign of Charles's father James I. He wrote that "The state of monarchy is the supreme thing on Earth... As to dispute what God may do is blasphemy, so is it treason in subjects to dispute what a king may do... A good king will frame his actions according to the law, yet he is not bound thereto but of his own goodwill." Needless to say, this point of view was not popular in Parliament, who began proceedings to wrench power back from the hands of the King.

money for a force capable of crushing these rebels, he needed Parliament's help. It was with great reluctance that he ended his 11 years of independence on 13 May 1640, but when they began to criticise the king for his spending rather than answering his call for money, he dissolved Parliament in a fit of rage.

Meanwhile, the Scottish rebels continued to advance south. Charles would have to set his pride and his anger to one side. He needed Parliament, and the members knew it. The Long Parliament was called to session in November 1640 and, as Charles watched and listened, Parliament aired their grievances from their years spent in the cold. They passed a law that ensured that they would have to be called at least every three years, they made sure that any tax that the king wanted to impose needed to be approved by Parliament, and they passed a law saying that the king could not dissolve Parliament without their agreement. Charles's unpopular friends and appointments also came under scrutiny, but the issue becoming clear

> As a small child Charles suffered from rickets. He was unable to walk until age four, from which point he wore reinforced boots

was that Scottish rebels were not the only ones worried about Charles' drift towards Catholicism.

After nearly two years, the king had had enough. He identified the five main troublemakers in the House of Commons, John Hampden, Arthur Haselrig, Denzil Holles, John Pym and William Strode and marched into the House on 4 January 1642 to arrest them. Humiliatingly, the five men had heard the news and had escaped before his arrival. "I see the birds have flown," he told the assembled members. He fled London himself shortly afterwards. He could read the signs. War was imminent.

The final line was crossed when Charles was refused entry to the garrison at Kingston upon Hull. Enraged, he laid siege to the city but was defeated. All that was left now was a formal declaration of war, which Charles delivered on the 22 August when he raised his standard at Nottingham. It was a challenge to all those who would oppose him and the Parliamentarians accepted. Led by Robert Devereaux, the Earl of Essex, the Roundheads gathered their troops to meet Charles's Cavaliers before he reached London. After a skirmish at Worcester, the first open battle took place on 23 October at Edgehill with both sides claiming victory. Bragging aside, actual victories went back and forth. Charles was forced to take up residence in Oxford and lost his general, but the Royalists claimed victory at several battles. When Charles declared a ceasefire in Ireland, more troops were able to join his cause and the Royalist troops gained much needed numbers.

Things looked bleak for the Roundheads but when the Puritanical Oliver Cromwell and his cavalry won the Battle of Marston Moor on 2 July 1644, Parliament found a second wind. In 1645 they passed the Self-Denying Ordinance, which meant that anyone serving in the Civil War could not also serve in Parliament, and won conclusive battles at Naseby and Langport. In 1646, Charles was captured and handed over to Parliament.

The king was down, but not out. He may have lost the war but he was still the man chosen by God to rule these people. When he promised the Scots Presbyterian church reform in December 1647 they agreed to back his counter-revolution. Royalist uprisings began all over the country, with

Cromwell at the Battle of Dunbar, 1650, where Parliimentary forces were victorious

Timeline

1639

The Bishops' War Begins
Charles attempts to force his English prayer book on the more Puritanical Scotland. The Scottish church is deeply offended but Charles refuses to negotiate, and dissent becomes rebellion.
1639

The Short Parliament
Needing money to finance an army to crush the Scottish rebels, the King calls Parliament for the first time in 11 years. However, Parliament has axes to grind and the King dissolves it on 5 May.
13 April 1640

The Short Parliament
After nearly two years of listening to Parliament's complaints, Charles enters the House of Commons to arrest the five men he believes to be the ringleaders, only to find that they have fled. He flees London.
4 January 1642

King's authority not recognised
When Charles attempts to enter Kingston upon Hull to access the city's garrison of weapons, Sir John Hotham does not recognise his authority and refuses to allow him entry. Charles begins an unsuccessful siege.
April 1642

War is declared
The Civil War begins in Nottingham when Charles raises his standard, declaring war on his own people. Parliament troops assemble and conflict begins in September.
22 August 1642

The King is captured
The Although the war has been over for at least year, Charles continues to attempt to find support until he is finally captured. He's passed from group to group until he is finally handed over to Parliament forces.
2 June 1647

Oliver Cromwell depicted imprisoning Charles I as painted by Alexander Christie

be allowed back onto the throne, word got out that Parliament was trying to negotiate with Charles.

The army that had fought so bitterly against their monarch could not and would not stand the idea of negotiation. Instead, they marched into Parliament and kept members out who were deemed to be sympathetic to Charles's cause. This was known as Pride's Purge, after the ringleader Colonel Thomas Pride. 145 men were not allowed into Parliament, and a further 45 were arrested. The 75 members who were allowed in were guaranteed to follow the army's agenda and voted that the king should be tried. The House of Lords refused to agree to pass the bill but Parliament continued.

There weren't any laws, any guidelines for how to deal with this kind of situation. Of the 135 judges chosen, only 68 were present at the trial. Charles refused to acknowledge the authority of the court and did not defend himself for the three days of evidence and depositions. The first British monarch to stand trial for treason was found guilty. It was only at this point that Charles, perhaps finally realising what had happened and what was going to happen to him, tried to speak. He was told that he could not. He would not be allowed to speak publicly again until his execution.

Charles I was beheaded on 30 January 1649. The death warrant was signed by the man who would take his power, if not his title: Oliver Cromwell. Standing on the scaffold, he caused many to take note of his calm and dignified demeanour as he delivered his final address. "I have delivered to my conscience; I pray God you do take those courses that are best for the good of the kingdom and your own salvation I go from a corruptible to an incorruptible crown where no disturbance can be."

> Like his father James I, Charles I loathed tobacco. It was forbidden to smoke in the presence of the King

a rebellion in South Wales looking like a real threat until Cromwell's cavalry arrived. Sir Thomas Fairfax put down a Royalist force in Kent, but was forced into a lengthy siege at Colchester. Charles may have been more desperate but the momentum was with the Roundheads and, perhaps more importantly, a large number of nobles who had fought for Charles during the first Civil War refused to rejoin him having pledged their allegiance to Parliament. After losing Cumberland, the Royalists were forced to march south through Carlisle and meet Cromwell's forces at Preston. The Roundhead forces overwhelmed them and they were forced to flee, finally surrendering to Fairfax and ending the Second Civil War.

There was no way for Charles to disguise what he had done. He had negotiated with the Scots to overthrow the rule of Parliament. He had connived and concealed with another nation, and by his actions he had caused the deaths of tens of thousands of men. But Parliament itself didn't know what to do with him. Clearly he had committed treason against them, but what was the solution? While they tried to decide whether or not he could

● **The King is dead**
After being found guilty of high treason, Charles I is beheaded. His manner was described as dignified and he impressed many who came to see him die. He becomes the first British monarch to be executed for treason.
30 January 1649

A crowd watches the execution of Charles I. Many were impressed with the dignified manner with which he went to his death

Portrait of Oliver Cromwell, Lord Protector of the Commonwealth of Britain

The life of Oliver Cromwell

A Puritan and a politician
With the excesses of Charles I's reign the stuff of legend, Oliver Cromwell was a sober, puritanical figure whose fierce beliefs propelled him to the forefront of the English Civil War. He came to prominence during the Short and Long Parliament in which he represented Cambridge with his unshakeable moral code.

A politician and a soldier
Cromwell came to prominence by leading the Roundhead cavalry and proving himself to be a formidable military leader, and assisted in the creation of a separate Parlimentary army with the New Model Army. He won crucial victories at Marston Moor and crushed the rebellion in South Wales.

Off with his head
Although it wasn't Cromwell who made sure that the Parliament that decided whether or not to executed Charles was rigged, he was one of the main driving forces behind the King's trial and signed his death warrant in 1649. His name is visible on the warrant.

No kingship for Cromwell
He was hungry for power but faced opposition after Charles's death. Still, Cromwell became Lord Protector and managed to keep hold of power so successfully that he was offered Kingship in 1657, despite cancelling Christmas. He refused, and died on 3 September 1658 following the death of his daughter.

Respect for the dead
When Charles II took the throne in 1661 the Royalists needed to make an example of those who had stood against them. Cromwell's body was exhumed, tried and hung from a gallows at Tyburn, while his head was stuck on a spike at Westminster.

1660

● **The King plots a rebellion**
While Parliament tries to decide what to do with him, Charles reaches out to the Scots and promises their Presbyterian church independence in exchange for their military support.
December 1647

● **The Second Civil War ends**
Parliament begins to negotiate Charles's surrender after crushing his forces. The King is imprisoned but, while the members decide what to do with him, he plots his escape.
15 September 1648

● **Pride's Purge hits Parliament**
Army troops march into Parliament and remove anyone sympathetic to Charles's cause under the leadership of Colonel Thomas Pride. 45 members are imprisoned and the Rump Parliament begins.
7 December 1648

● **Long live the King**
11 years after the death of his father, Charles II is crowned King of England on his 30th birthday. He orders the deaths of nine men associated with Charles's execution and symbolically executes Cromwell's corpse.
29 May 1660

During the First English Civil War, he was nominally placed in charge of a royalist army, aged only around 15

CHARLES II
England, 1630-1685

Brief Bio

Charles grew up in one of England's most turbulent periods, culminating in the Civil War that led to his father Charles I being deposed. After his return from exile in 1660, he retook his crown and so began the Restoration period. His reign was hampered by political upheaval, foreign wars and tense religious turmoil.

1660-1685
Charles II

One of England's most controversial kings was notorious for his numerous mistresses, calamitous wars and secretive religious beliefs

On 29 May 1660, the streets of London were lined with cheering crowds eager to see if the rumours were true - that Charles Stuart had finally returned to claim his throne. He'd left England 14 years earlier, when the tide of the English Civil War began to turn against the Royalist cause and his father, Charles I, who was executed by Parliament in 1649. As the king's eldest son, Charles was the lawful heir to the throne, but protectorate rule led by Oliver Cromwell made it impossible for him to return. After Cromwell's death in 1658, the possibility of the Stuart monarchy being restored became more likely and negotiations soon began with the exiled royal court.

On his 30th birthday, the man who had fled his country as a young Prince of Wales now returned to a hero's welcome. The restoration of the monarchy heralded a new era in English politics and culture. Many were keen to move on from the oppressive ropes of the old regime - theatres that had been closed during the rule of Parliament and Cromwell were reopened - and an Act of Indemnity and Oblivion was passed. In effect, this bill erased the interregnum's place in history, forbidding mention of it in public. It also offered a general pardon to all who had fought against King Charles I during the Civil War, except those directly involved in his execution. Several were tried and violently executed for their part in the king's death, some of whom had even been long dead - Cromwell's corpse was reportedly exhumed and hung at Tyburn for several hours before being decapitated. However, this was the extent of Charles II's vengeance for his father's murder - now he had to tackle the business of ruling.

The Great Fire of London started in a bakery in Pudding Lane

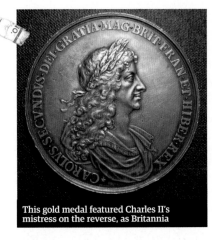

This gold medal featured Charles II's mistress on the reverse, as Britannia

While exiled in France, under the protection of his young cousin King Louis XIV, Charles had grown up among the customs of the French court, its culture and style. As king, Charles enjoyed a hedonistic lifestyle filled with parties, plays, as well as numerous and public affairs with many mistresses. One of the foremost of his lovers during his early reign was Barbara Palmer, who even had residence at Whitehall where the king could attend her more closely. He lavished his court with supporters who had accompanied him in exile, those who had accommodated his return to England, as well as numerous poets, musicians and playwrights. Famous among these was the Earl of Rochester, whose scandalous behaviour, witty satires and general debauchery were unparalleled.

As though by some divine retribution for the king's impious lifestyle, England soon became hampered by disasters. In 1665 a great plague took the lives of nearly 70,000 and on 2 September 1666 the Great Fire of London destroyed over 13,000 buildings. With over 100,000 Londoners made homeless, there was widespread anger, frustration and unrest. England was already financially crippled by ongoing wars with the Dutch republic and now there were loud cries of republican, Dutch and even French conspiracy in setting the fire deliberately. However, it was the age-old enemy, the Catholics, who were laden with most of the blame for the blaze.

The fear of Catholic conspiracy had been ever-present in England almost since the reign of

> Oak Apple Day commemorates Charles escaping England during the First Civil War, where he is said to have hidden up a tree

Elizabeth I and, following the infamous gunpowder plot to kill James I, the Catholic threat was a real terror in the minds of the English population. Charles II's mother, Henrietta Maria, was a French Catholic and had been disliked by many protestant and Anglican figures in power since she had been first married to Charles I. It was rumoured that while in exile she had put pressure on Charles II's siblings, including James (later James II), to convert to the Catholic faith. Certainly, while under the protection of their royal Catholic cousin Louis, the Stuarts had grown accustomed to their ways, so when Charles II returned he brought with him a far more friendly approach to the old faith. This unsettled many in government, as well as the surging protestant population of England.

After over 20 years on the throne, Charles had failed to sire any legitimate heirs. His many infatuations and promiscuous lifestyle had produced countless illegitimate offspring, but not one that he could name as an heir to the throne. This by itself was considered a crisis, but when the king's brother James publicly converted to Catholicism, it triggered outright panic. When Charles fell ill on 2 February 1685, many suspected poison and conspiracy once again, but three days later he called for a Catholic priest to come to his bed and there made his own conversion. On his death he left behind a treasury crippled by years of war, as well as his own extravagance; but worse, he left the crown teetering on the brink of utter chaos.

Life in the time of Charles II

Catholic conspiracy

Ever since the protestant Reformation in England, Roman Catholicism and Catholics in general had been treated with mistrust and often outright violence. Fears of Catholic conspiracy to overrun the country and bring it to heel had been rife ever since the Spanish Armada, and even into the 17th Century they were still very much real.

Forgetting the war

When Charles returned to England after his exile, many noblemen, MPs, landowners and businessmen had to change their previous opposition to the monarchy, at least in appearance. The king refused to restore lands stolen from royalist supporters, which angered them, but helped to ease the transition into his new reign and to keep the peace.

Restoration debauchery

Charles II's court was widely known for its drunkenness and bawdy behaviour, encouraged by the king himself. This made him the subject of much mockery from his friends, but hostile criticism from among the more conservative people in the country. Though the puritanical interregnum period was past, there were still many who saw the king's conduct as disgraceful.

Crisis of succession

When he failed to produce a legitimate heir by his wife, Catharine of Braganza, there was a crisis over the succession of the crown upon Charles's death. His brother James was lawfully next in line, but his Catholic faith made this prospect unthinkable. An Exclusion Bill was even raised by Parliament to exclude James from the succession.

The Great Fire of London

When the Great Fire started in 1666, many saw it as a divine judgement upon the king's debauched lifestyle, while others blamed one of the many enemies of the state. It left many thousands homeless and much of old London decimated, including St Paul's, triggering the construction of Christopher Wren's new cathedral that still stands today.

Wars with the Dutch

The Anglo-Dutch Wars dominated the politics and policies of the English government in the latter half of the 17th Century. With the first conflict starting during the interregnum period under Oliver Cromwell, the second sparked during the reign of Charles II. As a country rich in trade and colonial ambition, the Dutch republic was a fierce rival of England's. Also, without the knowledge of the English populace, Charles had signed a secret treaty with Louis XIV, promising to wage war against the protestant enemy of France. Not only did the wars cripple both countries financially, but they were also widely unpopular among protestants living in England.

During his role as the lord high admiral, James personally took part in the Battle of Lowestoft, where he was nearly killed

JAMES II
England, 1633-1701

Brief Bio

The second surviving son of Charles I, James spent many of his formative years in exile in France. Following his return to England with his brother in 1660, he became lord high admiral. James reigned for just three years before being ousted by William of Orange and would be exiled once again until his death.

1685-1689
James II

James's Catholic faith resulted in him being ousted by his own daughter and her Dutch husband

When Charles II died in 1685 he left numerous bastard offspring, but no legitimate heir to the throne. This meant his brother James, a Catholic convert, inherited the throne - it was what many Protestants in England had feared most. The new king was crowned on 23 April of that year, and during the ceremony his crown slipped on his head - seen as a bad omen by some. In the eyes of many English Protestants, the new monarch was not only a papist but also a supporter of the most traditionally loathed enemy, France, and was bound to enslave his people and withdraw religious liberties that had been enjoyed.

While in exile during the interregnum of 1649-1659, James and his family had stayed under the protection of Louis XIV. During this period the siblings picked up more than just an appreciation of French culture and the style of Louis's court; they grew ever closer to their Catholic roots. Their mother, Henrietta Maria, was a devout Catholic herself and encouraged the two to convert, which James duly did during the 1670s, and Charles much later on his deathbed. This conversion even caused Parliament

James and first wife Anne had two daughters, Mary and Anne

to try to block James from the succession, causing what became known as the exclusion crisis.

Shortly after James was crowned, James Scott, 1st Duke of Monmouth, launched a rebellion. Though he was Charles II's illegitimate son, Monmouth saw himself as the only rightful heir to the throne, and many of James II's enemies valued him as a viable Protestant alternative to the king's rule. Landing in the west country, the duke struck at the same time as Archibald Campbell, Earl of Argyll, sparked a simultaneous uprising in Scotland. Though Argyll failed to gather much support for his uprising, and was promptly executed without trial in Edinburgh after his defeat and capture, Monmouth raised an army of several thousand men.

With the support of Parliament, James raised his own army to crush the young pretender, which he succeeded in doing at the Battle of Sedgemoor on 5 July. He had his half-brother Monmouth executed for raising arms against him, but this would by no means be the last of his relatives to threaten his throne. Even worse, James struggled to form successful governments in both England and Scotland, where reactions to his favoured Catholic ministers often turned violent. The king also filled his own privy council, his closest and most trusted advisors, with Catholic lords, including Arundell, Belasyse, Dover and Powis, who were included in the council in July 1686.

> After his death, James's brain and heart were removed from his body and sent for burial at two separate churches in France

Perhaps most significant during his short reign was that James boosted the Catholic presence in the Irish army, supporting the native Gaelic-speaking population that by September 1686 formed 67 per cent of rank-and-file troops. His lord lieutenant of Ireland, the Earl of Tyrconnell, formulated a strong Catholic base in that country that would later prove useful in the Williamite wars.

On 10 June 1688 James's second wife, Mary of Modena, gave birth to a son, James Francis Edward. The news was met with delight by Catholics and supporters of the king, but with horror and outright scepticism by his opponents. Many believed that the king, desperate to secure his legacy and produce a surviving heir to the throne, had arranged for another child not of his own to be smuggled into his wife's bedchamber in a warming pan. In an attempt to crush this doubt, James even arranged a document including the accounts of 70 witnesses attesting to the authenticity of the birth. However, the king now had far more pressing issues. Just a month later, on 15 November 1688, William, Prince of Orange – James's nephew and son-in-law - landed in Devon in a bid to confront James and maybe even seize his throne.

What became known as the Glorious Revolution was over before it even really began. Within weeks of William's landing, James was in an all but hopeless position. Several planned uprisings all over the country threatened to march on London, while many of his own army officers defected to William. James left the capital on 18 December, the very day William entered it triumphantly. Although captured by Dutch soldiers while on his way to the coast, James soon evaded them and arrived in France on Christmas Day.

Though he would campaign several times to reclaim his throne, beginning the struggle of the Jacobite cause to see the Stuart dynasty restored to the throne, James would die in exile in France on 5 September 1701. Somewhat gruesomely, and as a last insult to the exiled monarch, his body would later be disinterred during the French Revolution and put on display by anti-monarchists.

James's ascension to the throne caused a constitutional crisis which ultimately turned into a revolution

Life in the time of James II

Religious toleration

Religious liberty was incredibly important to 17th Century populations, particularly in Reformist and Protestant nations. Any threat that it could be removed, by either a domestic ruler or foreign power, was almost always met with hostility.

Challengers for the throne

The unpopularity of James's accession to the throne meant numerous pretenders almost immediately sprung up to challenge his rule. The Duke of Monmouth, Charles II's illegitimate son, was the first of these to strike, but ultimately William, Prince of Orange would prove the most threatening.

Absolute monarchy

Since the Civil Wars, the relationship between Parliament and the monarch had been complex. The Stuart dynasty had a reputation for moving towards absolute monarchy, where the throne ruled independently of Parliament, without any accountability to the people, and with full control of taxes and policy.

Succession to the throne

Without a secure male heir to the throne, the king, government and by abstraction the whole country were steeped in uncertainty and insecurity about the future. Even when James's second wife Mary gave birth to a son, there was still widespread animosity that he would be raised as a Catholic heir.

The old enemy

James II's friendly attitude to France followed in suit after his brother and predecessor Charles II. This is just one of the reasons both their reigns became increasingly unpopular – not only was France an enemy of all Protestant nations, it had also been a traditionally loathed rival of England's for centuries.

"He had his half-brother Monmouth executed for raising arms against him"

American colonies

The New York colony, and the settlement of the same name, was renamed after James, the Duke of York at the time. The duke became the proprietor of the colony, nominally if not actually responsible for its governance. However, as king, James did take greater interest in the American colonies and formed the jurisdiction of New England out of the colonies of Massachusetts, Connecticut, New Hampshire and Rhode Island. He later incorporated New York and New Jersey and introduced laws allowing freedom of worship, as well as harsh tax laws to the colonies.

William III & Mary II

Ruling as joint monarchs, this husband and wife removed Catholic James II from the throne in the Glorious Revolution

On 15 November 1688, the last ever successful invasion of England began with the landing of thousands of soldiers at Brixham, Devon. They marched under the flag of William, prince of Orange, who had come to seize the English throne, all under the guise of saving the country from Catholic tyranny. Just a few days earlier he had bid a heartfelt farewell to his wife and cousin Mary, princess of Orange and daughter of James II, the incumbent King of England, Ireland and Scotland. Though he had left her behind across the Channel, as a skilled diplomat and daughter of the English king, she would lend crucial legitimacy to William's invasion.

Although still young at the age of 26, Mary had already been married to her husband for 11 years, but had not yet produced a surviving heir. Her match with the Dutch prince had been crucial for her own family's interests, as well as for young William, who had sought greater influence over the English court's foreign policy in his campaigns against France. As second in line to her uncle Charles II's throne, after her father James, her hand in marriage meant a lot to whomever she was married off to. In time, the match with the staunchly Protestant William would prove more important to the future of Europe than anyone could have guessed.

After Charles II died with no legitimate offspring in 1685, his brother, the broadly unpopular Duke of York, stood as the next in line to the throne. Years earlier, the duke had publicly declared his conversion to Catholicism, sparking the exclusion crisis of 1679-81 as the English Parliament sought to have James renounced as an heir to the throne because of his religion. Though the bill failed, upon James's accession 1685 there were already plans in place to supplant him. As nephew to both Charles II and James II, as well as being the latter's son-in-law, William was closely connected to the Stuart dynasty in England and took great interest in the developments and ongoing crises surrounding the new king. He saw England as a vital ally in the Protestant opposition to Catholic France, which was growing ever powerful under Louis XIV and was emerging as the prominent power in Europe. In order to protect his own interests at home, therefore, he had to ensure England maintained its age-old hostility with its neighbour across the channel - with a Catholic on the throne this became far less likely.

In England, opposition to James II's pro-Catholic policies steadily grew, and between 1687 and 1688 Prince William sent envoys to meet with English conspirators from among the clergy, as well as members of Parliament. Pamphlets were published denouncing James's policies, while declaring William's own desire to protect the Protestant religion in England. The Dutch prince was preparing the ground for a more aggressive

The anniversary of William's 1690 victory at the Battle of the Boyne is a national holiday in Northern Ireland

The Glorious Revolution was the last time the British Isles was ever successfully invaded

WILLIAM III
Netherlands, 1650-1702

Brief Bio Born the posthumous and only son of Prince William II of Orange in the Binnenhof Palace in The Hague, William ruled as the king of England, Scotland and Ireland for 13 years. He was also the stadtholder of Zeeland and the States of Holland from 1672, after what is now known as the Disaster Year.

MARY II

England, 1662-1694

Brief Bio

As the first daughter of James, Duke of York (later James II), Mary became the third in line to the English throne. She married Prince William of Orange at the age of just 15. She lived happily in Holland until her return to England in 1689, when she ruled as co-monarch with her husband until her death in 1694.

The Glorious Revolution

When William's army invaded England in 1688, James II initially remained in London in the hope that his nephew and son-in-law would be forced to march on the capital – a move that could well have galvanised the population against the invaders. However, William's consolidation in Exeter meant that the numerous conspirators and prepared insurrections had the time to come to full fruition. Within weeks, several officers of James's army defected to William, while rebellions in Nottingham and elsewhere took up arms for the prince of Orange's cause.

This invasion very shortly came to be known as the Glorious Revolution, suggesting the victory of liberty and the Protestant faith against the Catholic tyranny of James and his pro-French stance. Though for many in England and Scotland, William was accepted as a practical solution to the problems that James had posed in his stance as a Catholic monarch, he was not ultimately a legitimate one. His joint crown with his wife Mary was of the utmost importance, as it gave the government a legal standing in the line of the Stuart succession, through her father James II. William took many years to fully secure his authority in Ireland, before going on to use English resources for his ongoing war with France.

intervention, though he had to be certain of his own support in England, as well as widespread opposition to James, before he made his move.

On 30 June 1688, seven English conspirators sent an official invitation to William, asking him to invade England and save the nation from James. The prince was extremely anxious that his actions be seen as righteous to the English population, so even drafted a manifesto explaining his invasion, titled *Declaration of Reasons for Appearing in Arms in England*. This document was translated into several languages and distributed widely to appease not just English concerns, but also those of foreign courts who could have otherwise opposed his invasion. This carefully positioned him in the guise of a liberator and honest, law-abiding Protestant. It was with this air of authority that he marched from Brixham to Exeter on 15 November 1688, where he bided his time and awaited the reaction of the population. Within days, the support he had been promised began to gather at Exeter, several officers of James's army defected, while uprisings in the north of the country also sprung up. James's position was hopeless and he was captured in Faversham on 13 December. Five days later, William entered London triumphantly.

On 11 April 1689, the prince and princess of Orange were jointly crowned William III and Mary II of England and Ireland, then of Scotland the following month. The negotiations towards their thrones had been brief, with a push towards some form of stability being of the utmost concern, for fears that another civil war could have sprung up. Though there were mixed feelings about the new regime, with numerous clergy refusing to swear allegiance, most felt that this Protestant claimant, no matter how spurious his legitimacy, was preferable to James. With Mary at his side, William's credibility as a monarch was boosted.

However, majority Catholic Ireland was not so willing to accept what was already being dubbed the 'Glorious Revolution' in England. Although when they were jointly crowned rulers of England, they also acceded the throne of Ireland, the Emerald Isle would be far harder to win over.

When Richard Talbot, lord lieutenant of Ireland, declared his allegiance to James, it became clear that war in Ireland was inevitable. With 'Jacobite' forces rallying to the now exiled former king, propped up by troops and finance from Louis XIV, Ireland now became the battlefield where William and Mary's thrones would be won or lost. In June 1690 William landed at Carrickfergus, in the north of the country where he still commanded some support. He came with Dutch, Danish and English

William III, prince of Orange, winning a famous victory at the Battle of the Boyne in July 1690

Defining moment

Marriage of William and Mary
November 1677

On the night of 4 November, 15-year-old Mary Stuart is married to the Prince of Orange in her own bedchamber. She is given away by her uncle, King Charles II, rather than her father. As part of the match, she is gifted jewellery amounting to £40,000. Irrespective of this, she is said to be extremely distressed at marrying William, who is ugly and much smaller than her, at 5 feet 6 inches. Soon after their wedding she grows to love the Dutchman and is emotional when they are forced to separate, which they often are.

Defining moment

The Glorious Revolution
15 November 1688

After a long propaganda campaign, William lands at Brixham with a force of 21,000. Within weeks James II has fled London. With the declared intention of defending the Protestant faith and removing James's supposed evil advisors, William soon manoeuvres himself into an insurmountable position. In order to secure peace, and avoid another civil war, William is offered conditions for his ascending the throne. This is this last time that England is invaded by a foreign power.

Timeline

1650

Prince William born
William is born the posthumous successor to William II, prince of Orange. His mother, Mary, is the daughter of the late King Charles I of England.
1650

Mary Stuart born
Mary is born to James, Duke of York and future James II. She is named after her aunt Mary, princess of Orange, the mother of her future husband, William.
1662

William becomes stadtholder
Amid a series of violent uprisings by his own supporters, William is offered the stadtholderate of the States of Holland and Zeeland, which had remained empty since his father's death.
1672

William begins to plot
With the accession of James II to the throne, William begins to entertain the possibility of interfering in English politics in an attempt to make it more anti-Catholic and anti-France.
1685

"William's victory at the Boyne is one of the most significant in Irish history"

troops, seeking to quell the rebellion and secure his territories. By 11 July he had reached Dublin and engaged James's Irish forces at the river Boyne. William's victory here is one of the most significant in British and Irish history, and confirmed Protestant dominance on the island for the next two centuries. The battle is still commemorated to this day, with often controversial Protestant marches being held annually in modern Northern Ireland. With the Jacobite threat now quashed in Ireland, though resistance fighters continued to oppose William's rule for over a year, the king could now turn his full attention to his long-term goal: reducing French power in Europe.

In the king's absence, Mary was left as queen regnant in London, ruling with the help of a regency council. Though she had no formal training for such work, she proved to be a capable stateswoman, even managing to handle the regular infighting of her council members. Upon returning after his victory in Ireland, William was still absent from England for extended periods to visit the continent and his responsibilities there. Mary had to handle Jacobite conspirators, as well as a defeat to the French fleet at Beachy Head in June 1690, while her husband was absent and unreachable. In fact, from 1690 right up until her death in 1694, Mary was a de facto solitary ruler of the country at several points, sometimes for many months at a time.

> Mary suffered from regular migraines that were so severe that they prevented her from reading or writing

In her final year, she grew distant from her husband - not only geographically, with his prolonged trips to the continent, but also politically. While Mary was a supporter of the Tories in Parliament, William was more attached to the Whigs, who were in favour of reduced powers for the monarch and were against Catholic rule. Mary's ability to rule effectively gradually reduced as her health waned, so that her regency council took over the role. On 24 November 1694 she took a turn for the worse and began to show the signs of deadly smallpox, of which she died on 28 December. Though she had requested a simple and inexpensive funeral, £100,000 was spent on the event. The procession accompanying Mary's coffin was the largest for any monarch up to that point, and the first to include both Houses of Parliament.

William would go on to rule alone for the next eight years, handling turbulent parliaments, as well as more Jacobite conspiracies and assassination attempts. As ever, his main focus was on fighting Catholic France, and much of his dealings with both Whig- and Tory-dominated parliaments were for the benefit of this greater aim. By the time of his death in 1702, the party system in Parliament that we recognise today was beginning to emerge. In their relatively short reign, William and Mary had taken the British Isles out of the dark chaos following civil wars and into a new century.

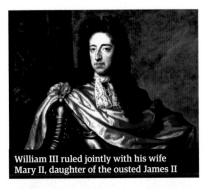
William III ruled jointly with his wife Mary II, daughter of the ousted James II

Life in the time of the monarchs

Whigs and Tories
Towards the end of the 17th Century two prominent factions emerged in parliament, seen as the first political parties. The Whigs were against absolute monarchy, while Tories broadly favoured a traditional monarchy and had greater tolerance for Catholics.

Jacobite conspiracy
After James II fled England he came under the protection of Louis XIV of France, who furnished him with finances and troops. Many Jacobite supporters who remained loyal to James continued to resist the rule of William and Mary and plot his return.

Catholic France
The struggle between Protestant and Catholic nations had shaped European politics since the Reformations of the 16th Century. As a Protestant ruler, William sought to weaken France, a strong Catholic nation, to prevent it from overpowering the Dutch republic.

Smallpox
Known simply as the pox, this virus was prevalent in the 17th Century, causing victims' skin to be covered in pustules, followed by severe nausea, vomiting and often death. William's father died of the disease before his birth, he himself survived it, but Mary succumbed to a more severe strain.

Regency and joint rule
When William was officially offered the crown, several conditions were set out. He would rule jointly with his wife Mary, though the executive power was given to William alone. The succession would also discount any children of William's other than with Mary.

Defining moment
Battle of the Boyne
11 July 1690
In one of the most significant engagements of the 17th Century, William's forces crush the Irish Jacobite army commanded by Richard Talbot, 1st Earl of Tyrconnell and lord deputy of Ireland. The earl had declared for James II soon after the Glorious Revolution and mustered the majority Catholic population, which had prospered under James II, to arms against William. The battle is fought just north of Dublin, over the river Boyne, and claims the lives of some 2,000 men from either side - a relatively small figure given the combined forces amounted to nearly 50,000.

Peace with France
After years of warfare, France and the Grand Alliance, including England and the Dutch republic, sign the treaty of Ryswick. This ends the period now known as the Nine Years' War.
1697

William and Mary crowned
A hasty coronation is held jointly crowning the new monarchs. After further negotiations with the Scottish parliament, they are crowned king and queen of Scotland the following month.
1689

William lands in Ireland
After his campaign against Jacobite resistance in Ireland stalls, William lands in the north of the country with over 15,000 extra troops. These are mainly Dutch and Danish soldiers, as English troops' loyalties are still under question.
1690

Battle of Landen
Facing a superior French force, William's English, Scottish, Irish and Dutch army is defeated in Neerwinden, modern-day Belgium. However, the French army fails to capitalise on its success and William escapes.
1692

Mary II dies
Suffering from smallpox, Mary dies on the morning of 28 December. Her body is quickly embalmed, because of the severe effects the virulent strain of the smallpox had on her skin, and she is finally buried on 5 March 1695.
1694

1702

William dies
Two days after suddenly collapsing with a fever, the king dies on the morning of 8 March. This is contrary to the myth that his horse tripped on a molehill and threw him.
1702

1702-1714

Queen Anne

The first queen of a united Britain, Anne came to power after the unpopular William III and during a time of political turmoil in Europe

The Stuart dynasty's final monarch was Queen Anne, whose reign oversaw several wars and the beginning of the unification of Britain. Born at St James's Palace in London on 6 February 1665, Anne spent most of her early life in France with her father James, who was the Duke of York and brother to the exiled English monarch of the time, Charles II. From an early age, the future queen was surrounded by Catholics in her family, but she was eventually brought up as a Protestant. This religious orientation would help her secure the English throne in the future.

The young Anne was raised as an aristocratic girl with a full education in languages and music. Being female, she was not given much of a grounding in law and military matters, which would ultimately go against her when she assumed the English crown. Anne was only 18 when she was married to Prince George of Denmark. The wedding was negotiated by Anne's father and King Louis XIV of France. The idea was that the marriage would create an Anglo-Danish alliance against the Dutch. This plan, however, never materialised. Just two years

> **Anne was the last monarch to practise the ritual of the 'royal touch', a form of laying on of hands thought to cure illness**

> **Anne had become so stout during her later years that when she died, her coffin was more of a square shape than a rectangle**

later in 1685, Anne's father James became king, followed by her sister Mary and her Dutch husband William in 1688. Short monarchies continued to be a trend in the Stuart age and Anne was thrust into the regal limelight aged 37 when she ascended to the throne on 8 March 1702.

Anne's reign began in a time of conflict. The War of Spanish Succession was well under way when she was crowned, as Europe entered a state of turmoil after the death of King Charles II of Spain. The Spanish Empire was now leaderless and without an immediate successor and all the major powers wanted a piece of the action. Britain waded in with all its military might and recorded a series of victories. This was partly due to the expert battle tactician John Churchill, the Duke of Marlborough, who would become an important member of Anne's regime. The English empire was growing in power and the nation was beginning to assume its role as the unofficial policeman of Europe. Its forces successfully expelled the French from the Netherlands and helped save Austria from invasion. English troops also captured Gibraltar in 1704 and recorded stunning victories

QUEEN ANNE

England, 1665-1714

Brief Bio The last of the Stuart monarchs, Anne held a strong desire for independent rule. However, intellectual and physical limitations meant she relied on ministers, particularly during the War of Spanish Succession. Questions over succession, combined with tensions between Whigs and Tories, characterised her reign.

While her formal education had been limited, Anne gained a mastery of the French language and spoke it fluently

John Churchill, Duke of Marlborough, was a key figure during Anne's reign and one of the greatest generals in British history

The War of Spanish Succession

The death of the childless Charles II of Spain and the end of the Spanish Habsburg line in 1700 sparked a scramble for power in Europe. On his deathbed, Charles decided that he wanted Philip, Duke of Anjou of the House of Bourbon, to be his heir. Philip was the grandson of the king of France, Louis XIV. This pleased the French but angered the other European powers, who moved swiftly to prevent the Bourbon takeover. The result was war.

The Grand Alliance against France, Bavaria and Spain was made up of Great Britain, the Holy Roman Empire, Austria, the Dutch republic and Prussia. A French advance in 1704 towards the Austrian stronghold, Vienna, was curtailed by the timely introduction of the Grand Alliance armies. Masterminded by Marlborough, this was a decisive victory for the Alliance that knocked Bavaria out of the war. Further victories across the continent, as well as the taking of Gibraltar, convinced Louis to consider peace proposals. The Allied powers did not take kindly to these suggestions and continued to advance until 1710, when the more French-inclined Tories replaced the Whigs in British Government. The war ended in 1714 with the signing of the Treaty of Utrecht.

at Blenheim (1704) and Ramillies (1706). The era is known by many contemporary historians as the Second Hundred Years' War due to the constant conflict over the Channel. As Churchill claimed these victories, Anne found herself under the growing influence of his wife Sarah. Friends such as Sarah would become big influences on her political outlook, especially as her own husband Prince George had no interest in such matters and preferred to indulge in his growing fondness for drink. Anne was so involved in the war that the American theatre of the War of Spanish Succession is often referred to as 'Queen Anne's War'.

The war ended in 1714. By this time England and Scotland had become a united nation (through the Acts of Union of 1706 and 1707) and Anne had signed the Treaty of Utrecht, which made France recognise her power. The queen's monarchy was one of gradual change in the newly formed Great Britain. She was already much more popular than her predecessor William after making a speech saying, "As I know myself to be entirely English, I can very sincerely assure you there is not anything you can expect or desire from me, which I shall not be ready to do for the happiness and prosperity of England."

In 1708, Anne became the last ever sovereign in British history to veto a bill as she decided against reorganising the Scottish militia. The new union gave Scotland 45 MPs and 16 elected peers in Westminster but this was not enough for the Scots, who would frequently lead skirmishes against the English for the remainder of the century and

> Gardening, hunting and horse racing were the queen's favourite pastimes. She founded Ascot race course in 1711

into the Georgian era. While Anne was queen, the biggest advocate for Scottish independence was Andrew Fletcher of Saltoun, who warned against the increasing amount of wealth going into London from other areas of Britain in what was an incorporating rather than a federal union.

The two political parties in Anne's era were the Whigs and the Tories. Anne originally pledged her support to the Whigs; it was this party that backed the involvement in the War of the Spanish Succession in which England made many gains. However, the queen slowly began to side with the Tory way of thinking (partly due to her growing friendship with Abigail Masham) but by the time of her death, the Whigs had become the dominant party under George I and the Tories would be out of Parliament for nearly a hundred years. The Tories were involved in financial scandals in this period, especially the 'October Club' of individuals who got their name from the strong ale they drank. The monarchy was now constitutional rather than absolute, but Anne still had a lot of input. Many believe that her involvement restricted a number of talented politicians having their say within Parliament. Anyone who went against Anne, no matter how valid their argument, would be banished from political matters. There were three politicians who benefited from Anne's iron grip on the cabinet. These were Marlborough, Sidney Godolphin and Robert Harley. Harley in particular was popular with Anne due to his strict religious beliefs, something very important to the Anglican queen. Although

Defining moment
Death of William
30 July 1700
Prince William, the Duke of Gloucester sadly dies a few days after his 11th birthday, after being gripped by a fever. His death and Anne's failure to provide any other offspring end the Stuart line. William was the longest-surviving child of Anne and George. Born on 24 July 1689, he was the future queen's seventh pregnancy. A sickly prince from the beginning, he was the House of Stuart's main hope to keep their dynasty intact. William was unable to walk or talk until the age of three and suffered from regular convulsions caused by hydrocephalus (fluid on the brain).

Defining moment
Battle of Blenheim
13 August 1704
On the banks of the river Danube, over 100 battalions of men enter battle in one of the decisive turning points of the War of Spanish Succession. Both sides have amassed huge numbers of infantry, cavalry and artillery. The cavalry is dominated by dragoon and hussar regiments while the infantry carry flintlock muskets. In a tough-fought battle, the military expertise of Marlborough shines through as he breaks the deadlock with a well-timed cavalry charge. 13,000 Franco-Bavarian troops are captured as the war starts to turn against Louis XIV of France. The centre of the Austrian empire, Vienna, is saved and the depleted French armies retreat towards the 1713 Treaty of Utrecht.

Timeline

1665

Birth of a queen
Anne is born at 11.39pm and is the second daughter of James, Duke of York. She is born in England but spends her early years in France in the care of her maternal grandmother.
6 February 1665

Marriage to George
At only 18 years of age, Anne marries Prince George of Denmark. The marriage is believed to be an attempt to create an Anglo-Danish alliance against the Dutch.
28 July 1683

The Glorious Revolution
King James II is ousted by William and Mary of Orange, who become king and queen of England. Rather than an invasion by force, they are invited by Parliament to become monarchs.
1688

Queen Anne of England
Aged 37, Anne succeeds the unpopular William III upon his death. Her reign begins in a time of conflict as the War of the Spanish Succession is raging on the continent.
8 March 1702

Victories on the continent
Britain takes the upper hand in the war, with victories at Blenheim and the capture of Gibraltar severely weakening French and Spanish forces. Peace, however, is still ten years away.
1704

Marlborough at Blenheim, 1704

all powerful, Anne was constantly manipulated by those close to her and this influencing would play a major part in the petty and squabbled politics of the time. Many believe that her poor appointments prevented Britain from gaining Canada from France. Her legacy is of a queen who meant well but was naive to political concerns due to her religious nature and friendships.

When Anne ascended to power, the age of Enlightenment was just beginning. Brilliant architect Sir Christopher Wren was putting the finishing touches to the new St Paul's Cathedral, an apple had landed on Isaac Newton's head, while Jonathan Swift and Alexander Pope were creating fascinating literature. The church also benefited under Anne's reign with the queen directing more funds to the clergy. Under Henry VIII in particular, all this income went straight to royalty. Britain as a unified nation grew much

stronger during Anne's reign. This era can be seen as the consolidation of British power, economy and culture in both the Old and New World. Gibraltar was put under British rule and new colonies like Newfoundland were acquired from the defeated France. Overall, the economy and military were in a good state for the next monarch, George I.

Throughout her life, Anne suffered from poor health. She regularly overindulged in both food and drink and became known in some quarters as 'Brandy Nan' due to her fondness for liquor. As she neared the end of her life, Anne suffered from gout and could barely walk. Her coffin at Westminster Abbey is more of a square rather than a rectangle, as she had put on vast amounts of weight in her later life. Her personal doctors attempted to cure her using the methods of the time (bleeding and hot irons) but predictably these just made things worse. She saw her failure to have children as God punishing her for the sins she had committed. Anne had 17 pregnancies but failed to produce any offspring that survived into adulthood. The oldest child was William, who died in 1700 at the age of 11 after contracting smallpox on his birthday. When her husband died in 1708, it was obvious that Anne would not have an heir. Determined not to have a Catholic monarch, the government passed the Act of Settlement in 1701. Anne eventually died on 1 August 1714 at Kensington Palace at the age of 49.

The result was the end of the Stuarts and the beginning of the Hanoverian era, with the German Protestant Georg Ludwig (George I) at the helm.

> She never held parties or entertainment and even struggled with extended conversation

Life in the time of Queen Anne

First race held at Ascot
Horse racing may be called the sport of kings, but it was Queen Anne who ordered the building of the famous Ascot racecourse in Berkshire, England. Anne spent much of her spare time riding and hunting. Completed in 1711, Ascot is now the only racecourse still partly owned by the crown.

St Paul's Cathedral
The second incarnation of this iconic London cathedral, designed by architect Sir Christopher Wren, was finally completed in 1710 after 35 years work. The first cathedral was burnt down in the Great Fire of London in 1666; it had been the first cathedral to be built following Henry VIII's Reformation.

The gin problem
Gin was the drink of choice for many in Britain in this era. Cheap and widespread, it was the staple drink for the lower classes, and was blamed for crime and other adverse social effects. The 'gin craze' was only reduced in 1751 when a very heavy tax imposed on the alcohol made it unattainable for many Britons.

Growing leisure industry
The upper classes flocked to spa towns such as Bath and Buxton as it was widely believed that spa water could cure illness. Seaside towns like Brighton and Bognor boomed with this newfound prosperity. Pleasure gardens were also very popular in the rapidly growing city of London.

Highwaymen
The roads of early 18th Century Britain were not a safe place. Highwayman lurked in the shadows and would hold up pedestrians and carriages and rob them for all they were worth. This helped usher in watchmen and posses to make the streets safer.

Defining moment
The Treaty of Union
1 May 1707
It is during Anne's reign that the United Kingdom of Great Britain is first formed. Scotland is integrated into the new kingdom with the promise of greater economic benefits from the global empire. However, these gains do not materialise and the Scots find the vast majority of power and decisions being made in London. The most despised is the malt tax that affects Scottish whisky production. This causes a huge rift that will continue throughout the century in a series of rebellions and conflicts. This is, in part, motivated by Scotland's Catholic roots and the Protestant leaning in England at the time.

St Paul's Cathedral reopened
Architect Sir Christopher Wren completes the new design of the cathedral. It is opened a year later and still stands today, despite being a major target in the Blitz of WWII.
1710

Arrival of the Old Pretender
James Edward Stuart arrives on British soil in an attempt to gain the throne. The ensuing Scottish rebellion is quashed. Over in Europe, British forces triumph at the Battle of Malplaquet.
1708

Bill veto
Anne becomes the last monarch to veto a parliamentary bill as she declines to reorganise the Scottish militia. The queen and her ministers are concerned that the Scots would be disloyal if there were a French invasion.
1708

New political power
Robert Harley and the Tory party take power in Britain after a Tory-Whig coalition is ended. The Tories are much more lenient to France as Britain loosens its grip on Louis XIV.
1710

The Treaty of Utrecht
The War of the Spanish Succession ends with Britain making significant gains in Europe and the colonies. France is forced to recognise Britain's imperial power.
1713

1714

End of the Stuart line
Anne passes away after a long battle with illness. She is buried at Westminster Abbey and with no direct heir, the Stuart dynasty ends. George I becomes king and the House of Hanover begins.
1 August 1714

Isaac Newton often visited the court of George and impressed the king's relatives and advisors with his knowledge of science

GEORGE I
Germany, 1660-1727

Brief Bio The first Hanoverian king, Georg Ludwig gained the throne by virtue of being the great-grandson of James I and, more importantly, a Protestant. His reign fell in a period of change in Europe known as the Age of Enlightenment, which preceded the industrial revolution and urbanisation of Britain.

1714-1727

George I

George didn't bother learning English but still found time to imprison his wife and war against the Scots

The House of Stuart came to a halt in 1714 with the death of Queen Anne after a long period of ill health. Into the void stepped a little-known German by the name of Georg Ludwig - or as we now know him, George I. A Lutheran Protestant from birth, George was by no means the first in line to the British throne. Around 50 Catholic members of the aristocracy had much closer ties to Anne, but the 1701 Act of Settlement ensured that a Protestant monarch would acquire the British crown and so began the House of Hanover, a dynasty that would rule Britain for the next 187 years.

George was born, in the duchy of Brunswick-Lüneburg, into the upper tiers of the European elite. His father, Ernest Augustus was the Duke of Brunswick-Lüneburg and after his death in 1698, George would take his place and also become prince elector of the Holy Roman Empire.

In 1701, Charles II of Spain died, beginning the War of Spanish Succession, which would last for 13 years. Seeing this as an opportunity to increase his stake in European affairs, George played an active role in the conflict assisting the British against the French, which gave him recognition in England. The ruling Whig party saw him as an ideal replacement for the soon-to-be-ailing Anne. Many of the English population at this time were Protestant, so the decision of a Lutheran king to replace an Anglican queen was a simple one and George was crowned, aged 54, on 20 October 1714 at Westminster Abbey.

Unfortunately, George's reign began with a splutter, as it emerged that the cohort he arrived with included two mistresses and no wife. This angered the religious English population, even more so after further allegations arose about the treatment of his wife.

Sophia Dorothea of Celle married George in 1682, but ended her days imprisoned by him in a castle

George married Sophia Dorothea of Celle in 1682, successfully unifying the regions of Hanover and Celle. Despite producing two offspring (George Augustus and Sophia), the marriage was troubled by both spouses having a string of affairs. The most famous of these, and perhaps the one that angered George the most, was his wife's relationship with Swedish count, Phillip von Königsmarck. After the association was made public, George divorced his wife and sent her to the Castle of Ahlden, where she spent the rest of her life as a virtual prisoner, dying in 1727. The Swedish count was never heard of again and some sources claim that he was disposed of by Hanoverian courtiers on the order of the vengeful George. The witty English were well aware of this and, according to old tales, named his two mistresses the 'Elephant and Castle' after their stocky appearances.

Within a year, England was on the warpath once again as the Jacobite rising broke out. The Scots were deeply unhappy about another Protestant monarch taking the British crown so marched south, demanding that the exiled 'Old Pretender' James Francis Edward Stuart be put on the throne instead. The rebellion was quashed by English

forces but relations remained at a low point in the Union and more rebellions broke out frequently throughout the 18th Century.

Despite being the country's king, George did not speak much English. Instead he preferred to converse with Parliament and his advisors in French or Latin. One of these advisors was Robert Walpole, who can be considered Britain's first prime minister although he did not hold the title in quite the role it is now. Instead he was lord of the treasury and his influence was keenly felt. George didn't associate himself too much with political affairs, so left many important matters to Walpole, chancellor of the exchequer James Stanhope and secretary of state Charles Townshend. As time progressed, George relied more and more on Walpole and the Whigs for guidance. This was demonstrated in the South Sea Bubble of 1720, a stock market crash that seriously affected the previously booming South Sea Company, of which the king was a governor. George was implicated for aiding the mismanagement of the company but bailed out by Walpole, who used his business and financial know-how to reschedule the firm's debts.

George was rapidly alienating himself from a position of power and spent more and more time in Hanover rather than the country he ruled. His leadership was increasingly questioned by his son, George Augustus, who was given next to no power or authority in his father's kingdom.

The king was not fond of literature and art, but enjoyed the German Baroque composer, George Frideric Handel

George's reign can be seen as a time when the political power of the monarchy greatly decreased and the political cabinet system we see today began to take shape. Under his leadership, both Hampton Court Palace and Kensington Palace were extended and improved by renowned architect William Kent.

The king died aged 67 years and 12 days in June 1727 after a stroke. 2014 marked the 300th anniversary of his rise to power. He is the sixth-great-grandfather to Her Majesty Elizabeth II and his daughter gave birth to a son who would later become Frederick the Great of Prussia. The short-tempered and extravagant George II succeeded his father as the House of Hanover continued.

George I spoke little English and preferred to converse with advisors in French of Latin

Life in the time of George I

The Age of Enlightenment
The era of George I can be seen as the beginning of reason over tradition. A belief in science and technology was rising and the influence of religion in day-to-day life, although still high, was waning. Great thinkers of the age included Denis Diderot and John Locke. In the 1720s, Britain was readying itself for the forthcoming industrial revolution.

Piracy is finally defeated
The golden age of piracy had threatened merchants and navies for centuries but by the Hanoverian era, their pillaging and plundering was starting to slow down. The expansion of European empires and improved ship technology allowed navies to keep tabs on illegal piracy and in 1718 the legendary pirate Blackbeard (Edward Teach) was killed.

The plague is no more
Major advancements in medicine were still some way off, but 1720 signalled the last ever plague outbreak in Europe, as bubonic plague arrived in Marseilles, France. Smallpox replaced plague as the major ailment in Europe, but this didn't stop London's population rising to 1 million in this period.

Seeds of industrialisation
As the century progressed, great swathes of the population began moving from rural areas to towns. While political and economic power was still in the hands of landowners, there was a rise of middle-class professionals. Jethro Tull invented the seed drill and Thomas Newcomen developed the steam engine as food began to be more readily available.

Unrest in Europe
The Holy Roman Empire was still dominating Europe, but the Spanish, Dutch and French empires began to prosper in this period too. There was much unrest in Europe, with the Great Northern War (1700-1721) and the War of the Quadruple Alliance (1718-1720) being the major conflicts of George I's era.

The Jacobite risings
Great Britain was established in 1707 when the kingdoms of England and Scotland joined together. Increased taxes meant famine spread across the highlands, while Queen Anne was replaced by George I and not the Catholic James Frances Edward Stuart. Supported by the French and led by former Union secretary of state John Erskine, the Jacobite uprising began in 1715 as thousands of Scots marched south to put James on the throne. It ended at the Battle of Sheriffmuir, where some 16,000 Jacobites were beaten by half the number of Union soldiers. The resistance was quelled, but conflict broke out frequently until 1801 when Ireland joined the Union. The most well-known uprising was the 1745 Jacobite rebellion.

1727-1760
George II

Marginalised by his father and loathed by his son, George II had to strike an uneasy balance with Parliament and see off an invasion from the Stuart claimant to the throne, Bonnie Prince Charlie

f George I was an unpopular monarch, then George II was determined not to be. He had plenty of reasons to hate his father, after all. In 1694, when the young George Augustus was only 11, George I – then simply Prince George Louis of the German Electorate of Hanover – had accused George Augustus's mother, Sophia Dorothea, of adultery and locked her up in Ahlden House – where she would remain until she died, never seeing her children again. One tragic tale of dubious veracity describes the young heir frantically trying to swim the moat of Ahlden House to get to her.

A prince's cruelty became a king's cruelty when he inherited the throne of Great Britain in 1714 by way of a legal act of succession that omitted over 50 closer relatives due to their Catholicism. The son – aged 31 and already a war hero, having led Hanoverian troops in the Battle of Oudenarde against the French – joined his father in London and took on the title of Prince of Wales.

Whereas George I conducted his affairs in German – baffled by the British political system and surrounded by advisers he'd imported from Hanover – the Prince of Wales and his wife Caroline of Ansbach held their court in English, surrounded themselves with British politicians and took every care to present themselves as the 'Prince and Princess of Hearts'.

> George II was buried next to his wife with the sides of their coffins left open so that they could be together

> Naturalist Sir Hans Sloane left his collection to George II in 1753; the British Museum was created as a result

Meanwhile, supporters for the deposed Stuart dynasty – known as Jacobites – circulated pamphlets denouncing these Teutonic interlopers and holding up George I's troubled private life to scrutiny – not only had he imprisoned his wife, but he was rumoured to have murdered her lover and now cavorted openly about London with his mistress. Songs were sung mocking him and effigies of the king in a cuckold's horns were strung up and burnt.

When George I died, his son's refusal to attend his funeral in Hanover was seen as a statement of his commitment to Britain, rather than a statement of just how dysfunctional the father/son relationship had become. With the crown cold on the old king's brow, the Jacobites made their move, stirring up unrest at George II's coronation as they had done for George I before him. But while the Jacobite rising of 1715 led to a pitched battle in Scotland (the homeland of the Stuart kings), isolated uprisings across England and mass arrests of Jacobite sympathisers, the coronation of George II went off with barely any unrest. It wouldn't be the last that Britain would hear of its royalist rebels and their would-be kings, plotting from their exile in Europe. Despite his efforts to adapt, George II may have left Hanover, but Hanover never truly left him and the king followed in his father's footsteps in

GEORGE II
Germany, 1683-1760

Brief Bio The last British king to be born outside of Britain, and the last to lead an army in battle (at Dettingen in 1743), George II had a scandalous family life and a thirst for foreign intervention. Ultimately, however, he managed to unite the British nation and helped define the role of the constitutional monarch.

George II married Caroline of Ansbach out of love, even visiting her father's court in disguise to find out more about her

The tragedy of Prince Frederick

George I didn't just take George II's mother, he also stole his son. While the Georges headed for England in 1714 to take their crowns, Prince Frederick – aged only seven – remained in Hanover as ruler (albeit with a regent, until he was old enough to rule for himself). Designed to emphasise George I's commitment to his homeland, it also served to drive a wedge between the first and second in line to the throne that would never heal as Frederick was increasingly groomed for greatness, while Prince George was increasingly denied responsibility. Without parental oversight, Frederick grew into a libertine – in contrast to his austere father and grandfather – and gained a taste for women, wine and gambling. The relationship scarcely improved with George II's accession in 1727 as history quickly repeated itself, with political opposition to the king rallying around the new Prince of Wales as its figurehead. Much as George II skipped his father's funeral, he forbade Prince Frederick from attending Queen Caroline's when she died in 1737. When Frederick himself died prematurely in 1751, His Majesty declined to attend the funeral and the cycle of intergenerational conflict continued well into the next century between Frederick's son and grandson, George III and George IV.

attempting to fight the Electorate's corner with British resources. With greater influence in foreign politics than domestic politics (treaties were conducted monarch-to-monarch, and diplomats were appointed directly by the king), George II involved Britain in a series of continental escapades with a view to increasing Hanover's territory, establishing it as the dominant Protestant state in Germany, or protecting its fragile borders from invasion by its aggressive neighbours (including his own nephew, King Frederick the Great of Prussia). Few of these were in the best interests of Great Britain and wherever possible, Parliament pulled George II back from the brink. While prime minister Walpole dug in his heels to keep Britain out of the War of the Polish Succession in 1733, leaving Hanover to go it alone (perhaps wrongly in this case, as the German states emerged victorious), George won the battle and dragged Britain into the War of the Austrian Succession in 1739 (which gained Britain nothing, at the cost of vast numbers that were left dead and wounded).

Perhaps validating the king's diplomatic meddling was the Seven Years' War, which began in earnest in 1756 over the French threat to Hanover and concluded after the king's death, with Britain seizing French territory in North America, India and the Caribbean (as well as Spanish Florida), accelerating yet further Britain's growth as an imperial superpower.

Though he increasingly lost interest in domestic politics toward the end of his life, George II initially alarmed many ministers with his keen interest

in the business of government. In contrast to the vicious conflicts waged between Parliament and crown across the previous century, George II witnessed the modern constitutional monarchy take shape, with functioning government relying on some accord between the king (who confirmed appointments presented by Parliament, and had great sway in the House of Lords, which confirmed or denied bills raised by the House of Commons) and his ministers, who often had the influence among MPs to corral the votes in the first place.

Forced to negotiate with ministers as king, yet largely unchallenged in his role as elector, George II opted to spend so much time in Hanover that on one occasion, after several months had passed with no sign of the monarch, some wry Londoners left a notice on the gates of St James's Palace that read "Lost or strayed out of this house, a man who has left a wife and six children on the parish."

Unsurprisingly then, when the Jacobites finally made their play for power, George II was in Germany and not in Britain. The last gasp of the Stuart claim to the throne, Charles Edward Stuart - also known as the Young Pretender or Bonnie Prince Charlie - landed in Scotland on 23 July 1745 to gather the clans to his cause.

Prince William Augustus - George's youngest son and the militaristic Duke of Cumberland - garrisoned in the Netherlands, pleaded with his father to be allowed back to Britain to tackle the Jacobite menace ("Let me come home with whatever troops are thought necessary, for it would be horrid to be employed abroad when my home was in danger") and it wasn't until 31 August

> Patriotic anthem 'Rule, Britannia!' was first performed in 1740 as part of a masque at the home of Frederick, Prince of Wales

Defining moment
Harsh beginnings
10 November 1683

George Augustus is born in Hanover, the eldest son of George Lewis (Ludwig) - Prince of Hanover and Duke Brunswick-Lüneburg - and Sophia Dorothea. Hanover is one of the Electorates, autonomous German principalities whose elector princes vote on the candidate for Holy Roman Emperor. George Augustus speaks only French - the language of court - until he is four, when he is taught German and then also English and Italian. In 1694, Sophia Dorothea is accused of adultery and imprisoned; young George Augustus will never see her again.

Defining moment
Hanoverian age begins
20 October 1714

Following the death of Queen Anne (daughter of King James II), there are no suitable Protestant Stuart heirs and so George Lewis and George Augustus of Hanover are summoned to London, to become king of Great Britain and Prince of Wales. George Augustus's son Frederick is forced to remain in Hanover, under the supervision of a regent, and the new Prince and Princess of Wales go on to have more children, further driving a wedge between the three generations. Meanwhile, riots break out in 20 towns across England in support of the Stuart claimant, the Catholic James Francis Edward Stuart - Anne's younger, Catholic half-brother, known as 'The Old Pretender'.

Timeline

The Hanoverian succession
With the current British monarch Queen Anne unable to produce an heir, the government agrees the Act of Settlement, omitting Roman Catholics from the succession and establishing the Hanoverian dynasty as the heirs to the throne.
1701

A royal wedding
George Augustus marries Caroline of Ansbach out of love, rather than politics. After a previous love match collapsed, he visited the court of Ansbach in secret to assess her suitability.
2 September 1705

Bloodied in battle
Hanover joins Britain and Austria to battle France in the War of the Spanish Succession. 24-year-old George Augustus leads the rearguard of Hanoverian cavalry, impressing the British commander.
11 July 1708

Treaty Of Utrecht
The Tory-dominated government makes peace with France, ending the War of the Spanish Succession and earning the ire of Britain's German allies – particularly Hanover's rulers, the future George I and George II.
April 1713

Breaking point
George Augustus insults one of the king's allies at the baptism of his second son. George I banishes the Prince and Princess of Wales from court.
November 1717

that George II returned from Hanover and then on 4 September, the prime minister requested Cumberland to return with his troops. Edinburgh, meanwhile, threw open its gates to the Young Pretender, and the rebels scored their first victory at the Battle of Prestonpans (21 September). On 8 November, the Jacobites crossed the border into England, taking Carlisle, Manchester, Preston and Derby, before news of Cumberland's force (as well as another, larger fictional army invented by a British spy in the camp) sent them back to Scotland to fight on home ground. The resulting Battle of Culloden (16 April 1746) was a crushing defeat for the Jacobites, ending all hope for the Stuart claim to the throne of Britain. The victory made a national hero of Cumberland in England and a monster of him in Scotland, where his brutal reprisals earned him the nickname 'Butcher Cumberland'.

The greatest threat to the Hanoverian dynasty had ended, with little direct involvement from the king himself, but indirectly George II saved his bloodline, and perhaps his nation. Expecting the Jacobite rising to continue into England (the French had held off supporting the Young Pretender too overtly unless he could prove support in the south), Bonnie Prince Charlie was winded by the lack of cheering crowds awaiting him and he was forced to line the route into the Lancashire town of Preston with his Scots followers. A song sung in London theatres, with its refrain of "God save the king", became a patriotic sensation and was later adopted as the British national anthem, although the anti-Jacobite 'Rebellious Scots to crush' verse was quietly retired soon after. A boorish German transplant with a toxic family he

may well have been, but the realities of a 31-year peace, unchallenged Protestant dominance, and a functioning Parliament under George I and George II had not passed the English by.

In the aftermath of the Jacobite rising, the powers of the Scottish lords were severely curtailed, but - to the shock of many - George II appointed a number of Scots to key roles in the army and with the growth of the British empire, many in Scotland became gradually more invested in the idea of Great Britain and its unifying crown.

That, more than anything, was George II's legacy. Though he spent much of his reign fussing over his homeland - Hanover was humiliatingly occupied by the French in 1757 and, continuing the father/son friction that had defined the dynasty so far, the king ostracised Cumberland for his failure to defend it - his gift to Britain was stability. George II redefined the relationship between the institutions of British government and redefined the monarchy, not as a driving force as the Stuarts were, but a rallying point for the nation.

On the morning of 25 October 1760, the king died from a rupture of the heart, leaving his grandson - the son of Prince Frederick, who had died some years earlier - to take the British throne as George III.

"With him our laws and liberties were safe," reflected writer and social reformer Elizabeth Montagu. "He possessed in a great degree the confidence of his people and the respect of foreign governments; and a certain steadiness of character made him of great consequence in these unsettled times.

"His character would not afford subject for epic poetry, but will look well in the sober page of history."

> George II was the last British king to lead an army in battle, at the Battle of Dettingen - in Bavaria - in 1743

Defining moment
George II is crowned
22 October 1727

After years of being increasingly marginalised by his father, George Augustus ascends to the throne upon George I's death in Hanover. He is crowned king of Great Britain to the sound of four new anthems from German composer George Frideric Handel at a service at Westminster Abbey. In contrast to the Jacobite backlash that greeted his unpopular father's accession, George II's coronation is marked by little public unrest. At the urging of Queen Caroline he retains George I's prime minister, the influential Sir Robert Walpole, in exchange for an allowance of £800,000 a year on the Civil List. Walpole goes on to become Britain's longest-serving PM at an incredible 20 years of service.

Life in the time of George II
Sweet teeth
Thanks to Britain's growing empire widening access to produce and bringing down prices, many of the previous century's luxuries became mass-market. Between 1690 and 1740, consumption of sugar doubled and cotton, rum and tobacco flooded into Britain. The sad truth is that much of this was the result of slave labour.

Whigs vs Tories
MPs were divided into Whigs (pro-Parliament) and Tories (pro-monarch). Thanks to their support for a treaty that left Hanover in the lurch in 1713 and perceived Jacobite sympathies, George I and II locked the Tories out of government for both their reigns.

Gin gets a tonic
Gin became the tipple of choice for the urban poor in the 1720s. Cheap to produce and mind-numbingly strong, by the 1740s an average of six gallons per person were being drunk, and by 1750 nearly half of Britain's total wheat harvest was used in gin production.

Birth of Canada
Thanks to one of George II's pro-Hanover wars against France, Britain took all of the latter's North American possessions in 1763. Moves to placate both the Native Americans, who supported Britain, and the French-speaking inhabitants of what is now Canada increased resentment in the original British colonies, paving the way for the American Revolution.

A to Z
First published 15 April 1755, Samuel Johnson's *A Dictionary of the English Language* remained the most comprehensive such volume for over 150 years and acted as the foundation for the development of language and learning in both Britain and North America. Johnson was paid 1,500 guineas for his trouble.

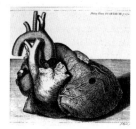

● **Hanoverian disgrace**
In a humiliating defeat, French troops occupy Hanover. The Duke of Cumberland is stripped of his command by George II for his failure to defend the homeland. **11 August 1757**

1760

● **Family reunited**
Frederick joins his parents in England and takes the title Prince of Wales. There's friction with George I thanks to his hedonistic lifestyle and Frederick becomes a focus for political opposition.
1728

● **The queen is dead**
Queen Caroline dies following a ruptured womb stemming from earlier problems in childbirth. A heartbroken George II swears never to remarry and refuses Prince Frederick permission to attend the funeral.
20 November 1737

● **Last warrior king**
George II becomes the last British king to lead his troops in battle. The Battle of Dettingen deprives the French of an early victory in the War of Austrian Succession.
27 June 1743

● **Jacobites strike back**
The most credible Jacobite insurrection of George II's reign is put down by his son, Duke of Cumberland, at the Battle of Culloden. Bonnie Prince Charlie – son of James Francis Edward Stuart – flees to France.
16 April 1746

● **Year of glory**
Victories against the French in the Seven Years' War lead to 1759 declared Annus Mirabilis – a year of miracles. The Royal Navy anthem 'Heart Of Oak' is written in commemoration.
1759

The king is dead ●
George II dies on the toilet, aged 76. The cause of death is aortic aneurysm, a rupture of the heart which causes shock and massive internal bleeding.
25 October 1760

"The king's penchant for patriotic remarks and foreign war, along with him being English-born, played well to the masses"

GEORGE III
England, 1738-1820

Brief Bio

Famous in history and popular tales as 'Mad King George', the king was probably suffering from a disorder known as porphyria, which manifests with severe neurological problems. Despite this, for much of his reign George was loved by his people thanks to his British birth, and knack of saying the right patriotic thing at exactly the right time. His reign saw British achievements grow.

1760-1820
George III

The first British-born king of England since James II, King George III was patriot and mad meddler in equal measure, leading to a reign arguably plagued by instability and financial mismanagement

George III was the King of the United Kingdom of Great Britain during one of the most tumultuous and disruptive periods in the power's history, with his reign witnessing the collapse of British control in the Americas, political instability in the British Parliament and near national bankruptcy. Despite this damning legacy however, for much of his reign George was well thought of among the commoners, with the king's penchant for patriotic remarks and foreign war, along with him being English-born, playing well to the masses. Even the king's famous 'madness', which grew more and more severe throughout his life did not seem to dent this view, with, as late as 1810 - near to the height of his insanity - the king popular among the people.

As one would expect however, George III was not as well thought of by the ruling political classes of England, with his reign leaving a disastrous legacy of political interference. Indeed, during his time as monarch, which began after his father Frederick,

> George had nine sons and six daughters, including Edward Augustus, the father of England's future Queen Victoria

> George used many titles throughout his reign, changing with the times and the countries he ruled

Prince of Wales died early from a lung injury and the crown passed from his Grandfather George II directly to him, George directly or indirectly caused the dissolution of the British government more than three times, with the most famous being the case of 1784, where George - dissatisfied with a bill setting forth the passage of powers in India from the East India Company to some of his parliamentary enemies - sent a message to the House of Lords that any member who voted for its passage would be considered 'his enemy'. The bill was rejected by the House of Lords and three days later the ministry was also dismissed. The subsequent election saw the then monarch-friendly William Pitt the Younger instigated as prime minister. This typified George III's attitude towards the elected parliament of his country during his reign, with the monarch frequently acting in his own interests or in the interest of the monarchy and overruling them. For example, during the tenure of William Pitt the

Younger as prime minister, George helped maintain his influence by creating an unprecedented number of new peers in the House of Lords, all of which - indebted to him as benefactor - voted in his favour whenever called upon. This not only disrupted the political establishment but, especially in the case of the American War of Independence, left Britain poorer financially and with less power overall on the world stage. Prior to the American War of Independence, Britain had been the leading military force worldwide, with its main rivals of France and Spain recently defeated in warfare and its cultural influence stretching throughout the Americas, Africa and even India. Thanks to George however, maintaining this at all cost would almost cripple the country.

In fact, with the American Revolutionary War, George III famously ignored the advice of his own ministers and voted repeatedly to keep Britain at war with the revolutionaries, even despite the fact that it was leading the country into a financial hole. According to the Victorian commentator George Trevelyan, George apparently wished to 'keep the

> During his reign Great Britain partook in the Seven Years' War, the American Revolution and the Napoleonic Wars

rebels harassed, anxious and poor by the indefinite prolongation of a war which promised to be eternal.' Of course, this kind of jingoistic flag-waving was often portrayed as merely the king being patriotic to the wider country, with public opinion staying firmly on his side right up until the early 1780s, when the desperate state of the country's finances began to become all too evident.

Indeed, George's financial mismanagement and lust for war meant that throughout the 1770s the national debt of the country rose to a level where it required an annual revenue of £4 million to service it and the king became famous for raiding the treasury to cover spiralling royal debts. This vast financial burden came courtesy primarily due to the costs of garrisoning and administering the large expansion of territory that control of the American colonies brought, a series of on-off wars with France and Spain, and huge annual loans payable to the East India Company to control Britain's interests in India. The country couldn't cope and eventually independence was won.

This loss of the American colonies hit George III badly and after the resignation of the then prime minister Frederick North he even considered abdication, with George bitterly resigned to the separation and loss of territory. While abdication

never came, the anxiety of losing the war seemed to place a great strain on George and throughout the following decades became increasingly ill, with bouts of his 'illness' making his appearances in public and participation in British politics more and more restrained. By the time he had a massive mental collapse in 1789 he was beginning to go blind and deaf and after relapses into illness in 1801 and 1804, was largely unfit to rule the country.

George's illness and decline reached a head in 1810, when after the untimely death of his youngest daughter, he mentally collapsed entirely and became completely deranged. As he was no longer fit to rule, the British Parliament passed the Regency Act of 1811 thereby allowing his son, the Prince of Wales George IV, to rule in his place.

For the last ten years of his life George III was largely confined to the interior and grounds of Windsor Castle, with his madness only punctuated by tiny moments of lucidity. His son George ruled the country in his place - albeit with none of the popularity that he had done during most of his years - the American revolutionaries established the young country of the United States of America - indicating that George was a tyrant in their Declaration of Independence - and, following his eventual death on 29 January 1820, views of his reign in Britain slowly altered from a stoic pillar of patriotic tradition in an age of unwanted revolution, to one wholly more negative.

> George III lived for 81 years and 239 days, while he reigned as monarch for 59 years and 96 days

Interestingly, today however, despite George III being largely remembered for just his madness, financial ineptitude and hunger for war, academically George's reign is increasingly being seen with a different, more positive perspective, one that highlights his learning and culture. In fact, it is true that George III was not only one of the most cultured English monarchs of all time, studying science throughout his childhood and

George (right) as a boy with his brother and tutor

> "George's reign is increasingly being seen with a different, more positive perspective"

Timeline

1738

Born to rule
On the 4th of June George William Frederick is born in London at Norfolk House two months prematurely. He was thought unlikely to survive however was baptised and lived.
1738

Marries Charlotte Sophia
After succeeding to the throne in October 1760, almost a year later George III marries Charlotte Sophia of Mecklenburg-Strelitz. He is crowned King of England 17 days later.
1761

Signs of madness?
Unhappy with the then prime minister's - George Grenville - continuous attempts to reduce the King's prerogatives, George III dismisses him after falling ill for a brief period.
1765

George's tea party
Following decades of meddling, including introducing the grossly unpopular Stamp Act, the British government begins to lose its grip on the American Colonies starting with the Boston Tea Party
1773

A cartoon from 1786 depicting George III and Queen Charlotte raiding the national treasury to cover royal debts. The prime minister, William Pitt the Elder, is seen handing him another money bag

The mad monarch

early adult life - he collected scientific instruments too, many of which can be seen in the London Science Museum today, and possessed his vary own observatory - but also taking a keen interest in the arts and agriculture. Indeed, it was George III who founded and paid the initial costs of the British Royal Academy of Arts and it was also George III who funded the construction and maintenance of famous astronomer William Herschel's ground-breaking 40-foot telescope. He was, rather cruelly, also comically referred to as 'Farmer George' by his opponents due to his keen interest and love of agriculture, writing numerous articles under a pseudonym in agricultural texts and pamphlets.

In fact, George's learning became rather quite famous in contrast to many earlier kings - and especially so in light of his stupid and unlearned son - with him accruing a royal collection of books that numbered the tens of thousands and opening his collection freely to learned scholars who wished

to gain the knowledge held within. 65,000 of these books were later donated to the British Museum and now form the heart of its collection.

Whether or not this contribution to the arts and sciences can be seen as redeeming features capable of permanently redressing the perception of George III's reign is open to debate, however there is one thing that all commentators, both modern and historical alike, agree on and that is that his rule was no where near as bad as his son's, with George VI acting throughout his short reign with a wanton disregard for Britain and its people, while bringing the monarchy to an historical low. Writing in his diary, contemporary of George VI Charles Greville said of the king that, 'He only wishes to be powerful in order to exercise the most puerile caprices, gratify ridiculous resentments, indulge vulgar prejudices, and amass or squander money; not one great object connected with national glory or prosperity ever enters his brain.'

> George's reign is now seen as a very positive time for British arts and sciences, which flourished under his aegis

Today, as in the 18th Century, why George III regressed into madness is not fully understood, with records from the time of his 'illness' vague or nonexistent. Obviously, in the 18th and early 19th Century, mental illness was nowhere near as understood as it is today, with those affected typically just locked up. One thing is clear though, the recurring nature of George's illness – with the first record of it coming as early as 1765 – does seem to indicate it was more mental than physical.

A few hypotheses have since been postulated by historians, the most prominent being that the king suffered from the blood disease porphyria, a rare inherited series of enzyme disorders that can often lead to neurological problems. This cannot be confirmed however for sure, albeit with records of his madness and later dementia tallying well with the hypothesis. An analysis of a few surviving strands of George's hair in 2004 also revealed a high level of arsenic, which is also known to precipitate attacks of porphyria.

Arguably the worst recorded case of George's madness was the relapse that led to his death. Starting at Christmas 1819, George spoke nonsense for 58 hours straight before falling exhausted into a coma. He never recovered consciousness and was dead within a month.

1820

George chooses Pitt
George III causes Parliament to be dissolved due to a dispute over the India Bill, with the subsequent election giving his own monarch-friendly candidate, William Pitt the Younger, a solid mandate.
1784

Ministry of All the Talents
After George's long-time bete noire William Grenville had taken back control of Parliament after Pitt the Younger's death in 1806, setting up his famous Ministry of All the Talents, George once more causes Parliament to be dissolved.
1807

Amelia dies
After a decade of decline in the health of his youngest and favourite daughter Princess Amelia, she suddenly dies at the age of just 27, sending the near-blind George into 'scenes of distress and crying every day'.
1810

Prince Regent
George finally accepts the need for the Regency Act of 1811, allowing his son to take over the official duties of king as Prince Regent. He does so until George's death.
1811

Mad man of Windsor
Following the Regency Act of 1811, George became increasingly mad, confined at all times to Windsor Castle. In 1818 his wife dies and he is too insane to realise.
1818

58 hours of insanity
Following a bad bout of insanity where he talked nonsense for 58 hours, George III collapses and never recovers. He dies on 29 January 1820 and is buried in St George's Chapel, Windsor Castle.
1820

© Getty

George IV

The truth about the son of the mad king who is better known as a caricature than a ruler of his country

It's easy to paint a caricature of King George IV. Debauched, gluttonous, lecherous, drunken, short-tempered, impulsive, profligate and careless, the laundry list of the man's defects paint an extremely unflattering picture of the king. But who was this man who incited such contempt, mockery, and outright hatred?

George was born on 12 August 1762, the oldest of King George III and Queen Charlotte's fifteen children. He was a bright and thoughtful child but by the age of six his natural intelligence was beginning to be countered by some of the less flattering aspects of his character. He was short-tempered and easily distracted, so the young Prince of Wales and his brother Frederick were sent to a stricter house of learning that made free use of capital punishment to correct any laziness or insubordination. Despite the prince's apparent need for frequent beatings, it was obvious that he was clever and his ability to master language and music was truly impressive.

However, this promising young man had not won the respect of his father. George III was a harsh taskmaster indeed, and viewed any failing or shortcoming in his son as a sign of a weakness of character. He was not impressed by the progress his son was making in his studies, and he was particularly disappointed by the lack of interest he showed in religion, which the king thought bordered upon contemptuous.

It was his all-too-public womanising, which grew and grew throughout his teens, which would continue to land George in serious trouble. His impulsive nature, aided by his powerful love of wine, led to a series of affairs that quickly gave the Prince of Wales a reputation. He bedded married women, well-known actresses, and even one of the Queen's maids of honour. Sometimes he was so overcome with lust that he even promised payment in exchange for becoming a faithful mistress, such as the £20,000 he pledged to Mary Robinson to give up her acting career.

His notoriety wasn't limited to his womanising. He was known for associating with Whig politicians (much to the irritation of his conservative-leaning father) and for his extraordinary talent for mimicry (which inevitably created as many enemies as it did friends). Naturally, all this socialising needed financing, which was yet another cause of conflict between the prince and his father. King George III and his wife lived relatively simply, and his son bitterly resented being forced to make do with the meagre allowance he was given. King George had even rejected the allowance proposed by Parliament, stating that it was irresponsible to give £100,000 a year to his son.

The endless spending only grew worse when the prince became 21 and took possession of Carlton House at Pall Mall. With furniture from China, craftsmen from France, and neighbouring houses

> Regent for nine years as his father struggled with illness, George wouldn't become king until he was 57 years old

George was notoriously bad with money, spending thousands of pounds on his estate and on his debauched lifestyle

GEORGE IV
British, 1762-1830

Brief Bio

From a charming rogue to a bloated national joke, the life of George IV was one of tremendous appetites and frustrated ambition. A disappointment to his father who spent his life in trouble, George's path to the throne was a torturous and very public one and by the end of his life his reputation lay in tatters.

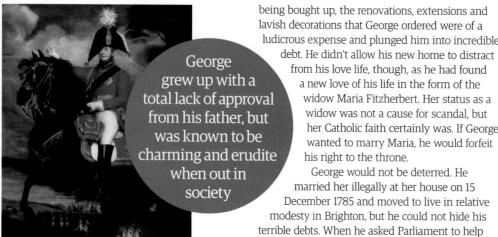

George grew up with a total lack of approval from his father, but was known to be charming and erudite when out in society

An 1809 depiction of King George IV

British arts in bloom

Despite his many failures as a King and, frankly, as a human being, the major redeeming factor for King George IV has been his love for and patronage of the arts. While his work on Carlton House can be reasonably seen as a selfish endeavour, George made his collection of incredible art available for viewing by the public. Artists such as Constable, Gainsborough, Reynolds, Stubbs and more were on public display. The National Gallery in Trafalgar Square, London was created in large part due to his efforts and patronage. In the field of architecture, John Nash worked not only on Carlton House, but all over London as his work defined the look of the era.

His efforts and interests were not strictly limited to the visual arts. This was a boom time for English literature, with Shelley and Byron defining the poetry of the era while Mary Shelley wrote Frankenstein. George became a patron of Jane Austen, who was invited to visit Carlton House. Austen was not at all taken with her sponsor and spoke of supporting his wife Caroline because the King was so awful.

His character defects certainly can't be ignored, but his patronage of the arts and the extraordinary work created during his life should not be either.

being bought up, the renovations, extensions and lavish decorations that George ordered were of a ludicrous expense and plunged him into incredible debt. He didn't allow his new home to distract from his love life, though, as he had found a new love of his life in the form of the widow Maria Fitzherbert. Her status as a widow was not a cause for scandal, but her Catholic faith certainly was. If George wanted to marry Maria, he would forfeit his right to the throne.

George would not be deterred. He married her illegally at her house on 15 December 1785 and moved to live in relative modesty in Brighton, but he could not hide his terrible debts. When he asked Parliament to help him, the question of his marriage to Maria was raised and denied, much to her distress. The prince was bailed out, this time, but a bigger problem was on the horizon.

In 1788, the king became seriously ill. What would later be revealed to be porphyria provoked a shocked and confused reaction from his family and a parliament that didn't know what to do in the face of this apparent mental illness. When Prince George went to visit his father, he reacted by slamming his son's head into a wall.

It was clear that the king was unfit to rule, but the crisis that followed showed that many in the country did not believe that his son was either. The Tory government, led by Prime Minister William Pitt, believed that if Prince George came to power

then they would lose theirs, as he would almost certainly instate a new government made up of his Whig friends. George was thrilled at the possibility and plotted away while both parties lobbied the issue. The Whigs praised the brilliant young man, while the Tories painted him as a debaucherous idiot. Finally a Regency bill was passed in Parliament that would seriously limit his powers, but the king recovered before it passed before the House of Lords.

Faced with this bitter disappointment, George's behaviour became worse and worse, and it did not go unnoticed by the national press. He took more mistresses, abandoned Maria, and finally married his cousin Caroline on 8 April 1795 to get rid of a new and massive set of debts. There was no love involved in the match and no love lost between the two. It was such a shambles that he drunkenly fell into the fireplace on their wedding night. George back in the arms of Maria by the time Caroline gave birth to Charlotte almost exactly nine months later. To make matters worse, George III was far more fond of his granddaughter than he had ever been of his eldest son, while Caroline soon as notorious for her love life as her husband.

The day Prince George had waited so long for finally came in 1810 when his father succumbed to his illness and the Regency question could no longer be avoided. However, he surprised many when he came into power on 5 February 1811 by keeping the Tory government in power, which his Whig friends took as a betrayal. George would soon find that

Maria Fitzherbert, George IV's wife

Defining moment
George marries Maria Fitzherbert
15 December 1785

Despite a life littered with mistresses, George could be incredibly committed to the pursuit of one woman, as proved by his relentless courtship of widow Maria Fitzherbert. Marrying her was out of the question, due to Acts that made it impossible for anyone married to a Catholic to become the monarch, and for a Prince or Princess to marry without the King or Queen's consent. George and Maria married illegally with only a few of her relatives present. Maria was embarrassed by the necessary secrecy, but it would be her arms that George would return to after his failure of a royal marriage.

Defining moment
The Regency Crisis
1788-1789

Prince George must have thought that his time had come early when his father became ill in 1788. Doctors later diagnosed George III with porphyria, at the time it was assumed that he had gone mad. The question of whether a Regency bill was the answer was made difficult by the uncertain diagnosis and the fact that the in-power Tories believed that Prince George would give power to his Whig friends. The crisis dragged on as both sides used George as the centre of their publicity campaigns, but by the time an extremely restrictive Regency bill had been approved, his father had recovered.

Timeline

1762

● **The Prince is born**
In August, 1762, Queen Charlotte gave birth to her first son, George August Frederick. He would be King George III's first child but by no means the last, as the young boy would have 14 siblings.
12 August 1762

● **A home for a Prince**
At the age of 21, George took possession of Carlton House and it soon became one of the free-spending Prince's biggest expenses. His expansions, improvements and furnishings were colossally expensive and plunged him into debt.
1783

● **Bailing out Prince George**
With the matter of Prince George's debts becoming increasingly problematic, he appealed to his Whig friends in Parliament to help him out. Having denied that he was married to Maria Fitzherbert, George was given money to pay his debt and finish Carlton House.
1787

● **A Royal Wedding**
At his father's insistence, Prince George finally agreed to a marriage that George III approved of: his cousin Princess Caroline of Brunswick. The pair loathed each other and George drank heavily throughout his wedding day and night.
8 April 1795

friends were in short supply, as he realised that being king meant that much was expected of him and public opinion now meant a lot. He turned to drink, while Caroline went abroad, leaving him with the wilful Charlotte. He forced her to break off her relationship with the Prince of Prussia and saw her married Prince Leopold of Saxe-Coburg-Saalfeld in 1816, but she was dead within two years and the public accused the Prince Regent of not caring. Public perception was becoming an increasingly massive issue, as he was held responsible for the government's mistakes, including the brutal events of the Peterloo Massacre.

In 1820, King George III died, and the 57 year old Prince George was now king. However, any happiness at this was short-lived as Caroline returned to claim the power that was rightfully hers and to make life hell for her husband. George desperately tried to prove that she had committed adultery and have her not only divorced but also charged with high treason. The result was inconclusive, however, despite the obvious veracity of the claim, and Caroline's popularity soared. The public was on her side.

That is, until the coronation. When George was crowned King George IV, the public rallied behind him at his magnificent occasion and Caroline was booed as she left after failing to gain access to Westminster Abbey. The period following the coronation was a glorious time for George. Caroline died shortly after this very public humiliation and George suddenly found himself with the people's support behind him.

Parliament would prove to be another matter. After trying to reconcile with the Whigs, George lost the support of the Tories and failed to regain the friendship of the men he had betrayed when he became regent. The amount of real power he possessed dwindled, despite his friendship with the Prime Minister Canning. Even that friendship would be short lived when Canning died in August 1827, and soon after George found himself with the Duke of Wellington as Prime Minister, someone who had no interest in dealing with an eccentric, bad-tempered king.

George's behaviour became increasingly erratic. He told Wellington that he had not only fought at the Battle of Waterloo but had been responsible for victory at the Battle of Salamanca. When Wellington finally forced him to pass the Roman Catholic Relief Act that he was vehemently opposed to, George's mental state was clearly in a decline. He raged against the bill passing, threatening to fire members of Parliament despite lacking the power to do so, and slipped into a state that would lead to his death.

Ever one for over-indulgence, the king shocked his visitors and staff with the amount that he was now eating and drinking, compounded by the huge doses of laudanum he was taking. He suffered from gout and various other sicknesses, for which he was given leeches and was bled, and he grew obese. He died on 26 June 1830, with his reputation as bad as it had ever been. As the years passed, George's legacy would prove to be one of indulgence, bad judgement and unpleasantness.

> He was morbidly obese when he died and was consuming an obscene amount of painkillers, alcohol and food

Life in the time of George IV

Wellington and Waterloo

On 18 June 1815, Wellington's forces took on Napoleon at Waterloo and won. It would be the decisive victory against the French and would propel Arthur Wellesley, first Duke of Wellington to greatness. However, Wellington could not stand George IV, who insisted on claiming that he fought at Waterloo.

A king without power

From his time as Regent to his death, King George IV was inconsistent when it came to demanding the power that was owed to him. When the Catholic Emancipation Act was being forced upon him, he threatened to dismiss all who stood in his way, a threat that nobody took seriously.

Social unrest and bloodshed

Shortly after the death of George III, a group of political reactionaries attempted to kill the members of the Cabinet. In 1819, George approved a violent suppression of a group demanding Parliamentary reform at St Peter's Field in Manchester.

Metropolitan Police Force

In the 1820s the London police force was disorganised and rising crime rates were repeatedly raised in Parliament. Finally, in 1829, Home Secretary Sir Robert Peel founded the Metropolitan Police Force, with a 10-mile radius covered by six divisions. Over time, it expanded to become the force it is today.

Georgie Porgie, Pudding and Pie

Despite a brief flirtation with popularity, the general public did not look upon George IV kindly. He was often the subject of grotesque caricatures, his obituary in *The Times* chalked him as friendless. It's even thought that the *Georgie Porgie* nursery rhyme is about him.

The Prince Regent
After George III relapsed towards the end of 1910, Parliament passed a Regency Act and Prince George finally found himself in a position of power. However, he found himself with precious few friends in Parliament after keeping the Tories in power.
5 February 1811

Defining moment
King at last
1820 - 1821

After decades of living in his father's shadow and with his disapproval, the time had come for George IV to rule. George III died in 1820, after Prince George had been regent for nearly 10 years. After roughly a decade of very public ridicule and being ignored (at best) in Parliament, George IV suddenly enjoyed a moment of popularity after a stunning coronation. He also had the last laugh in his toxic relationship with Queen Caroline, who was barred from entering Westminster Cathedral despite her best efforts to claim her rights as his wife.

1830

Death of Princess Charlotte
George IV's relationship with his strong-willed daughter Charlotte had always been strained. When she died in childbirth two years after marrying the Prince of Saxe-Coburg-Saalfeld, he found himself blamed by the public.
6 November 1817

The Queen on trial
Following the death of King George III, the Prince began legal proceedings to keep his hated wife from becoming Queen, accusing her of adultery and high treason. While there was certainly evidence for the former, the bill was withdrawn before reaching the Commons.
17 August 1820

A Royal Scottish visit
Following George's coronation, the King was enjoying a popularity he'd never known before, as exemplified by his visit to Scotland in 1822, where he enjoyed a surprisingly warm reception, a rare thing indeed for a Hanoverian monarch.
August 1822

Catholic Relief Act
Throughout his time as regent and King, George had fought against any form of relief or emancipation for Catholics, alienating him from the Whigs, but he was finally pressured into passing the Catholic Relief Act in 1829 to his great frustration.
13 April 1829

The King is Dead
The fact that George IV was in ill health was no secret, as visitors remarked on his obesity, terrible gout and gruesome eating, drinking and laudanum habits. When he finally expired his reputation was at its lowest point.
26 June 1830

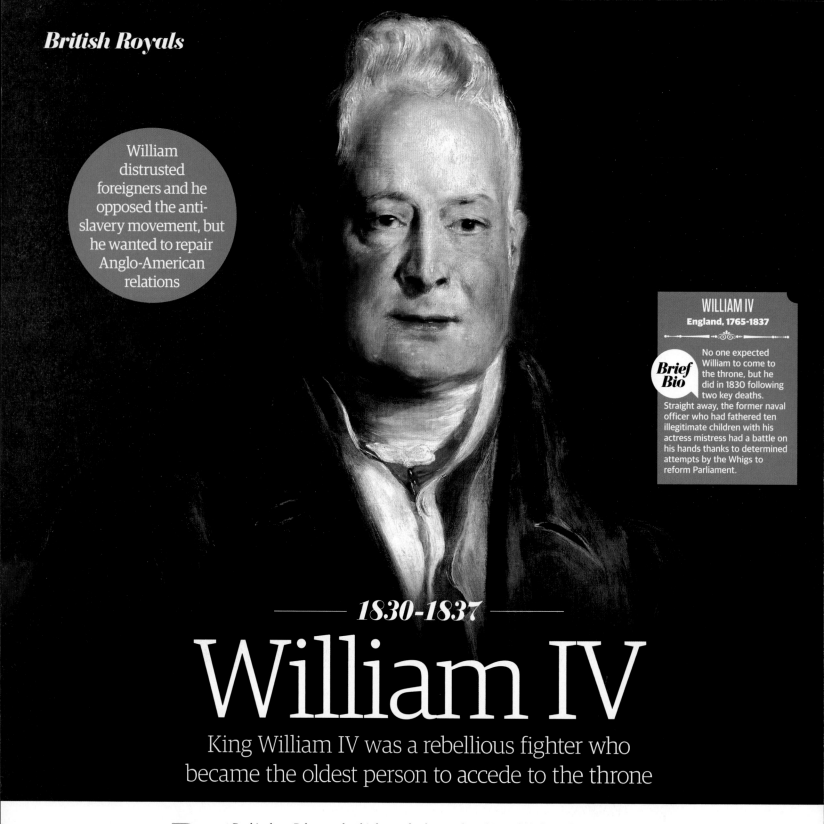

William distrusted foreigners and he opposed the anti-slavery movement, but he wanted to repair Anglo-American relations

WILLIAM IV
England, 1765-1837

Brief Bio No one expected William to come to the throne, but he did in 1830 following two key deaths. Straight away, the former naval officer who had fathered ten illegitimate children with his actress mistress had a battle on his hands thanks to determined attempts by the Whigs to reform Parliament.

1830-1837

William IV

King William IV was a rebellious fighter who became the oldest person to accede to the throne

orn at Buckingham Palace as the third son of George III and Queen Charlotte, William took to the throne on 26 June 1830 at the age of 64. He was the younger brother of George IV whose only legitimate child, Princess Charlotte of Wales, had died in 1817 as well as Prince Frederick, Duke of York and Albany, who'd died in 1827. Almost immediately, William found himself embroiled in a tricky political situation.

William had had a strict upbringing thanks to the disciplined nature of his father and, because he wasn't expected to become king, he had entered the Royal Navy in 1779 at the age of 13, serving against the Spanish in the Battle of St Vincent a year later. He also served in New York during the American War of Independence which lasted until 1783, during which

he was the subject of a kidnap plot that, despite being approved by George Washington, had been discovered and foiled.

When William returned to Britain in 1788, he was eager to become a duke, but his father refused the request, fearing it would lead to political opposition. This led to resentment and William hit back, threatening to run for Parliament by contesting the constituency of Totnes in Devon. William threatened allegiance with the Whigs (his father was allied with the Tories) and this act of rebellion forced George III to back down. In 1789, William IV was created Duke of Clarence and a year later he left active service in the Royal Navy as a rear admiral.

During the 1790s, William settled in the royal residence Bushy House with his pretty and

"He set up home with Dorothy Jordan, a famous Anglo-Irish actress with whom he had ten illegitimate children"

intelligent mistress Dorothy Jordan (real name Phillips), a famous Anglo-Irish actress and courtesan with whom he had ten illegitimate children, each of whom took the surname FitzClarence.

The relationship came to an end in 1811 with William giving her a yearly stipend and granting her custody of their daughters while he looked after his sons. Dorothy Jordan's life took a turn for the worse following the separation when she was forced to return to the stage to help pay debts incurred by a son-in-law. William cancelled the stipend and took custody of his daughters. Dorothy died in poverty in France in 1816.

A year later, the death of Princess Charlotte of Wales led to a string of marriages for members of the royal family, who were eager to produce heirs to safeguard the succession. William married the Protestant Princess Adelaide of Saxe-Meiningen on 11 July 1818 after meeting just a week earlier. They wed in a double ceremony in Kew Palace with William's brother Prince Edward, Duke of Kent, and bride Victoria, dowager Princess of Leiningen. Their first daughter, Charlotte, lived for just a few hours and Adelaide suffered a miscarriage during her second pregnancy. Her second daughter, Elizabeth, died four months after birth and the couple had stillborn twin boys in 1822.

When William took to the throne in 1830, the Duke of Wellington's Tory government had lost ground in the general election to the Whigs, informally led by Earl Grey. The Tories had 250 seats to the Whig's 196, which meant they did not have a stable majority. A series of defeats forced Wellington and his cabinet to resign and go into opposition, with Sir Robert Peel becoming the Tory leader of the opposition in the House of Commons. Earl Grey became the Whigs' formal leader, with the 1831 general election seeing his party win 370 seats to the Tories' 235.

William was crowned king on 8 September 1831 in Westminster Abbey in a rather low-key, inexpensive

ceremony. He was sympathetic to the Whigs, especially their determination to bring in reform of the traditional electoral system. But every attempt was defeated in the House of Lords. A political crisis ensued, leading to an outbreak of riots and William knew he had to act.

Key to the 1832 Reform Act was the abolition of electoral system abuse. There were 'rotten boroughs', constituencies that had small electorates and yet could return an MP or two. At the same time, large industrial cities such as Manchester and Birmingham had no Parliamentary seats at all. Earl Grey threatened to resign unless William created more Whig peers in the Lords. The king agreed but, before it went ahead, the Lords became frightened and agreed to pass the Reform Act.

The king wasn't entirely happy with this and he felt that he had been pressurised to take action. He was also upset that his early popularity was dwindling and at the raft of changes being made. He had opposed William Wilberforce's attempts to abolish the slave trade, but the Slavery Abolition Act was passed in 1833.

So when Grey resigned in 1834 and Lord Melbourne took over, he seized an opportunity. The leader of the House of Commons and chancellor of the exchequer John Charles Spencer, Viscount Althorp, inherited a peerage, forcing Melbourne to find a replacement. Melbourne suggested Lord John Russell, whom William found to be radical and therefore unacceptable. In a controversial but not unconstitutional move never since repeated by a monarch, the king dismissed the entire government and handed power to Peel, even though it meant hampering the new prime minister with an unworkable Tory minority. This prompted, in 1835, yet another general election; retaining a majority, Melbourne became prime minister again.

William IV died on 20 June 1837, aged 71, of heart failure and he was succeeded by his niece, Victoria.

A much loved 'man of the people', William would walk around London and Brighton unaccompanied

The Age of Reform was all encompassing during William IV's entire reign and it led him to dissolving parliament at one point

Life in the time of William IV

There was political unrest
During the 1830s, the UK had four prime minsters, starting with Tory Arthur Wellesley, the first Duke of Wellington, Whigs Charles Grey, second Earl Grey and Lord Melbourne, and Tory Sir Robert Peel. Calls for reform caused much of the flipping back and forth and there were general elections held in 1830, 1831, 1832, 1835 and 1837.

Children worked in cotton mills
Young children were employed in cotton mills as the industrial revolution got into its stride. In 1833, a professional Factory Inspectorate was established, with children under nine banned from being employed in textile manufacture (except in silk mills) and forbidding work after 8.30pm and before 5.30am.

Trade unions were growing in strength
Workers rights in general were a hot topic, with protests rife among employees. The Merthyr Rising of 1831 was the bloody culmination of unrest among coal miners in South Wales who were angry at their wages having been lowered and of a lack of work. The British government called in the army.

Marriage outside of church
Before the Marriage Act 1836, marriage had to be performed in an official ceremony in a religious setting that was recognised by the state. But now civil marriage in nonconformist churches was allowed. A Registrar General of Births, Marriages and Deaths was also established at this time.

Seeds of universal suffrage sown
Prior to 1832, only men aged 21 and over who owned a property of a certain value in a particular location could vote. But demand for all adults to be given a voice gathered pace. The Reform Act made the system fairer but Chartism grew in popularity, demanding that every man be able to vote in secret ballots.

Sir Robert Peel

Born at Chamber Hall, Bury in 1788, Robert Peel served as prime minister for a very short period of time under William IV's reign – just 100 days, from 10 December 1834 to 8 April 1835. Prior to the king's coronation, Peel had been home secretary, creating the modern police force – whose officers became known as 'bobbies'. He would frequently oppose and then support policies such as the Reform Act of 1832, but his Tamworth Manifesto of 1834 was crucial: it laid down the main points from which the Tories would become the Conservative party. Modest reform was central to this.

1837-1901
Queen Victoria

How a tiny island and its queen came to own an empire so large that the sun never set on it

The date was 22 January 1901 and the British Empire was the largest of any in human history, but the monarch who reigned over it would not live another day. As Queen Victoria lay dying in Osborne House on the Isle of Wight she looked back on a reign that spanned over 63 years. She had seen her empire grow from a collection of scattered isles, separated by vast plains of lands and insurmountable oceans, to the greatest the world had known. It had reached over India, plucked its riches and mounted it as the glimmering jewel in her crown. It had butchered its way mercilessly across Africa at the cost of thousands of British corpses and countless natives who had tried in vain to stand in its way. It was powered forward both by Christian values and colonial greed, so as Victoria drew her last breath, she left a world forever transformed by the empire she had built.

When a young Princess Victoria ascended the steps of Westminster Abbey on her coronation day, few would have foreseen the mighty empire she would eventually rule over. The British public were increasingly disenchanted with the monarchy and her grandfather, the mad king George III, had failed to protect British interest in the Americas, and her uncle George IV's terrible relations with his wife and reckless spending had tarnished the monarchy's prestige. At a mere 18 years and barely 150 centimetres (five feet) tall, Victoria hardly seemed a fitting patron for the vast ambitions of British expansion from the 17th century. But this blue-eyed, silvery-voiced lady possessed a stubborn will of iron and her reign would become the longest in British history. Her ascension marked not the death of the British Empire, but the new dawn of a kingdom so massive that none could ever hope to challenge it.

The world was changing as Victoria took her place on the throne. The tiny, scattered rural villages of England were being abandoned en masse and the cities were transforming into sprawling metropolises. Great towering concrete chimneys rose from the ground and the whirr of

Queen Victoria

"The British Empire had the might, ingenuity and limitless ambition to conquer the world"

QUEEN VICTORIA
British, 1819-1901

Brief Bio Victoria served as monarch of the United Kingdom from 20 June 1837 until her death on 22 January 1901. At 63 years her reign is currently the longest in British history, and is associated with the Industrial Revolution, economic progress and most notably, the expansion of the British Empire to the largest domain of all time.

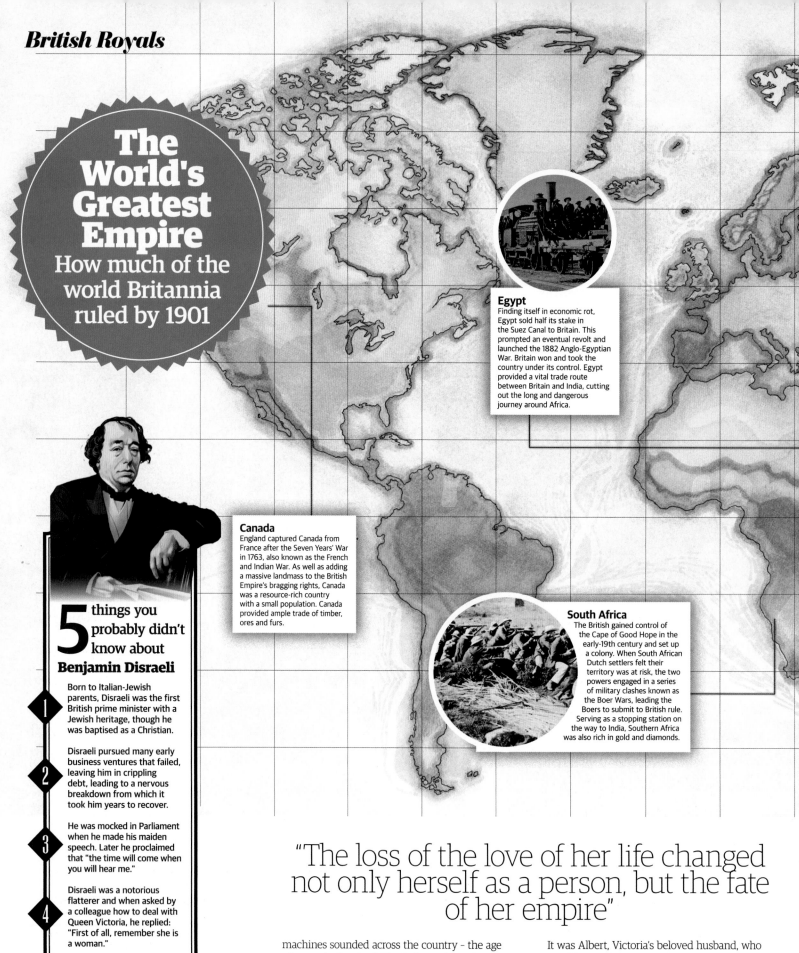

The World's Greatest Empire
How much of the world Britannia ruled by 1901

Egypt
Finding itself in economic rot, Egypt sold half its stake in the Suez Canal to Britain. This prompted an eventual revolt and launched the 1882 Anglo-Egyptian War. Britain won and took the country under its control. Egypt provided a vital trade route between Britain and India, cutting out the long and dangerous journey around Africa.

Canada
England captured Canada from France after the Seven Years' War in 1763, also known as the French and Indian War. As well as adding a massive landmass to the British Empire's bragging rights, Canada was a resource-rich country with a small population. Canada provided ample trade of timber, ores and furs.

South Africa
The British gained control of the Cape of Good Hope in the early-19th century and set up a colony. When South African Dutch settlers felt their territory was at risk, the two powers engaged in a series of military clashes known as the Boer Wars, leading the Boers to submit to British rule. Serving as a stopping station on the way to India, Southern Africa was also rich in gold and diamonds.

5 things you probably didn't know about Benjamin Disraeli

1 Born to Italian-Jewish parents, Disraeli was the first British prime minister with a Jewish heritage, though he was baptised as a Christian.

2 Disraeli pursued many early business ventures that failed, leaving him in crippling debt, leading to a nervous breakdown from which it took him years to recover.

3 He was mocked in Parliament when he made his maiden speech. Later he proclaimed that "the time will come when you will hear me."

4 Disraeli was a notorious flatterer and when asked by a colleague how to deal with Queen Victoria, he replied: "First of all, remember she is a woman."

5 He introduced much legislation that benefited the poor, such as the 1877 Artisans Dwelling Act that provided housing, as well as the Public Health Act the same year.

"The loss of the love of her life changed not only herself as a person, but the fate of her empire"

machines sounded across the country - the age of steam had arrived. The Industrial Revolution changed Britain from a quaint maritime nation on the edge of Europe into a manufacturing colossus. Railways and steamships brought the British overseas territory closer to the mother country, opening up opportunities for trade and commerce that were previously unfathomable.

It was Albert, Victoria's beloved husband, who opened her and Britain's eyes to the ideas that went on to shape her empire. Fascinated by mechanisms and inventions, Albert organised The Great Exhibition at the Crystal Palace - a temple to the ingenuity of the rapidly developing modern world. Inventions from around the world were displayed, but this was Britain's show, first and foremost. The

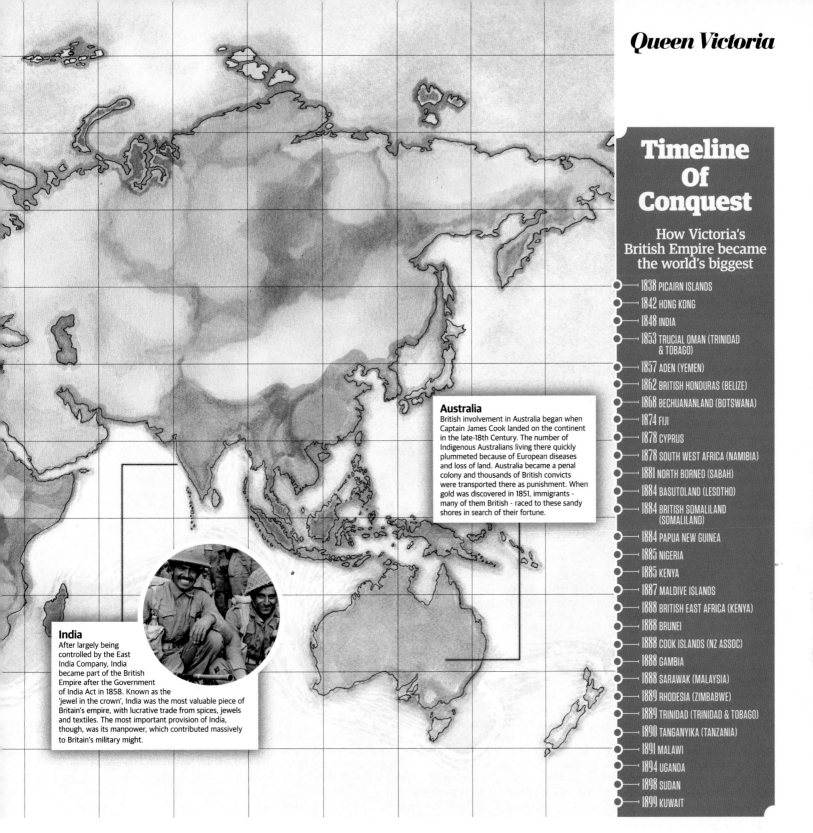

- 1838 PICAIRN ISLANDS
- 1842 HONG KONG
- 1848 INDIA
- 1853 TRUCIAL OMAN (TRINIDAD & TOBAGO)
- 1857 ADEN (YEMEN)
- 1862 BRITISH HONDURAS (BELIZE)
- 1868 BECHUANANLAND (BOTSWANA)
- 1874 FIJI
- 1878 CYPRUS
- 1878 SOUTH WEST AFRICA (NAMIBIA)
- 1881 NORTH BORNEO (SABAH)
- 1884 BASUTOLAND (LESOTHO)
- 1884 BRITISH SOMALILAND (SOMALILAND)
- 1884 PAPUA NEW GUINEA
- 1885 NIGERIA
- 1885 KENYA
- 1887 MALDIVE ISLANDS
- 1888 BRITISH EAST AFRICA (KENYA)
- 1888 BRUNEI
- 1888 COOK ISLANDS (NZ ASSOC)
- 1888 GAMBIA
- 1888 SARAWAK (MALAYSIA)
- 1889 RHODESIA (ZIMBABWE)
- 1889 TRINIDAD (TRINIDAD & TOBAGO)
- 1890 TANGANYIKA (TANZANIA)
- 1891 MALAWI
- 1894 UGANDA
- 1898 SUDAN
- 1899 KUWAIT

Australia
British involvement in Australia began when Captain James Cook landed on the continent in the late-18th Century. The number of Indigenous Australians living there quickly plummeted because of European diseases and loss of land. Australia became a penal colony and thousands of British convicts were transported there as punishment. When gold was discovered in 1851, immigrants - many of them British - raced to these sandy shores in search of their fortune.

India
After largely being controlled by the East India Company, India became part of the British Empire after the Government of India Act in 1858. Known as the 'jewel in the crown', India was the most valuable piece of Britain's empire, with lucrative trade from spices, jewels and textiles. The most important provision of India, though, was its manpower, which contributed massively to Britain's military might.

symbols of British might, which occupied half of the entire display space, served as clear examples of what the British Empire was capable of and fostered the ideas of national supremacy in the eyes of Victoria, the government and the majority of the British population. The Great Exhibition proved that far from the crumbling remains of a once-powerful nation, the British Empire had the might, ingenuity and limitless ambition to conquer the world.

The opportunity to pave the road for this empire arose in 1857 with the Indian Mutiny. India had been ruled by a private entity - the East India Company - from 1757. The rebellion manifested the discontent felt by the Indian people for the blatant disrespect of their beliefs and customs. The

company showed disregard for the Indian caste system and issued new cartridges greased with cow and pig fat that had to be opened with the mouth, highly offensive to Muslim and Hindu soldiers. These actions opened the eyes of the Indian people to the daily injustice they were being subjected to, and unrest snowballed into mass riots and an uprising. Although the mutiny was eventually quelled, the rebellion led to the dissolution of the company, the passing of power to the British state and the creation of what Victoria would call the jewel in her crown - the British Indian Empire.

Queen Victoria welcomed the country to her empire in a lavish ceremony, promising that Indian native customs and religions would be

respected and that she would "draw a veil over the sad and bloody past." She presented herself as a maternal figure and a crusader for peace, justice and honest government - ideals largely inspired by her husband. Albert had instilled in her mind the vision of King Arthur's Camelot, an empire ruled not by tyranny but by justice, where the strong serve the weak, where good triumphs over evil, bringing not oppression and bloodshed, but trade, education and welfare. His influence on Victoria was immense and when on 14 December 1861 he died of suspected typhoid fever, the empire veered into an entirely new direction.

When Albert drew his last breath in the blue room at Windsor Castle the queen was

What was the East India Company?

Emerging from humble beginnings, the East India Company began as a simple enterprise of London businessmen who wanted to make money from importing spices. The company was granted a royal charter by Queen Elizabeth I in 1600, and in 1601 James Lancaster led its first voyage. The company set up trade outposts in Indian settlements that slowly developed into commercial towns. Steadily increasing its territory, the company claimed vital trading ports from Aden to Penang. As its control extended, the company became the most powerful private company in history, with its own army established by Robert Clive, the first British governor of Bengal. With its great military power behind it, the company controlled India with a combination of direct rule and alliances with Indian princes. The East India Company eventually accounted for half the world's trade and specialised in cotton, silk, tea and opium.

Lancaster was an Elizabethan trader and privateer

The Argyle and Sutherland Highlanders before the 1899 Battle of Modder River during the Second Boer War

inconsolable; the loss of the love of her life changed not only herself as a person, but the fate of her empire. As she donned the mourning clothes she would wear until her own death, she drew a veil over Albert's vision and pursued a different path for her kingdom - one of world domination.

An emerging figure in Parliament would come to foster her views - Benjamin Disraeli. The ambitious and rebellious leader of the Conservatives was led by a passion for imperial power and glory. Inspired by tales of imperial adventures, Disraeli believed Britain should pursue an empire of power and prestige. His most direct political opponent represented everything Albert dreamed the empire could be. William Gladstone, the leader of the Liberals, thought the empire should serve a high moral purpose, to follow not a path of conquest but one of commerce, sharing their moral vision with the world.

These two fiery and driven men fought over these opposing visions in Parliament as Victoria continued to mourn. Without Albert she felt incompetent and unable to face the immense duty that her role dictated. With her strong conservative views she found Gladstone and

A British marketing poster promoting the Suez Canal - the waterway was an important factor in the growth of the empire

"The Industrial Revolution changed Britain from a quaint maritime nation into a manufacturing giant"

his liberal reforms dangerous and unpredictable. Disraeli, suave, coy and dripping with forthright confidence, enchanted the lonely queen. With his constant flattery and sharp wit, Disraeli reignited her interest in politics and captivated her, as Albert had done so previously, with his vision of just how mighty the empire could be. However, Gladstone's liberal vision and Albert's quest for Camelot had not completely faded. The British people, led by strong Protestant beliefs Victoria herself had instilled in them, felt it was Britain's role - their duty even - to civilise people around the world. They believed the British cause was to export not only trade, but also gospel values of morality and justice.

It was in pursuit of this lofty goal that many missionaries turned their attention to Africa. Little was known of the 'Dark Continent', but the common perception was that it was a place of pagan worship ravaged by tribal wars. One missionary in particular would capture the attention of the British nation. Tall, handsome and heroic, David Livingstone embodied everything the British believed their nation to represent. A medical

missionary, Livingstone's daring adventures around the continent were followed by a captivated British public. Fighting vicious beasts, battling through dense jungles and suffering a multitude of illnesses, Livingstone was the heroic face of the empire's Christian ideals.

Livingstone's horrific confrontation with African chain gangs was to drive the British cause of expansion. The slavery rife in Africa was abhorrent to Livingstone and the British public, as the practice had been abolished across the empire in 1833. The queen and government united behind Livingstone's quest to find a suitable trade route, hoping that by doing so, the African people would find ways to make a living that wasn't built on the backs of slaves. Livingstone's journey was a failure and he returned to scathing criticism - something the imperialist Disraeli leapt on with glee. His flattery of Victoria had completely won her over and the monarchy and government became united in pursuit of one goal - the expansion of the empire.

The perfect opportunity to begin this new empire emerged as another nation struggled to

How Queen Victoria came to rule the word

Dominance of the seas
Britain employed a 'two-power standard' in 1889 which called for the Royal Navy to maintain a force at least equal to the combined strength of the next two largest navies in the world. This policy ensured British dominance of the seas with a string of naval bases encompassing the whole world. The pure size and strength of the navy served its purpose - deterring any would be competitors and confirming its position as ruler of the waves.

The Industrial Revolution
Britain was the first nation to harness the power of steam and the first to undergo an industrial revolution. This resulted in mass production of low-cost goods to trade around the world. It also gave Britain's military an array of resources like rifles, steamships and trains, equipping it to defeat any possible enemies. Medical advances also allowed British explorers to penetrate remote areas without fear of tropical diseases.

The quest to spread democracy
Land grabbing aside, the British Empire was led by a strong Protestant desire to improve the world. Britain saw itself as an agent of civilisation - one they wanted to spread worldwide, bringing peace, order and stability. This belief that they were doing genuine good led men like David Livingstone to travel to Africa to spread the word of God, and with it, the British Empire.

Taking advantage of the competition
As major powers of the world such as Spain, France, the Netherlands and the Ottomans were losing power, the British began to peak in strength. Britain was able to take advantage of the European wars that had weakened other nations as it enjoyed a period of relative peace, allowing uninterrupted expansion of its empire. Any threats that did emerge, such as Russia, just gave Britain new zeal to cement its powerful hold on the world.

Strong leadership
Britain was ruled by a single monarch throughout most of the 19th century - Queen Victoria. The record-breaking length of her reign brought a sense of stability and contributed to the unconquerable notion of the British Empire. Although Victoria did involve herself in government, her role was symbolic rather than one of direct power, which ensured stability of British politics. While other nations were dealing with socialist movements, Britain enjoyed a long period of relative domestic peace.

The anatomy of the HMS Prince George

How Britannia ruled the waves

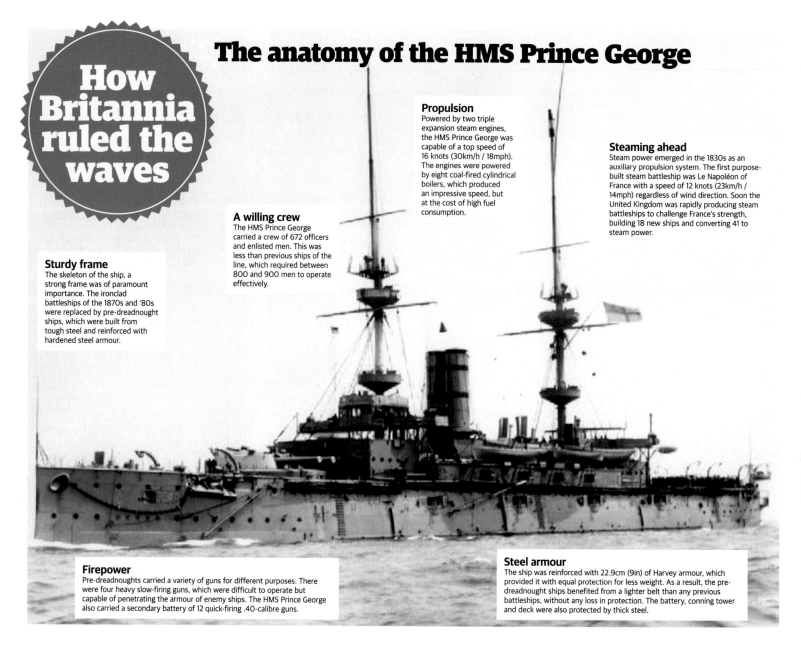

Propulsion
Powered by two triple expansion steam engines, the HMS Prince George was capable of a top speed of 16 knots (30km/h / 18mph). The engines were powered by eight coal-fired cylindrical boilers, which produced an impressive speed, but at the cost of high fuel consumption.

Steaming ahead
Steam power emerged in the 1830s as an auxiliary propulsion system. The first purpose-built steam battleship was Le Napoléon of France with a speed of 12 knots (23km/h / 14mph) regardless of wind direction. Soon the United Kingdom was rapidly producing steam battleships to challenge France's strength, building 18 new ships and converting 41 to steam power.

A willing crew
The HMS Prince George carried a crew of 672 officers and enlisted men. This was less than previous ships of the line, which required between 800 and 900 men to operate effectively.

Sturdy frame
The skeleton of the ship, a strong frame was of paramount importance. The ironclad battleships of the 1870s and '80s were replaced by pre-dreadnought ships, which were built from tough steel and reinforced with hardened steel armour.

Firepower
Pre-dreadnoughts carried a variety of guns for different purposes. There were four heavy slow-firing guns, which were difficult to operate but capable of penetrating the armour of enemy ships. The HMS Prince George also carried a secondary battery of 12 quick-firing .40-calibre guns.

Steel armour
The ship was reinforced with 22.9cm (9in) of Harvey armour, which provided it with equal protection for less weight. As a result, the pre-dreadnought ships benefited from a lighter belt than any previous battleships, without any loss in protection. The battery, conning tower and deck were also protected by thick steel.

survive. The Egyptian ruler, Isma'il Pasha, was confronted with crippling debts after reckless spending on lavish ceremonies and a costly war with Ethiopia. In an act of desperation he made an offer to sell to the British Egypt's shares in the Suez Canal. The canal was more than a mere trading port; it opened up a short route to India across Egypt and down the Red Sea, cutting out the lengthy journey around Africa. The Egyptian ruler's offer would give the British controlling influence over the jugular of the empire, so Disraeli urged Victoria to accept. She immediately did and the Suez Canal fell into British hands.

With control of India, Britain was already the most powerful nation on Earth and three-quarters of the world's trade was transported in British ships, but this control was being threatened. The Russian Empire had been steadily expanding east and south and was getting uncomfortably close to Victoria's prized jewel - India. The Middle East was largely controlled by the Turks, but they were

busy dealing with violent rebellions. The Turkish treatment of their Christian subjects was shocking and atrocious, but as Russia backed the rebels the British had no option but to support the Turks. The British public, to whom Russia stood for everything Britain opposed - ignorance, slavery and subjugation - largely supported this choice. Facing the prospect of imminent war with the strongest nation on the planet, Russia agreed to peace talks and thanks in part to the charisma and negotiation skills of Disraeli, agreed to stop their advance on the Middle East.

Imperial spirit rushed through the public as the might of British muscle flexed and proved itself again. As the empire continued its steady expansion across the continent it came face to face with the most powerful African nation - the Zulus. The British, with a bloated ego, underestimated the strength of their spear-wielding enemies and suffered a crushing initial defeat. In the end it took 16,000 British reinforcements to prise the Zulus'

independence from their grip. Expecting to return to a wave of praise for their daring exploits, the victorious army were surprised to discover that British opinions were changing once again.

Gladstone, the "half-mad firebrand", as Victoria dubbed him, preached his outraged opinions about the mass slaughter of Zulus and rampant destruction of their homes. Victoria was outraged but the public sided with Gladstone and, much to the queen's dismay, the power of the government switched hands once more. Liberal leader or not, all of Europe's attention was firmly fixed on Africa as nations began a scramble to establish colonies there. In amongst this mad rush to establish new territory by European powers, it was arguably one man's actions that would determine the ultimate fate of Victoria's empire.

Led by Muhammad Ahmed, revolution was tearing through the Sudan as tribes rose against their corrupt rulers. As this holy war drew uncomfortably close to the Suez Canal, Victoria

"They believed the British cause was to export not only trade, but also gospel values of morality and justice"

urged Gladstone to utilise the British troops stationed there to defend it. The liberal leader refused. In order to buy time he sent one man, General Charles Gordon, to secure the evacuation of loyal civilians and soldiers.

Like Livingstone, Gordon was a national hero. He was brave, dashing, popular and his decorated military career had painted him in the British public's eyes as a gleaming knight of old. Despite these qualities Gordon was also wild and unpredictable. When he reached the Sudan he was horrified by the slavery rife in the region and decided to face the Mahdi in battle. With limited forces, Gordon soon found himself besieged in the city of Khartoum. His appeals for aid, to the adoring public's outrage, fell on deaf ears in the government. It took more than eight months of public fury to finally force Gladstone's hand, but it was too late – Gordon, the nation's hero of Christianity, was dead.

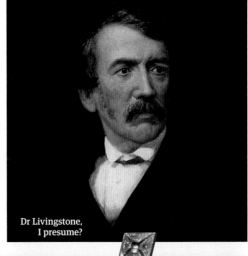

Dr Livingstone, I presume?

The Great Exhibition of 1851 boosted Britain's national confidence

Paintings of Victoria in her youth are a world away from the traditional austere depiction of her

Main competitors

Three countries that were battling with Britain for territory

Russia

As England expanded its territory, so did Russia. For a hundred years Russia expanded east and south, narrowing the gap between the British and Russian Empires in Central Asia. Britain soon became obsessed with protecting India which was a rich source of goods and manpower. The competition for dominance of the states that separated them – Iran, Afghanistan and Tibet – became commonly known as The Great Game. The looming, but unlikely, threat of Russia's attack led Britain into largely unnecessary military involvement in Afghanistan and Tibet.

Germany

From 1850 onward, Germany began to industrialise at an astonishing rate, transforming from a rural nation to a heavily urban one. In the space of a decade Germany's navy grew massively and became the only one able to challenge the British. Although the German Empire of the late-19th century consisted of only a few small colonies, the newly unified state slowly moved toward colonial expansion in Asia and the Pacific. As Wilhelm II rose to power, his aggressive policies in achieving a 'place in the sun' similar to Britain was one of the factors that would lead to WWI.

France

Britain's age-old rival France was still licking its wounds after the loss of most of its imperial colonies in the early part of the 19th century. However, French leaders began a mission to restore its prestige in 1850, seeking to claim land in North and West Africa as well as in Southeast Asia. After the defeat of France in the Franco-Prussian War, it still continued with zeal to expand its empire, acquiring land in China and all over Africa. Unlike most of its rivals, France would continue expanding after WWI, well into the 1930s.

7 Eye-watering empire facts

458 million
people ruled over

23%
of the world's surface
was ruled by Britain

13.01 million
square miles of land
belonged to the empire

113
ships in the Royal Navy

63 years & 21 days
the length
of Victoria's
reign

165,000
convicts sent to Australia

7,010,000
total goods shipped by Britain in
one year (1881)

General Gordon organised a year-long defence of Sudan but a relief force arrived two days after the city had fallen and he had been killed

"The monarchy and government became united in pursuit of one goal – the expansion of the empire"

In an instance the liberal vision was shattered, Gladstone was voted out and his moral influence departed with him. The renewed crusading spirit of British imperialism found its poster boy in a man who would lead the empire down a dark and dangerous path. Moving from England to Africa to work on a cotton farm, Cecil John Rhodes had become outrageously wealthy from the diamond rush, but he wanted more – the whole of Africa. Driven by greed and lust for power, Rhodes wished to create a British colony across Africa, not for the betterment of its people or to spread Christian values, but for profit and business.

Using the tenacity and cunning that had elevated him to success, Rhodes tricked and butchered his way across the continent with the British government backing him every bloody step of the way. Rhodes made it his purpose to make the

world English and famously said: "If there be a God, I think that what he would like me to do is paint as much of the map of Africa British Red as possible." His path of colonial greed led Britain head-first into a conflict now known as the Boer Wars.

Gold had been found in Transvaal in northern South Africa and Rhodes worried that this would prompt an alliance with the Germans, thus cutting off his route to the north of the continent. Rhodes planned an uprising to overthrow the Boer leaders, but it did not go as planned – far from the naked, spear-wielding foes he had previously conquered, the Boers had guns, and they fought back hard with skill and courage.

Outrage tore across Europe against what was seen as an unprovoked attack on an independent state, but not in Britain. Fully convinced of their noble mission, the British people believed the Boers

"As more British bodies piled up, British confidence in their own unconquerable might began to wane in Africa"

to be vicious and uncompromising. More soldiers poured into the region into a war they believed would be short and glorious, but as more British bodies piled up - Victoria's own grandson among them - British confidence began to wane.

As British reinforcements continued to flood into the territory the tide slowly began to turn. Rhodes had managed to squeeze a win from the jaws of defeat and the Boer territories became British colonies. The empire had grown, but at a cost. Rhodes' controversial actions during the war - including forming what would come to be known as the first concentration camps - had been a step too far for the British public. What had begun as a noble quest of Christianity had transformed into a greedy and brutal scramble for power. When Rhodes died his merciless version of imperialism was buried with him in the dry African dirt.

When Victoria passed away she was finally rid of the black mourning clothes she had worn for 40 years and was dressed entirely in white. Spring flowers were scattered around her body and her wedding veil was placed on her head as she prepared to reunite with the dearest love of her life. She was, however, leaving another behind; the Empire she had mothered now stretched across the globe with large swathes still coloured in the pink of British rule. As the sun set on the quiet room in which she lay in Osborne House, it was rising on the bustling spice markets of India, and soon the vast plains of British land in Africa would be bathed in warm golden light. Victoria had died, but the legacy she left behind continued to expand over the face of the planet. Even without their driver, the cogs of the British Empire whirred steadily on for another half century at least.

1892 caricature of Cecil Rhodes, after he announced plans for a telegraph line and railroad from Cape Town to Cairo

A satirical cartoon from 1876 poking fun at the relationship between Queen Victoria and Benjamin Disraeli

Edward's social life was very much public knowledge; he was renowned for his drinking, and womanising

EDWARD VII
England, 1841-1910

Brief Bio

Known for his womanising and his excesses, Edward lived with the disapproval of his mother Queen Victoria until her death, but as king he became more popular than she ever had. He used his easy-going nature and friendliness to forge new relationships with Britain's European neighbours.

1901-1910

Edward VII

The prince who disappointed Queen Victoria became one of Britain's most popular monarchs

Every monarch lives in the shadow of their predecessor, but few kings have taken the crown from so fearsome a ruler as Queen Victoria. Edward VII, born Albert Edward in 1841, sat on the throne for the first time at the age of 59, having spent most of his life living with the disapproval of his mother. However, having enjoyed the benefits of his royal standing throughout his life, he would go on to win the hearts of his people and make the monarchy more popular than it had been in a very long time.

Born to Victoria and her beloved Prince Albert on 9 November 1841, Edward was held to an incredibly high standard from a very early age. Victoria and Albert were determined that the boy would work hard and be given the very best education, but it became apparent that he did not work best within

the guidelines that his parents had set out for him. He was desperate to play a role in the army, but that was declared absolutely forbidden. He would later be given a rank that was purely honorary, much to his chagrin.

During his teens, Edward improved academically but his talents were far more social, and he began to create a reputation for himself as a society figure. When the time came for Edward to marry, he fell for Princess Alexandra of Denmark, a match that was created by his sister Victoria while mostly disapproved of by his parents. However, while visiting Ireland in 1861 during the marriage preparations, Edward had a fling with an actress called Nellie Clifden. Word got out and, despite the fact that he was extremely ill, Prince Albert visited his son to scold him in person. Albert died shortly

Nine European Sovereigns at Windsor for the funeral of King Edward VII

afterwards, which Victoria blamed entirely on her son and his terrible appetites.

Following Albert's death, the queen was devastated and excluded her son from any royal business. She began to withdraw from the public eye and therefore it fell to Edward to become the face of the monarchy. It was a role he took to like a duck to water, as his natural charm and amiable nature made him extremely popular on his visits through Europe, helping to restore relations that had become seriously frayed. As well as enjoying his visits and the luxury in which he did so, Edward held some progressive views for the time in which he lived. During a visit to India in 1875, he was strongly critical of the way in which the British colonial officers treated the locals. Edward was known to be strongly opposed to any form of racial or religious prejudice.

Princess Alexandra married him in 1863, but Edward's lifestyle changed very little following their wedding. His affairs were numerous and well documented, despite his attempts at secrecy. The list of his mistresses included, but was in no way limited to, Winston Churchill's mother Lady Churchill, actresses Lillie Langtry and Sarah Bernhardt, and Alice Keppel - the great-grandmother of Camilla, duchess of Cornwall. Despite Victoria's hatred of her son's philandering, it is believed that Alexandra knew about her husband's extramarital love life and accepted it. Indeed, she bore him six children. A scandal over

illegal gambling was a little more serious, as the prince was subpoenaed as a witness. However, the press were fairly easy on Edward and he made it through with his popularity relatively unscathed.

In 1901, Queen Victoria died and Edward took the throne at aged 59. His parents had intended for him to be crowned Albert Edward, but the new king decided instead that he would be King Edward VII, declaring that the name of Albert should stand alone in respect to his late father.

Once king, Edward threw himself into the business of rule. He was known as the 'Uncle of Europe', only in part due to the familial ties he had created via his children's marriages. His visit to France in 1903 proved such a success that he is credited with helping to pave the way for the Entente Cordiale a year later, which smoothed over a history of arguments over territory abroad and, perhaps more importantly, positioned both powers against Germany as both countries were already wary about that nation's expansion and growing military power. He also made a groundbreaking visit to Russia in 1908, the first reigning British monarch to do so. Finally able to involve himself in military affairs, Edward also played a large part in reforming the army and expanding the navy in the wake of the Boer war.

As his reign progressed, the changes in British society did not go unnoticed by the king. He made more and more of a point to be seen in public by his subjects. "We are all socialists now," he is reported to have said, and he grew increasingly frustrated at the obvious class divide and struggle in the Houses of Parliament, which culminated with a constitutional crisis in the last year of his reign when the Liberal budget was vetoed by the Conservative majority in the House of Lords. The times were changing and when a Parliament reform bill was introduced in April 1910, Edward reluctantly returned from Biarritz, but his health was poor. On 6 May 1910 he died at Buckingham Palace, and was given a splendid royal funeral of the kind of pomp and elegance he would have approved of.

> Edward's bronchitis in later life was mainly due to his colossal smoking habit of more than 20 cigarettes and 12 cigars a day

Edward's flamboyance was very much part of his public image, but it was a style of monarchy that died with him

Life in the time of Edward VII

Jack the Ripper
In 1888 London was gripped by a series of brutal, grisly murders committed by a seemingly uncatchable lunatic calling himself Jack. The victims were five prostitutes, whose corpses were gruesomely mutilated, sending the nation's press into a frenzy. While the true identity of the killer remains unknown, some believe that King Edward's eldest son Albert Victor was in some way linked to the murders.

Man takes to the skies
Wilbur and Orville Wright made history on 17 December 1903 when they made the first manned aircraft flight. For 12 seconds, they soared 20 feet above a North Carolina beach. 1909 would see the first cross-Channel flight as Frenchman Louis Blériot made the trip from Calais to Dover.

Triple Entente
While the Entente Cordiale may have been the first step towards an alliance against Germany, Britain and France would make their position clear in 1907 with the signing of the Triple Entente with Russia, bringing Britain's 'splendid isolation' to a definite end.

Votes for women!
Despite his progressive views on race and equality, King Edward VII did not show any support for the Women's Suffrage movement. The cause gathered momentum and public awareness during the first decade of the 20th Century and became increasingly hard-fought after the king's death until the outbreak of the First World War.

The Order of Merit
The Order of Merit had been conceived in the early 19th Century, but it was Edward VII who finally established it in 1902 to reward "exceptionally meritorious services in Our Crown Services or towards the advancement of the Arts, Learning, Literature, and Science."

The Entente Cordiale
In 1904, both France and Great Britain were becoming increasingly wary of Germany's rising power, due to its growing military strength and its alliances in Western Europe. Both countries saw an urgent need to put an end to their squabbling and create some kind of agreement for the sake of security. Thanks in part to King Edward VII's openness to a French alliance and the hard work of foreign secretary Lord Lansdowne and French ambassador Paul Cambon, Britain and France reached an agreement on the foreign territory issues that had dogged the process. While the agreement had no mention of a military alliance, it could not escape Germany's notice that these two powers were suddenly on good terms, and tensions continued to escalate.

1910-1936
George V

George V saw Britain through the horrors of the First World War and he reigned over a period of great social and political change

George V was born in 1865 as the second son of Albert, Prince of Wales (later Edward VII) and Alexandra of Denmark. His elder brother Albert, Duke of Clarence was second in line to the throne and, as such, George wasn't expected to become king. Instead, he was able to join the Royal Navy as a cadet at Dartmouth and kick-start a wonderful career in the armed forces, one which he greatly enjoyed and excelled in.

But when his elder brother died of pneumonia in 1892, George was promoted to heir presumptive and so forced to leave his career in preparation. He was given the title Duke of York and also became a member of the House of Lords. He began to better understand the ins and outs of British politics as he prepared himself for the throne.

George was religious man, reading the Bible daily and attending Sunday morning service. He was also slim, well dressed and handsome. He was soon engaged to Princess Victoria Mary of Teck, who despite being born and raised in England was the daughter of Francis, Duke of Teck, a man of German extraction. She was originally engaged to George's older brother Albert, but she had become close to George during their period of mourning and romantic feelings had developed. With the approval of Queen Victoria, George's grandmother - who was a big fan of Princess Mary - the pair married on 6 July 1893, at St James's Palace.

The Duke and Duchess of York lived happily on the Sandringham estate in Norfolk and had four children - Edward, Albert, Mary and Henry - by the time George's father took to the throne in 1901. The couple, who at this stage were the prince and princess of Wales, had a further two children - George and John - before George V became king upon his father's death in 1910. Unknown to him at the time, he was about to lead the British Empire through a period of incredible change.

George's first task was to tackle the constitutional crisis that had flared up in 1909. Conservative peers in the House of Lords had rejected the Liberal government's budget, causing an uproar. It led to the calling of a general election in January 1910 to get a mandate to pass the budget, but the result was a hung parliament with the Liberals winning 274 seats, just two more than the Conservatives. The Liberals entered into a coalition with John Redmond's Irish Parliamentary Party and, in April 2010, the Lords passed the budget.

Anger simmered, though, and the ruling government decided to conjure up laws that would strip the Lords of any power to reject financial legislation approved by MPs while restricting the peers' veto on ordinary legislation. This formed the Parliament Bill, which was hated by the Lords.

But with George V agreeing to create more Liberal peers, pressure was put on the existing members of the upper house. In December 1910, a second general election was called with the Liberals winning 272 seats to the Conservatives' 271, but it was enough for the Lords to pass the Parliament Bill in 1911 without the mass creation of peers materialising, proving to be an early, stabilising victory for George V.

Yet trouble was brewing as war loomed in Europe. Two days before Britain entered the war, George V and his foreign secretary Sir Edward Grey were understood to have met. The king informed

> George was given a rather limited education. As a result, he could barely speak German or French, unusual for a British king

GEORGE V
England, 1865-1936

Brief Bio George V was forced to abandon his naval career when he became second in line to the throne, eventually finding himself king in 1910. Thrust into a tricky political situation and with war looming, George oversaw periods of gloom, boom and downturn and yet remained ever popular throughout.

Even though he was in the Royal Navy, he suffered from seasickness. At the time his elder brother Albert died, he had typhoid

The death of Emily Davison

George V loved sporting occasions and so it was on 4 June 1913 that he attended the annual Epsom Derby along with Queen Mary. Unknown to him – as his own horse, Anmer, galloped around the track – was that Emily Wilding Davison, a leading militant in the Women's Social and Political Union, was also in attendance and about to make a dramatic political gesture.

Davison was a key figure in the suffragette movement pushing for women to be given the vote in Britain. She had been imprisoned on nine occasions and force-fed 49 times, but she was about to make her last protest. At 2.10pm, she ran on to the racecourse and was hit by the king's horse. As the animal fell and the jockey was flung to the ground, Davison lay unconscious. She never recovered and died of her injuries in hospital four days later. The king, meanwhile, was said to have inquired about the health of his jockey – who, it transpired, had suffered no broken bones.

Over the years, there has been a huge debate over whether Davison intended to kill herself or merely disrupt the race. There is a degree of uncertainty about the exact events on that day, even though British Pathé's cinema cameras were there to capture the moment. Most newspaper reports afterwards focused on turning the public against the suffragette movement, calling it a moment of madness. But Emily's death was not in vain. Women over the age of 30 were given the right to vote in 1918. The voting age was subsequently lowered to 21 in 1928.

"A canny king, George changed the Germanic name of his royal house to make it sound more English"

Sir Edward that it was "absolutely essential" that Britain went to war with Germany to prevent it from achieving "complete domination of this country." He went on to urge Sir Edward to find a reason for war.

Despite that, the king said nothing publicly in the run-up to the conflict in 1914, but in his diary on 4 August 1914 he wrote: "I held a Council at 10.45 to declare war with Germany. It is a terrible catastrophe but it is not our fault." That day he had gone on to the balcony with Queen Mary – informally known as May because of the month in which she was born - to address a large crowd gathered outside Buckingham Palace. "Please God it may soon be over," he added in his notes.

It would not be. The war lasted for four years. George did all he could to keep his citizens and soldiers motivated, visiting hospitals, factories and dockyards and seeing soldiers on the front line. He would boost morale with his straight-talking manner and impress soldiers with his knowledge of military positions. But on one of these visits - to see the First Army at Labuissière - he was thrown from his horse and fractured his pelvis. Reeling in pain and shock, his injuries would stay with him for the rest of his life.

And yet if his visits were a public relations exercise, they hit the right spot. He appeared to be a canny king, changing the Germanic name of his royal house - Saxe-Coburg and Gotha - to Windsor to make it sound more English, and denying political asylum to his cousin Tsar Nicholas II despite getting the go-ahead from the British government. The tsar had been deposed during the Russian revolution, but he and his Russian imperial family had ruled with an iron fist. George figured the British people would come to resent him if he agreed to the move and effectively cast his cousin adrift.

The tsar's fate was horrific, executed with his family by the Bolksheviks. Similar fates awaited the monarchies of Germany and Austria-Hungary following the end of war in 1918. And yet, despite being victorious in the war, George was in no doubt that the world was changing fast and that the British empire was creaking. Ireland had been demanding home rule and in 1916, the Easter Rising in Dublin led to a civil war and the setting up of the Irish Free State in 1922, leaving just six northern

> During WWI, George V wore uniform and ensured that, in solidarity, he lived a frugal lifestyle in Buckingham Palace

Defining moment
Prince Albert Victor dies 1892

Prince Albert Victor, the duke of Clarence and Avondale, dies of pneumonia in 1892, thereby promoting Prince George to second in line to the throne after his father. George's elder brother was a naval cadet like him but, as heir presumptive, did not take part in military duties. Albert was also viewed as being rather unintelligent, but kind and considerate. Surprising then that, in 1970, British physician Dr Thomas EA Stowell wrote an article in *The Criminologist* linking the duke to the Jack the Ripper murders, claiming he was driven mad by syphilis; the evidence is considered flimsy, however.

Defining moment
Prince of Wales 1901

George visits Australia where, on 9 May 1901, he opens the new Commonwealth parliament in Melbourne before heading off to Brisbane, Sydney and New Zealand. On the way to Australia, he stops at Aden, Ceylon and Singapore and, on the way back, visits Mauritius, South Africa and Canada. It is a mammoth tour - the most comprehensive one made by a future monarch at that time. On his return to Britain at the age of 36, George is made the prince of Wales and the earl of Chester. He visits Berlin in 1902 and 1908 and, from October 1905, he spends seven months visiting India.

Timeline

1877

Joins the Navy
Following a childhood spent mainly at Sandringham where he has been privately educated, George is sent at age 12 with his brother, Albert, to the Royal Navy training ship HMS Britannia.
1877

Commander of HMS Torpedo
George excels in the Navy. He has a terrible time at sea between 1880 and 1882, during which several crew members are killed. But by 1889 he is commanding HMS Torpedo.
1889

George gets married
On 3 May 1893, George becomes engaged to Princess Mary of Teck and they are married on 6 July of that year. Mary had intended to marry Albert before he died.
1893

Queen Victoria dies
Queen Victoria dies on 22 January 1901. George's father becomes Edward VII, king of the United Kingdom, emperor of India and king of the British Dominions. George is now heir apparent.
1901

George becomes king
When Edward VII dies on 6 May 1910, George becomes king at the age of 44 and his wife is now Queen Mary. He is crowned on 22 June 1911.
1910

counties as part of the UK but retaining the Irish Free State as a dominion, under the king's control.

Growing demands for independence in India also grew, with tension mounting in the Punjab region (India was eventually allowed a certain level of self-determination following the passing of the Government of India Act in 1935). In 1922, Egypt was granted formal independence and put it on the path towards a complete separation with the British Empire.

But even domestically, things weren't going well. The ten-day general strike of May 1926 - just two years after the country had seen its first, brief Labour government - saw 1.7 million workers down tools. George V intervened, persuading the Conservatives to refrain from an aggressive stance against the unions. He enthused over Britain's exceptional handling of the strike. "Not a shot has been fired and no one killed," he wrote in his diary. "It shows what wonderful people we are."

In 1929, there was a severe worldwide economic depression. Industry in northern Britain began to collapse. Exports fell and unemployment during the early part of the 1930s rocketed. In 1931, George asked the leaders of the Conservative and Liberal parties to meet with both him and Labour prime minister Ramsay MacDonald. The four discussed the best way forward, with George pushing for the three parties to form a national government to restore the budget and restore confidence. At the same time, dominion parliaments were allowed to form their own laws independently of the UK. This led to Canada, Australia, New Zealand, South Africa, the Irish Free State and Newfoundland becoming independent of British legislative control.

Personally, however, George was scandal free. And while he became involved with politics to a degree, he was far more hands-off than his predecessors, preferring - most of the time - to represent his people rather than try to exert overt influence on the direction of the country. He threw himself into British life, becoming a regular presence at sporting events such as cricket test matches at Lords, tennis at Wimbledon and the football FA Cup final at Wembley. He even agreed to record a Christmas message, beginning a radio broadcast in 1932 following a request by the founder of the BBC, Sir John Reith. It resonated with the 20 million listeners who tuned in and so George agreed to make it an annual event.

Had people been able to watch on television, they may well have seen him with a cigarette in hand. He was a keen smoker, loving it almost as much as he did collecting stamps. But it would be his eventual undoing.

In 1925, George was diagnosed with chronic obstructive pulmonary disease and he developed a serious chest infection. He became rather ill from this point but he remained king until, in 1936, aged 70, his health deteriorated. Close to midnight on 20 January, he died. His funeral was held at St George's Chapel, Windsor, eight days later and he was succeeded by his eldest son, Edward VIII.

The funeral procession for suffragette Emily Davison

Defining moment
A libel case opens 1911

The French reporter EF Mylius writes an article in *Liberator* claiming that George V is a bigamist who had married an admiral's daughter, Mary Culme-Seymour in Malta in 1890. Copies of this are circulated around parliament and George is incensed, particularly because, if it were believed, it would make his children with Queen Mary illegitimate. It is also damaging his otherwise clean reputation given that the public is showing great interest in the allegation. George takes the unusual step in suing Mylius, who is found guilty of criminal libel and imprisoned for a year.

Irish Free State established
Ireland is partitioned in 1922 and the Irish Free State established. The British empire is beginning to break up, with other dominions being given their own powers.
1922

Life in the time of George V

Traditional family life
In the 1910s, Britain was a conservative country with clearly defined family roles. Although working-class women would often work in factories, middle-class women stayed at home to look after the children and ensure the family abode was kept in a good state. Men would be the breadwinners: railway and dock work, mining and building were typical jobs for working-class males.

The Roaring Twenties
Following the gloom of the 1910s, a decade marked by the frugality and horror of the First World War, prosperity began to return to Britain. People began to enjoy themselves in clubs and bars and women felt more free than ever before, thanks to the success of the suffragette movement which had gained them the vote in 1918.

The Education Act
The Education Act 1918 raised the school leaving age from 12 to 14 and it also allowed young workers the right of access to day-release education. However, the new rules weren't actually implemented until a further 1921 act was passed. Even so, in the 1920s, schooling became a hot topic for politicians and educationalists.

Mass unemployment hits the kingdom
As the successful 1920s turned into the 1930s, so all that was prosperous about the post-war United Kingdom came to a sudden jolt due to a global depression. In 1932 unemployment was as high as 3.5 million. The lack of jobs, hunger and desperation saw the rise of extremist political parties, not least the British Union of Fascists led by Sir Oswald Mosely.

Science was advancing
There had been great advances in science and technology throughout George V's reign. From the pop-up toaster, shortwave radio and stainless steel to the first robot, insulin, and 3D movie to the jet engine, cat's eyes and radar. Nuclear fission, which would be used to create devastating weapons in the 1940s, was discovered in 1938.

Crisis in parliament
With the Liberals pushing for reform of parliament and the Lords knocking back the party's budget, George's early reign is spent dealing with the ensuing constitutional crisis.
1910

War in Europe
Believing strongly that Britain has to go to war, George throws his support behind the troops, visiting them regularly on the Western front and handing out 50,000 awards for gallantry.
1914

House of Windsor
On 17 July 1917, the king announces that all descendants of Queen Victoria should bear the name Windsor rather than Saxe-Coburg and Gotha, making the house appear infinitely more English.
1917

Labour Party wins
George appoints the first Labour prime minister, Ramsay MacDonald. Two years later, the general strike sees millions of workers walk out in protest at wages and worsening conditions.
1924

National government formed
As economies nosedive into depression across the world, George encourages the leaders of the main parties to unite to form the National government. The civil list is reduced, cutting royal costs.
1931

1935

Silver jubilee
George celebrates his silver jubilee and famously says of the public affection shown to him, "I cannot understand it, after all I am only a very ordinary sort of fellow." He dies in 1936.
1935

© Alamy

January-December 1936

Edward VIII

Edward VIII shocked the world in 1936 when he announced to Britain and her empire that he was abdicating his throne for an American socialite named Wallis Simpson

In the late Thirties, Britain was facing its darkest hour. Hitler and his fascist thugs were rattling the sabre across Europe, quashing the rights of free men and women everywhere. Italy and Spain had fallen to the oppression of right-wing dictatorships and it wouldn't be long before war would sweep through the last free countries of the European continent. This was a time for stout hearts and stiff upper lips, for every British soul to look to the defence of the country and face these evil forces valiantly. Meanwhile Edward, Duke of Windsor, who until very recently had been King of Great Britain, sat in his villa in Antibes, France.

Edward's childhood and teenage years were a preparatory education to groom him for the day he would become King of Great Britain. He had one-to-one tuition with the best tutors in the land and attended renowned military schools - yet he was deeply unhappy. His father George, later to be crowned King George V, stood as a domineering and at times terrifying figure to Edward and his two siblings. George ran his household like a military operation, the children were forced to always be on time, to dress correctly and behave properly. Punishments included frightening confrontations with George in his study; a harsh prospect for Edward who was small and shy.

At just 12-years-old, Edward's father felt he needed a military education in order to prepare him for public life. He was sent to the naval college at Osborne on the Isle of Wight. Edward's

> According to his biographers Edward had an unhappy childhood; his nanny would deliberately hurt him

shy nature meant that he struggled to fit in with the other boys and bullying was an almost inevitable consequence. He did eventually find his feet and settled into this regimented life, passing the naval examination board for Dartmouth officer school in 1909. Edward continued to be a shy young man. During his cadet training, his parents threw a party for him at Buckingham Palace about which he recorded in his diary, 'I had to dance, a thing I hate, the whole thing was a great strain.' The 19-year-old Edward was still struggling to find his place in the world outside of the ritual of royal protocol.

It was clear that Edward lacked direction but World War I would see to it that all men of his age would be given a chance to prove themselves. Edward wanted to serve with the men of his army regiment on the frontline, he yearned to make a difference and war afforded him the opportunity. Unfortunately, the Secretary for War Lord Kitchener refused his request stating that it would be too dangerous for the young man. Edward continued to insist on being allowed to go and in the end toured the front regardless.

His admiration for the troops was shown in a correspondence he sent back to England, 'I'm very keen on the fighting troops being made as comfortable as possible always... the poor devils have a bloody enough time in the trenches... they are absolutely marvellous.' The war years had given Edward a sense of freedom he wouldn't normally have been permitted, he could meet other

"He continued to make horrendous errors in judgement, conducting a tour of Nazi Germany in 1937 and allowing himself to be photographed with Hitler"

During World War I Edward visited the trenches and saw first-hand the devastation and suffering caused by modern warfare

Wallis Simpson was the love of Edward's life, though it was known that he had other mistresses previously

EDWARD VIII
Britain, 1894-1972

Brief Bio

Playboy prince Edward never really wanted to be king, but the death of his father forced it on him. The rigours of an unhappy childhood resulted in a man who pursued pleasure and he struggled to combine this with his royal duties as Prince of Wales. His affair with Wallis Simpson sounded the death knell for his kingship.

A dark connection

The dark connection between Hitler and the British royal family in the Thirties begun in 1935 when the Fuhrer used Karl Eduard, the Duke of SaxeCoburg-Gotha as an informal ambassador of goodwill to the royal family. Eduard seemed to have succeeded in persuading Edward that Hitler was the only defence against communism. The connection grew stronger when Edward decided to visit Germany in 1937. A clandestine meeting between Edward and committed Nazis Rudolf Hess and Martin Bormann took place in Edward's hotel in Paris before the visit. An impression of the meeting written by Hess informed Hitler that, 'the Duke was proud of his German blood' and there was 'no need to lose a single German life in invading Britain. The Duke and his clever wife will deliver the goods.' Hess fully expected Edward to regain power in Britain and persuade the populace to seek peace. The visit to Germany then went ahead, Hitler was charming and Edward enjoyed his tour. As the war progressed, a secret memorandum to American president Roosevelt from J. Edgar Hoover claimed, 'that the Duke of Windsor entered into an agreement. If Germany was victorious [Herman Goering] would install the Duke of Windsor as King of England.' While it seems unlikely Edward did agree to this, he must have maintained links with the Nazis for this type of rumour to circulate.

men his own age under the guise of these tours and drop the cold protocol normally required of official visits.

After the armistice it was as if this new-found freedom had disappeared with the rifles and bayonets. He commented in 1919, ' I mixed with men... I found my manhood.' His father was quick to clip his new found self-confidence sternly informing him, 'don't think you act like other people.' He longed for the freedom given to him during the war and found his new life of state openings and formal banquets smothering. He drifted through his university career failing to make an impact academically and then went on an extended tour of the empire. While this should have offered him the adventure he yearned for, he quickly saw that he was just as much a prisoner abroad as he was at home. Every step he took was closely monitored, and he became frustrated and depressed. His frustration made him angry and he began to display the bigotry and dismissive nature inherited by many English aristocracy of the time. He was appalled by the Australian aborigines describing them as, 'the most revolting form of living creatures I've ever seen.' He also began to hate communism with unrelenting zeal.

It was during this unhappy time that in 1931 he met the woman that would change his life forever - Wallis Simpson. Edward had already had a number of affairs but they were fleeting. In Wallis he found something that he hadn't seen in other women, a strong independent character that knew

her own mind and refused to stand on ceremony. He quickly became infatuated by her, it was said by observers that he lost 'all sense of reason' when he was around her. He lavished her with jewellery, gold or whatever she wanted, it seemed as if Edward had finally found someone to give his life meaning. There was however a complication as far as Edward's position as the Prince of Wales was concerned; Wallis was a married woman. When she became Edward's mistress she promised to give up her second husband for him but this wouldn't soothe the sensibilities of his family. To compound the issue she wasn't from a royal household, she was an American socialite from Baltimore. When it became obvious to Edward's father in 1934 that this wasn't another casual relationship he was furious; he angrily told him to get rid of her.

On 20 January 1936, George V died and the question of Wallis's status was immediately brought into question. Would she become queen? The short answer was absolutely not - she was twice divorced and unpopular with the British establishment. Absurd rumours circulated about the spell she had placed Edward under, her devious manipulation, her dark hold over the new king. The issue was becoming even more serious, especially considering that the country was edging ever closer to another world war. The nation needed leadership, not uncertainty, but Edward did not see the two issues as related. He wanted to marry Wallis, and everything else was of secondary importance. Besides, Adolf Hitler would defeat the

> Edward gained his pilot's licence and founded the 32 Royal squadron, used for royal flights to official engagements

Defining moment
Tour of the empire
5 August 1919

After the war, Edward spends the next five years touring the empire and representing his father abroad. He does a number of public relation events including presenting the Prince of Wales cup to the Canadian hockey league and visiting the politically sensitive city of Quebec where he receives a warm welcome. His charm and good looks serve him well and he becomes a popular figure. Not all of his visits went so smoothly however; in a high-profile visit to Australia he wrote of the Aborigines, 'they are the most revolting form of living creatures I've ever seen'.

Defining moment
Royal family meet Wallis
November 1934

Edward's less than discreet affair with Wallis Simpson comes to a head in 1934 when Edward invites Simpson to an evening party at Buckingham Palace. Edward's father had originally struck her name out of the list of invitations but Edward invited her, regardless. When George finds out, he becomes outraged and shouts his disapproval. Simpson is subsequently frozen out of all royal family functions. This puts enormous strain on the relationship between Edward and his father, lending more fuel to the suspicion that Edward will abdicate when George dies.

Timeline

1894

A prince is born
Edward Windsor is born at White Lodge, Richmond Park London to George and Mary, the Duke and Duchess of York. He is given the title His Highness Prince Edward of York.
23 June 1894

The Prince at Dartmouth
On the wishes of his family, Edward joins the navy as an officer cadet at Dartmouth Navy College. He spends two years there before becoming a Midshipman.
September 1909

Prince of Wales and heir apparent
On the death of Edward VII, Edward's father becomes the King of Britain and her empire. Edward is immediately invested as the Prince of Wales and is now next in line to the throne.
23 June 1910

War
At the outbreak of World War I, Edward joins the Grenadier guards and asks to serve at the front. This request is refused by the Secretary of State for War Lord Kitchener.
28 July 1914

Time magazine story
Time magazine publishes a story in which Edward is reported to have said that he would abdicate the throne. This is officially denied, but the story serves as an insight into his thoughts.
29 April 1929

communists and the world would be at peace - there was really nothing to worry about as far as he was concerned.

The fact that Edward was for the appeasement of Hitler was not unusual; many members of the British establishment were in the late Thirties. What was compounding the issue was the Nazi party was seen to be influencing the king through Wallis. Whether this was true or not is debatable but many influential people saw it so; the American ambassador commented, 'many people here suspect that Mrs Simpson is actually in German pay.' The situation was looking bad and as an illustration of the tense atmosphere, Edward suffered an assassination attempt when a lone gunman apparently working for an undisclosed foreign power tried to pull a gun on him. When Edward returned to Buckingham Palace the first sympathy call was from Hitler.

Then in November 1936 Edward told Prime Minister Stanley Baldwin that he was going to marry Wallis. Baldwin rejected the proposal, stating that it would be unacceptable to the British cabinet if the head of state married a twice-divorcee. Wallis herself expected full marriage, and Edward refused to give her up. He saw no option; on the 11 of December he announced to Britain and the empire, "I have found it impossible to carry the heavy burden of responsibility and to discharge my duties as king... without the help and support of the woman I love." He abdicated the throne, passing the duty to his brother Albert, the father of Queen Elizabeth II.

Edward and Wallis were now in limbo. They were granted official titles, the Duke and Duchess

Edward was stanchly anti-communist and feared the communist takeover of Europe during the Thirties

of Windsor, but were frozen out of much of the public salary they should have received for the role. Once again Edward fell into a deep depression, he relied on the hospitality of friends abroad and used the Château de Candé in France to marry Wallis. He became an embittered and ungrateful guest, running up huge phone bills and refusing to pay for anything. He also continued to make horrendous errors in judgement, conducting a tour of Nazi Germany in 1937 and allowing himself to be photographed with Hitler.

In 1940, as a way of preventing any more embarrassment to the royal family, Winston Churchill gave the Duke a governorship in the Bahamas. Edward saw it for what it was - a way to get him out of the way. He conducted his duties, made inroads into improving the situations of the workers on the islands but hated his current position none the less. He had become increasingly estranged from his family.

By the time the war was over and the dust had settled over his relationship with Wallis, the Duke was content to live quietly. He established himself in France at the 4 Route du Champ d'Entraînement Paris, later to be known as Villa Windsor, where he spent the rest of his days in retirement. He had lived a privileged life but it was a life he did not want, in the end he gave up the power he inherited at birth for the woman he loved.

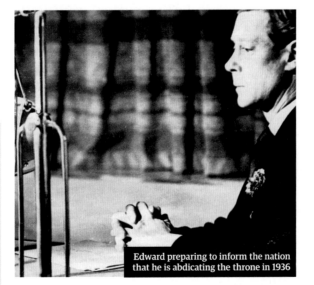
Edward preparing to inform the nation that he is abdicating the throne in 1936

The British Empire
The British Empire still remained the single biggest empire on the face of the planet during the years leading up to the war. Many of its dominions like Canada, Australia and New Zealand governed their own affairs but still held political ties with Britain through the British monarchy. Other countries like Burma and India were governed directly as colonies.

An age of extremes
The huge social upheaval caused by the Great Depression created a credibility gap between liberal governments and their citizens in Europe. This gave rise to extremist governments from the communist left and fascist right. Adolf Hitler in particular was starting to make a name for himself as an uncompromising totalitarian leader.

Role of the monarchy
The role of the monarchy in Britain and throughout the Commonwealth was changing in the wake of the mass media. It was no longer enough for the monarch to simply open Parliament once a year, the Royal family was expected to set an example of British values in the country and take on a leadership role in times of national need.

Colonial unrest
The Thirties gave rise to independence movements in many imperial colonies. The most vocal of these movements came from India and Mahatma Gandhi's freedom group. While the British government doggedly hung on to its empire in India, the British people started to wonder if it was worth it

Britain, a waning power?
No-one could dispute that British influence throughout the globe remained strong during the Thirties, but the government's reluctance to rearm and prepare for war in the face of fascist and communist threats was said to be indicative of an waning power that no longer had the stomach for military commitments.

● **Governor of the Bahamas**
In an effort to prevent Edward and Wallis, now Duke and Duchess of Windsor, from embarrassing the British government even more, Edward is given the governorship of the Bahamas.
18 August 1940

● **Retirement**
With the war won and the new world order establishing itself in Europe, France becomes safe again for British citizens. Edward and Wallis retire there comfortably.
November 1952

Defining moment
Abdication
10 December 1936

Edward makes it clear to Prime Minister Stanley Baldwin that he will not change his mind about marrying Wallis as soon as her second divorce is finalised. Baldwin informs Edward that the cabinet and the imperial parliaments will not accept his marriage to Wallis if he still wishes to be king. With Edward finding it impossible to reconcile his personal life with his duty as a future monarch, he finally decides to abdicate and signs the act at Fort Belvedere in the presence of his younger brother Albert the Duke of York who is next in line to the throne.

1972

● **Succession to the throne**
George V dies and Edward is immediately put forward for the succession. It also becomes known within the government that he intends to soon marry Wallis.
20 January 1936

● **Assassination attempt**
A man called George McMahon pulls a gun on Edward and is quickly set upon by police. He testifies that he was working for a foreign power although this is never proved.
16 July 1936

● **Marriage to Wallis**
Edward and Wallis marry at the Château de Candé in France. While the service is attended by a number of high-profile socialites, none of the royal family attends.
3 June 1937

● **Visit to Germany**
Against the advice of the British Government, Edward and Wallis visit Nazi Germany and are warmly welcomed by Adolf Hitler. It is reported that he almost gives a Nazi salute.
October 1937

Death of a Duke ●
Edward dies peacefully in his sleep aged 77. His body is flown back to England and a funeral service is attended by Queen Elizabeth II. His body is buried at the royal burial ground at Frogmore.
28 May 1972

1936-1952
George VI

George VI was the stammering sovereign who saw Britain through a terrible war with Nazi Germany

In 1932, George V had delivered the royal family's first Christmas Broadcast, a short message beamed around the UK via the new medium of radio, on the invitation and persistence of the BBC's founding father Sir John Reith. This fledgling tradition would have been assumed by Edward VIII who took to the throne on 20 January 1936 following his father's death, but just three weeks before Christmas, on 11 December 1936, Edward VIII abdicated in order to wed his American socialite mistress Wallis Simpson.

Taking his place that same day was George VI, Edward VIII's younger brother. With too little time to prepare for the Christmas speech in 1936, it was cancelled, a move that would have proven to be a mighty relief for the new king. George VI had a stammer which, some have said, resulted from a tough relationship with his father, and it appeared to get worse when he was nervous. But, while the stammer was the subject of an acclaimed film, *The King's Speech* in 2010 and has come to define him in the eyes of many ever since, there was far more to this brave and dedicated man than talk alone.

Formally known as His Highness Prince Albert of York, the future king was a sickly child who suffered with a lack of affection from his father, George V. Albert wasn't particularly close to his mother, Mary of Teck, either and his cold-natured, harsh upbringing had made him into a rather unassuming fellow, with the now-famous stammer that had developed at the age of eight proving doubly unhelpful in his desire, and later, need, to overcome his shyness.

To make matters worse, Albert also struggled at school, where he was forced to write with his right-hand despite being left-handed. As a result, he faired poorly in exams and while, in 1909, he graduated from the Royal Navy Academy at Osborne, he had been bullied and he had also

come bottom of the class in his final exam. But he went on to join the Royal Navy as a midshipman, serving on HMS Collingwood in the first world war and fighting as a young naval officer at the Battle of Jutland in 1916. He became a pilot with the Royal Air Force in 1919 - the first of his family to learn to fly - and he showed great braveness and determination; qualities that would be evident throughout his reign.

In 1920, he met the Scottish aristocrat Elizabeth Bowes-Lyon. She was an attractive woman who garnered the attention of many men. Prince Albert was smitten and he chased her relentlessly, proposing to her in 1921 and 1922, on each occasion suffering the humiliation of being turned down. He eventually persuaded her, though, and they married on 26 April 1923 in Westminster Abbey. She became Her Royal Highness the Duchess of York and the couple had two children, Elizabeth on 21 April 1926 and Margaret on 21 August 1930.

Shortly after Elizabeth was born, the prince had been to see a maverick Australian speech therapist called Lionel Logue. They had met for the first time in Logue's consulting room in Harley Street, London, on 19 October 1926 and they struck up a friendship while the therapist attempted to cure the royal of his stammer following incredible embarrassment and silence during the closing address of the British Empire Exhibition at Wembley in 1925.

Logue attempted to inject confidence into Prince Albert, making him believe that the stammer was a physical rather than psychological condition and the pair met frequently, striking up a friendship that lasted for life. It was a hard battle (the stammer continued to afflict him even at the time of his coronation on 12 May 1937) but was one he persevered with, showing a level of bullishness that would stand him in good stead for his reign.

> Many changes to the Empire took place during George's reign. He was the last King-Emperor of India

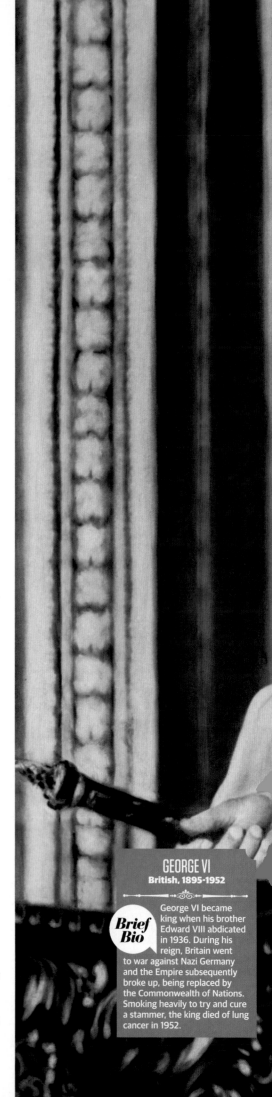

GEORGE VI
British, 1895-1952

Brief Bio George VI became king when his brother Edward VIII abdicated in 1936. During his reign, Britain went to war against Nazi Germany and the Empire subsequently broke up, being replaced by the Commonwealth of Nations. Smoking heavily to try and cure a stammer, the king died of lung cancer in 1952.

Queen Elizabeth and King George VI at the 1939 New York World's Fair

Life in the time of George VI

Frequent air raids
The first few months of the Second World War have been referred to as the Phoney War because, until the Battle of France in May 1940, there had been a very long period of inactivity. But that changed eventually, and from 7 September 1940, the Germans bombed London. Heavy blitzing caused many casualties in Birmingham, Manchester, Coventry, Bristol, Portsmouth and Plymouth.

Food and clothes rationing
With supplies of food cut and ships bringing supplies attacked, imports fell dramatically and it was necessary to ration the fewer resources that were available in Britain. Brits were handed ration books that kept a check on what each person would receive. Rationing continued after the war with meat, butter, lard, sugar, tea, clothes and fuel in scarce supply.

Booming picture houses
The first television programme – a bulletin of the *British Movietone News* – was broadcast on 2 November 1936 but the BBC's TV service closed down on 1 September 1939. With victory in sight, it returned on 7 June 1946, broadcasting from Alexandra Palace but very few people had TV sets at the time. Cinemas proliferated in Britain and people would visit at least once a week.

Black Market fear
Cinemas would show a short film that warned against a flourishing black market trade in food which had emerged thanks to rationing. It did not stop enterprising people from buying produce from illicit sources, though. Indeed, the film was just one of many that were produced on behalf of the government to encourage certain behaviour.

Freezing British weather
The winter of 1946 to 1947 was particularly harsh with heavy snow causing chaos on the road and rail. Temperatures only reached 14 degrees Celsius, falling to as low as -21 degrees Celsius and further restrictions on life were put in place as a result of low supplies of coal. Home-grown food became even scarcer.

A heavily bomb-damaged street in Valletta, Malta in 1942

Siege of Malta

During the Second World War, the tiny Mediterranean island of Malta was part of the British Empire but its strategic proximity to Axis shipping lanes made it a prime target for the air forces and navies of Italy and Germany. The first bombs fell on 11 June 1940, the day after Italian dictator Benito Mussolini declared war on Britain and France.

The island was devastated over the coming months with the heaviest sustained bombing taking place in 1942 during the so-called Siege of Malta. For 157 days and nights, 6,700 tons of bombs fell on the population. Winston Churchill's government sent the Royal Navy and Royal Air Force to help defend the island while Malta's people held out and, in 1943, with victory secured, the Allies used the island as a launch pad for an invasion of Sicily.

Impressed by their bravery and resilience, King George VI awarded the entire people of Malta the George Cross. In a message to the island's governor, the king said the award was "to bear witness to a heroism and a devotion that will long be famous in history."

King George VI fires a Bren gun during a visit to a small arms factory

Defining moment
King meets Lionel Logue 1926

The self-taught therapist Lionel Logue had arrived from Australia in the UK in 1924. He met His Royal Highness The Duke of York for the first time on 19 October 1926 at his Harley Street practise, noting his "acute nervous tension which has been brought on by the defect", a nod to the future king's stammer. When word got out that Prince Albert was seeing Logue, the medical profession was up in arms, considering the therapist as an amateur. But Albert was strong-willed and the pair continued to meet. His help was deemed so useful that the Queen Mother wrote a handwritten letter of thanks to Logue.

Defining moment
Birth of two children 1930

In 1926, Albert became a father to Elizabeth Alexandra Mary, who would go on to become queen. In 1930, Princess Margaret, Countess of Snowdon was born. Elizabeth and Margaret were close and they spent the Second World War at Windsor Castle. After the war, however, Margaret went down a path that the royal family did not approve of. She fell in love with divorcee Group Captain Peter Townsend who proposed to Margaret, aged 22. The Church of England would not marry Margaret to a divorced man and so, instead, she wed Anthony Armstrong-Jones. The couple divorced in 1978.

Timeline

1895

● **Albert Frederick Arthur George is born**
Prince Albert was born on 14 December 1895. The date was, significantly, the 34th anniversary of the death of Prince Albert, consort to Queen Victoria – the newborn's great grandfather.
1895

● **Naval college beckons**
Prince Albert was sent to naval college. He would see action as a junior office at the Battle of Jutland in 1916 but he was bullied by fellow officers during his early years and became increasingly withdrawn.
1909

● **A romantic liaison**
When Albert met Elizabeth Bowes-Lyon, he fell in love but it would take until 1923 before he could persuade her to marry him. She became known as the Smiling Duchess for her beaming face.
1920

● **Keen tennis player**
Partnered by tutor Louis Greig, the Duke of York played in the men's doubles championship at Wimbledon - although a convincing, heavy defeat ensured he did not appear in public with a racket again.
1926

● **Accedes to the throne**
When Edward VIII abdicated to pursue a marriage to Wallis Simpson, George VI became king on 12 December 1936. He was crowned in May of the following year.
1936

"Like his father, George VI had to lead the Empire into a mass, global conflict soon after taking to the throne"

For in 1938, prime minister Neville Chamberlain had failed to appease Adolf Hitler, leader of the National Socialist German Workers Party. As chancellor of Germany and dictator of Nazi Germany, Hitler was dismissive of George VI, referring to him as a simpleton on many an occasion and being equally disparaging of his wife who, incidentally, had come to be known as Queen Elizabeth the Queen Mother so as to avoid confusion with the couple's daughter.

But Hitler was nevertheless shocked and annoyed when, on 3 September 1939, Britain declared war with Germany. For George VI, it meant, like his father, he was having to lead the Empire into a mass, global conflict so soon after taking to the throne. The silver lining to this cloud was the king's ability to deliver a clear, calm radio speech that day while standing at a lectern in an anteroom at Buckingham Palace with only Logue for company. Sailing through with barely a stammer, George VI was pleased with himself, putting his triumph down to Logue's hard work as well as his heavy chain-smoking which, the king had been told, was helping him to relax.

Following the outbreak of war, Winston Churchill was appointed first lord of the Admirality (the political head of the Royal Navy) and he was admitted as a member of the War Cabinet. It was a role he had taken on during the First World War as a member of the Liberal party. During the interwar years, Churchill had crossed the floor and become a Conservative party member and while he lost his Tory seat in 1929, he was still vocal. He had warned Chamberlain that appeasement was a bad move that would lead to war and, when Chamberlain resigned in 1940, Churchill was chosen to succeed him, becoming prime minister of an all-party coalition government.

George VI worked closely with - and ultimately admired - Churchill whose endearing, stirring speeches had spurred a nation. Maybe the king felt a pang of jealousy at his new PM's impeccable oratory but he certainly, in the long run at least, bore Churchill no ill will for the support he had shown to Edward VIII during the abdication crisis. Indeed, George VI was becoming a confident king who was making some shrewd decisions, chief among them the insistence that he remain at Buckingham Palace for much of the war despite the building being bombed nine times as the conflict rolled on to 1945. It showed incredible solidarity with the suffering of the British population and it headed off a potential uprising from Londoners who were suffering greatly during the Blitz.

Like his father, George VI spent time abroad visiting his troops, checking on morale and gaining a firm tactical understanding. He instituted the George Cross and George Medal; the former replacing the Empire Gallantry Medal in becoming the highest gallantry award for civilians. It shared equal precedence with the Victoria Cross. The George Medal was created as an award for those performing acts of bravery in the UK. When the war was won in 1945, he was relieved and yet exhausted. He worried about the state Britain would find herself in for the next few years.

He was right to be concerned. The Second World War had been bloody and genocidal - costing the lives of some 70 million people, two-thirds of whom were civilians - and on top of this, it had also proved to be hugely disruptive with populations forced to flee their home countries, a refugee crisis and thousands of bombed out properties.

The economy had taken a battering and the Empire was on its knees. The Commonwealth of Nations replaced the British Empire as, for the remainder of the king's reign, nationalisation and decolonisation was taking place.

What's more, rationing was extended, further restricting the sale of various essential and non-essential food, clothes, fuel and furniture. The king also clashed at times with Clement Attlee, the Labour prime minister returned by British voters in 1945. Attlee supported increased nationalisation of key industries such as steel and coal mining. He also moved Britain towards socialism which the king opposed. Yet the post-war era brought the introduction of the National Health Service and it brought the Bank of England under public control.

The war and the subsequent changes left George VI feeling the strain and it was taking its toll on his body and mind. His heavy smoking caught up with him and his health deteriorated. Princess Elizabeth took up many of his royal duties. In 1951, the king was diagnosed with lung cancer and arteriosclerosis and it meant he had to have his left lung removed. On 6 February 1952, at Sandringham, George VI died aged 56. His body was buried at St George's Chapel in Windsor.

> Lord Haw-Haw mocked George VI in broadcasts, calling him "your stammering king" for his faltering speech

Defining moment
Chamberlain and Hitler
1938
In September 1938, Nazi dictator Adolf Hitler wanted to take a part of Czechoslovakia called Sudetenland, an area in which three million Germans were living. An uprising by Sudeten Germans was quelled by the Czech police who Hitler accused of killing some 300 of the protestors. German troops were then placed along the Czech border. Alarmed by this, the British prime minister visited Munich to meet Hitler, securing his signature on a non-aggression pact that stated the German leader would not war with Britain.

Timeline

War breaks out
Chamberlain and George VI had appeared on the balcony of Buckingham Palace to herald the attempt at appeasement of German aggression. But in 1939, it had evidently failed.
1939

Britain is bombed
With Winston Churchill now prime minister, backed fully by George V, England is bombarded by the German Luftwaffe, blitzing London and other major cities.
1940

American allies join war
In 1939, George VI had visited America for the New York World's Fair and he had struck a strong bond with President Franklin D. Roosevelt. That helped when the US entered the war in 1941.
1941

Cold War begins
Although victory was Britain's, more troubled brewed. The "Iron Curtain" split Western Europe from the Communist East and the Cold War with Russia in particular began in earnest.
1946

National Health Service established
The Labour Party ruled the UK following the war and socialist policies were enacted. The NHS was established. But rationing continues and the economy was in a poor state.
1948

George VI dies
His mind shattered and his body ravaged by cancer, George VI's health deteriorated and he died in the winter of 1952. His eldest daughter, Queen Elizabeth II, took to the throne.
1952

1952

© Getty

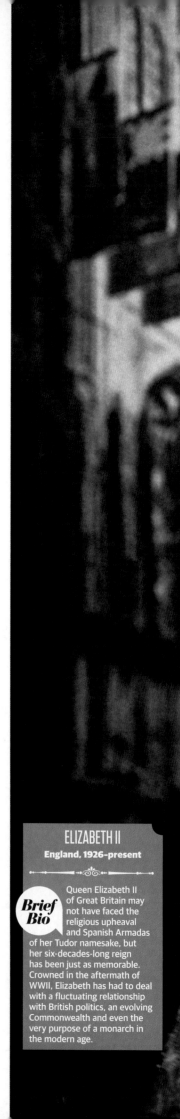

1952-present

Elizabeth II

After more than 60 years on the throne, Her Majesty Queen Elizabeth II remains one of history's most popular monarchs

Her Majesty the Queen may not have led armies into glorious battle or faced down bloodthirsty rebellions in far-flung corners of her realm, yet she remains one of the most popular and beloved rulers to have ever worn the crown. Her reign as queen is also one of the longest the nation has ever known. Such a lengthy tenure may seem less noteworthy in an age removed from murderous plots and usurping royal relatives, but Elizabeth has nonetheless sat resolute in her duties through the latter half of the 20th Century and the burgeoning years of the 21st – a time when the Western world metamorphosed in the wake of two world wars. Britain and her many territories have undergone quite the transformation, and the role of monarch and the royal family has changed drastically along with it.

After more than six decades as the head of state, Elizabeth has faced the perils, challenges and benefits of being a monarch in the modern age. Gone are the threats of invasion, intrigue and insurrections, replaced instead by satire, media scandals and the weight of public opinion. She remains the most well-travelled of any British monarch and her tireless work with hundreds of charities around the world set a precedent that has typified the role of a modern-day royal.

It seems bizarre then, when you consider the extent of her future reign, that the young Princess Elizabeth was barely a consideration for the throne as a child. Born on 21 April 1926, the daughter of Prince Albert, Duke of York, Elizabeth was at the time third in the line of succession behind her uncle, the Prince of Wales, and her father. However, as was royal protocol, it was assumed that her uncle would almost certainly father children of his

own, pushing Elizabeth further down the line. She was never expected to become queen.

But to the young princess, such trivialities were of little concern. Nicknamed 'Lillibet' by her family, she enjoyed a close relationship with her father, her mother Lady Elizabeth Bowes-Lyon (later the Queen Mother) and her grandfather, George V. The king's health was already deteriorating by the time Elizabeth was born, but her regular visits and playful relationship with the ailing monarch were said to have buoyed his spirits far more than any medicine. Her positive effect was even covered by newspapers – a taste of just how obsessed the media could, and would, become with its own monarchy. Still, Elizabeth got to enjoy the pomp and privilege of being a royal without the pressures of being an heir apparent or an heir presumptive. However, no one could see the turn of events that came next.

The king was dead. George V had finally passed away from a worsening bout of septicaemia on 20 January 1936, with the throne then passing to his eldest son, the Prince of Wales. Crowned King Edward VIII, it was apparent from the very start that Edward wasn't going to be a conventional king. Known for his vocal dislike of court protocols and politicians, the new monarch even broke convention by watching the proclamation of his own ascendancy from a window in St James's Palace. By his side stood Wallis Simpson, an American socialite whom the 41-year-old king had been courting for some time. Edward's association with the once divorced and still married (to her second husband) Simpson was already causing outrage in royal and political circles alike, but it would take his decision to propose to her a few months later to tip the balance.

> After WWII, the young Elizabeth saved up her ration coupons to afford the material for her wedding dress

The Queen sent her first email in... 1976. She sent the message over ARPANET, a small-scale precursor to the internet

171

The annus horribilis

1992 was an eventful and difficult year for Queen Elizabeth II

There have been a number of challenging years in Elizabeth's considerable reign, but 1992 proved to be one her worst. Despite it marking the 40th anniversary of her ascension to the throne, those 12 months were littered with political issues and startling catastrophes that likely pushed the normally resolute monarch to her limits. Elizabeth named the period her 'annus horribilis' (likely a reference to John Dryden's poem of the same name that describes London in the grip of the Great Plague and Great Fire of London in 1666).

It all started in March when her second son, Prince Andrew Duke of York, separated from his wife Sarah Ferguson duchess of York. The couple made an official announcement stating the separation was amicable, but speculation was rife that all was not so rosy behind the scenes. These rumours seemingly sprung to life a few months later when photos of the duchess topless with her lover appeared all over the tabloid newspapers. It was an incredibly embarrassing episode for the royal household and it didn't bode well for the rest of the year.

The incidents continued a month after the duke and duchess' split in March with another member of the royal family. Her daughter Anne, the Princess Royal, had married Mark Phillips, a lieutenant in the 1st Queen's Dragoon Guards, in 1973 and it seemed another fairy-tale royal union to captivate the public. However, the couple decided to separate in 1989, citing years of strain stemming from Phillips' military commitments. In April 1992 the couple officially divorced, further adding to a media-fuelled story that the royal family was splintering under the strain of being in the public eye.

In June, things got even worse. The journalist Andrew Morton had just released his biography of the princess of Wales, *Diana: Her True Story*, and it was filled with sensational stories regarding Diana and her deteriorating relationship with Prince Charles. The couple's fairy-tale relationship had been falling apart as early as the mid-1980s and the two were openly seeing other people despite still being married. Diana's affair with Major James Hewitt, Charles's liaison with Camilla Parker-Bowles and Diana's supposed suicidal thoughts were sensationalised in gruesome detail and it caused the Queen, and her whole royal family, a great deal of embarrassment for years to come.

To top it all off, one of the Queen's favourite residences was badly damaged by a raging inferno in the same year. On the 20 November – a mere four days before the Queen would give her Guildhall speech in which she referred to her year as her annus horribilis – Windsor Castle caught fire, causing severe damage to the whole structure. So bad was the damage that it cost an estimated £36.5 million to repair over the following five years. The blaze started when a spotlight caused a curtain to catch alight and it soon spread through the entire castle in a matter in minutes. There were no serious injuries and no deaths as a result of the blaze, but the royal administration was forced to open Buckingham Palace soon after in order to help fund the castle's restoration program.

As the first female monarch in 51 years, Elizabeth knew many challenges faced her in a rapidly changing world

Mounting pressure from the rest of the royal family and Parliament forced the king to choose between his duties as a monarch and his love for a woman judged too politically troublesome to be his queen. Edward, forever the rebel, chose his heart over his crown and abdicated on 10 December 1936 after 326 days as king (among the shorter reigns of British monarchs). This unforeseen decision threw Edward's younger brother, Elizabeth's father, onto the throne. With her father crowned George VI on 12 May 1937, the 11-year-old princess was no longer a carefree child, but an heir presumptive to the British throne. (An heir presumptive is someone who is first in line to the throne, but whose position can be superseded by a stronger claim - conversely, an heir apparent is someone in the same position, minus the chance of a challenge.)

It was during her early teens that Elizabeth met Prince Philip of Greece and Denmark. The two began a slow courtship, with Philip travelling regularly as part of his service in the Royal Navy - eventually the young couple announced their engagement on 9 July 1947. Her choice of fiancé caused friction with some members of the royal court. Philip had very little financial standing and his family had marital ties to the Nazi party in Germany, but his conversion from Greek Orthodoxy to Anglicanism and the taking of his mother's family name, Mountbatten, helped ease the union in the eyes of his detractors. The two married later that year on 20 November at Westminster Abbey. Despite the hundreds of presents the couple received from around the world, Elizabeth refused to allow the wedding to be a lavish affair.

Despite his royal responsibilities as both a duke and then a king, George VI enjoyed a close and positive relationship with his two daughters

With her reign spanning over six decades, Elizabeth has become an intrinsic part of Britain's cultural identity

As the health of King George VI began to deteriorate, Elizabeth and Philip's first two children were born - Prince Charles, born on 14 November 1948 and Princess Anne born on 15 August 1950. Elizabeth was enjoying her new role as mother, yet her responsibilities on behalf of the king were becoming more time-consuming as she travelled Europe on his behalf to visit those countries still recovering from the scars of World War II. On 6 February 1952, the king eventually succumbed to the melting pot of cancers and tumours that were robbing him of life. And, just like that, the 25-year-old princess became the new monarch of the realm.

Elizabeth was crowned at Westminster Abbey on 2 June 1953, following over a year's worth of national mourning for the late king. Elizabeth chose to retain her given name as her regnal title and, under the advisement of prime minister Winston Churchill and her mother, the surname of Windsor (instead of her husband's family name). Upon her ascension she was officially crowned Queen Elizabeth II of the United Kingdom, Canada, Australia, New Zealand, Union of South Africa, Pakistan and Ceylon (modern-day Sri Lanka).

The Commonwealth Of Nations, as it would come to be known, was an idea that began to form before Elizabeth was even born, yet it was under her reign that the Commonwealth swelled in size and became more than a gathering of former British territories. Many of these overseas nations were beginning to crave autonomy from Britain and the new queen embraced the idea fully. She and Philip, now the Duke of Edinburgh, began a six-month tour of the Commonwealth almost immediately following her coronation. With Europe still in a state of physical, economical and political recovery from World War II, Elizabeth's arrival had an almost talismanic effect. She even travelled further afield, becoming the first British reigning monarch to visit both Australia and New Zealand.

In 1956, Elizabeth experienced her first political misstep. Following the rise of nationalism in Egypt, Britain made a joint attempt with France to take control of the Suez Canal in Egypt. It was a short-lived effort and Britain was forced to withdraw as the USA attempted to appease the situation diplomatically. It was an embarrassing episode for the Conservative administration at the time, made worse by rumours that Elizabeth had been against invasion from the start. The prime minister, Anthony Eden, denied such a claim, but it was enough to undermine his position and he soon resigned. At this time, the Conservative government had no formal process to appoint a new prime minister in the middle of a parliamentary term.

The decision fell to Elizabeth who, under advisement, appointed Harold Macmillan as Eden's replacement. The decision, along with the Suez Canal fiasco, led to considerable criticism of the Queen from MPs, lords and the media. It was a stark reminder that the days of the monarch as a ruler were firmly resigned to the history books.

The Queen has two birthdays: an official one celebrated in June by the Trooping the Colour ceremony, and her real one on 21 April

Life in the time of Elizabeth II

Empire to Commonwealth
During her reign, the realm has evolved from the British empire into the Commonwealth of Nations. This transition is the result of the decolonisation of the empire into an intergovernmental organisation that consists of 53 nations (mostly former British colonies) that are recognised as equal member states.

A shift in power
The actual power the king or queen of England can enact upon the realm is a shadow of its former self. The time of absolute royal authority is a thing of the past and Elizabeth II is bound by a constitutional agreement with Parliament that limits her influence over policies and legislation.

Travelling the globe
Elizabeth II remains one of the most well-travelled monarchs in British history. As the head of the Commonwealth, she flew to Canada in 1958 and opened the 23rd Parliament there, which served as just one of the ways that the crown has recognised the semi-autonomy of its member states.

Silver jubilee
In 1977, Elizabeth II celebrated the 25th anniversary of her accession to the throne. To mark the occasion, she and Prince Philip visited 36 counties – no monarch had visited so many parts of the UK within such a small amount of time.

Media frenzy
Public interest in the royal family had always been high, but the media's focus on royals took an alarmingly sensational turn in the 1980s. The media ran endless stories about how the Queen disapproved of prime minister Margaret Thatcher's often unpopular policies, fuelling rumours of a division between crown and government.

So what were Elizabeth's political powers? Well, while Parliament holds autonomy from the crown in terms of its infrastructure, the king or queen still holds some administrative (be they mostly ceremonial) authorities. Elizabeth has the power to open and dissolve Parliament prior to a general election, as well the right to consult the prime minister on issues of state at any time. That's not to say that Elizabeth's position as queen is simply a figurehead - as monarch, Elizabeth must ratify all bills passed through Parliament. This is known as Royal Assent, and it's a political procedure that's not been refused since its creation in 1707. Even the Queen's speech (not to be confused with the Queen's Christmas message), delivered in Parliament every year, forms an important role, signifying royal approval of a new year in legislation.

Despite all her travels, the Queen doesn't have a passport. Since the crown issues them, Her Majesty is exempt from needing one

While the 1960s and 1970s were a transformative period for Britain and the Commonwealth, with over 20 countries gaining independence, the 1980s were a mixed affair. Despite issues with rising unemployment, the nation was united in celebrating the union of Elizabeth's eldest son, Prince Charles with Lady Diana Spencer in 1981. It was a lavish affair and the presence of the bright, young princess-to-be was a breath of fresh air for the royal family's public image. Sadly, the jovial public mood was curtailed when the Falklands War broke out the following year. Even the Queen's middle child, Prince Andrew, took part in the Royal Navy's conflict with Argentinean forces in the South Atlantic. Despite her concerns, Elizabeth wanted Andrew to remain

Once Elizabeth became queen, she travelled tirelessly across the world, including this trip to West Germany in 1965

The abdication
20 January-1 December 1936

1936 is a very tumultuous year for the royal family. In January, King George V (Elizabeth's grandfather) dies. The throne then passes to his eldest son Albert, who becomes Edward VIII. However, the uncrowned Edward chooses to abdicate less than 12 months later and his brother (and Elizabeth's father) the Duke of York becomes King George VI. With her father now presiding on the throne, Elizabeth becomes first in line to the throne at the age of ten. During this period, Princess Elizabeth is also referred to by the official title of 'heir presumptive'.

Elizabeth is crowned
2 June 1953

Following the death of her father, George VI, towards the end of 1952, the 26-year-old heir presumptive is finally crowned Queen Elizabeth II. Despite the tradition that the husband's surname is taken, it is decreed that Elizabeth will retain her family name of Windsor instead of Philip's name Mountbatten. At the time, Philip complains that, "I am the only man in the country not allowed to give his name to his own children." To appease the situation, the name Mountbatten-Windsor is adopted in 1960 for any male-line descendants who do not carry royal titles.

Timeline

1926

Elizabeth is born
Born Elizabeth Alexandra Mary Windsor, the young princess is the daughter of George, Duke of York (later George VI) and Elizabeth Bowes-Lyon (later Queen and then Queen Mother).
21 April 1926

Young love
In 1934 and 1937, the young princess meets with Prince Philip of Greece and Denmark. In 1939 they meet for a third time at the Royal Navy College in Dartmouth, with the 13-year-old Elizabeth remarking that she has fallen in love with the 18-year-old prince.
22 July 1939

Marriage to Philip
Princess Elizabeth marries Philip at Westminster Abbey after almost 15 years of slow courtship. Since tensions are still running high from the global catastrophe that was World War II, Philip's German relatives are not permitted to attend.
20 November 1947

Prince Charles is born
A month prior to the arrival of Elizabeth's first son, Charles, her father George VI decrees that any of her children will retain the title of prince or princess. This overturns the rules set out by George V that restricted such titles to children of the monarch or the monarch's son.
14 November 1948

For over 70 years the Queen Mother remained a source of guidance and inspiration, up to her death in 2001

in his original posting - a public decision that showed her pride as a mother as much as her commitment as queen. (A fact made all the more chilling when you consider Argentina planned to assassinate the prince during the conflict.)

Despite the high points of the previous decade, the 1990s were a challenging time for Elizabeth and the rest of the royal family. A fire at Windsor Castle at the tail end of 1992 caused catastrophic damage and destroyed priceless royal heirlooms, while the script for the Queen's speech was leaked and published by *The Sun* newspaper a year later. To make things even

worse, the very public disintegration of Charles and Diana's marriage had become regular fodder for the British and international media. The publication of the Diana biography *Diana: Her True Story*, with its claims of an ongoing affair between the princess of Wales and Major James Hewitt, brought further strain on the royal family. Charles and Diana's eventual separation in 1993 would lead to years of criticism of the royal family's conduct as Diana rose to prominence as a charity worker. This scrutiny would fail to abate, even when Diana was tragically killed in a car crash in Paris in 1997.

The last decade and a half has seen the royal family enjoy a far more positive reception in the public eye. The death of the Queen Mother and Elizabeth's younger sister, Princess Margaret, in the space of two months in 2002 saw an outpouring of public support for the Queen, which flowed seamlessly into celebrations for the golden jubilee later that summer. Not one to let personal feelings affect her royal duties, Elizabeth set out on an extensive tour of the Commonwealth and returned to mass celebrations that surprised many, most notably the media. Her diamond jubilee a decade later further cemented the nation's more positive relationship with the crown, with celebrations across the land merging with excitement for London's hosting of the Olympics in 2012.

And now, aged 88 and on track to become the longest-reigning monarch in our country's history, the Queen still exudes the same principles of character she learned in those early years of her

> Elizabeth II is the second longest-reigning British monarch. Queen Victoria holds the record at 63 years and 216 days

rule. She's a monarch who understands her place in the anatomy of a modern nation, less concerned with how history remembers her, but how she can serve the realm. As generations of younger royals continue to attract most media attention away from her, Elizabeth still remains an iconic figure in the identity of Britain and the Commonwealth.

The Falklands War

In comparison to the World War she lived through as a princess, the confrontation over the Falklands, South Georgia and South Sandwich Islands was a relatively low-key affair. Nonetheless, Great Britain's involvement in the ten-day crisis was covered in meticulous detail by the media, including the deployment of her second son, Prince Andrew, into the conflict.

The war itself was fought over the sovereignty of a number of islands in the South Atlantic, most notably the Falkland Islands (an archipelago consisting of two large islands and 776 smaller ones) with a population of just under 3,000 people. The Falklands had been a crown colony since 1841, but nearby Argentina refused to recognise Great Britain's claim, believing the islands to be Argentinian soil. On 2 April 1982, Argentina landed on the islands with a contingent of 600 troops and proceeded to take control of the whole area. Considering, though never officially stating, the invasion an act of war, the British government responded by sending the Royal Navy to engage the Argentinian navy and air force, as well as landing an amphibious assault on the island. The conflict lasted for two months, one week and five days and ended with Argentina's surrender. While 258 British sea and airmen were killed during the conflict, almost 650 soldiers died on the Argentinian side.

"She understands her place in the anatomy of a modern nation"

The diamond jubilee
2-5 June 2012

In the summer of 2012, Elizabeth celebrates a whole 60 years as Queen of the United Kingdom and the Commonwealth. In a speech on Accession Day, Elizabeth says: "In this special year, as I dedicate myself anew to your service, I hope we will all be reminded of the power of togetherness and the convening strength of family, friendship and good neighbourliness." She and Philip tour the country extensively as part of the celebrations, with their children and grandchildren travelling across the Commonwealth on her behalf. A month later, Elizabeth officially opens the 2012 Olympic Games on 27 July and the Paralympic Games on 29 August.

● **Prince Edward is born**
Four years after the birth of Andrew, Elizabeth gives birth to third son Edward. The young prince is third in line to the throne at his time of birth, but in 2015 is now eighth in the order of succession; he's now known as the Earl of Wessex.
10 March 1964

2015

● **Prince Andrew is born**
At the beginning of 1960 - almost seven years into her reign as queen - Elizabeth gives birth to her second son, Prince Andrew, in the Belgian Suite of Buckingham Palace. He is baptised three months later.
19 February 1960

● **The silver jubilee**
In 1977, Elizabeth celebrates the first major anniversary of her accession. A monarch's jubilee is based on the date they were proclaimed king or queen rather than that of their coronation. To celebrate, festivities and parties are held all across the Commonwealth during the year.
1977

● **Charles weds Diana**
After a widely publicised courtship, Prince Charles marries Lady Diana Spencer at St Paul's Cathedral in a ceremony that captivates Great Britain and the wider world. The marriage will produce two sons, Prince William and Prince Harry.
29 July 1981

● **Diana passes away**
Just as her wedding had captured the hearts and minds of the nation, the death of Diana, Princess of Wales is just as publicly scrutinised. Despite Elizabeth II requesting the divorce of Diana and Charles in 1995, Diana still remained a hugely popular figure.
31 Aug 1997

● **The Golden Jubilee**
In 2002, Elizabeth marks the 50th anniversary of her accession to the throne. Despite the celebrations across the Commonwealth, the event is bittersweet, as the Queen Mother and Elizabeth's sister Princess Margaret have died a few months previously.
2002

DISCOVER

Churchill's Toyshop
7 unbelievable inventions from the secret war lab of Winston Churchill

ALL ABOUT HISTORY

VIKING RAIDERS
How heathens from the north turned seas red with blood

TERRACOTTA WARRIORS

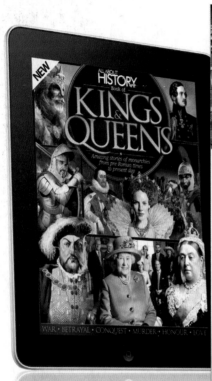
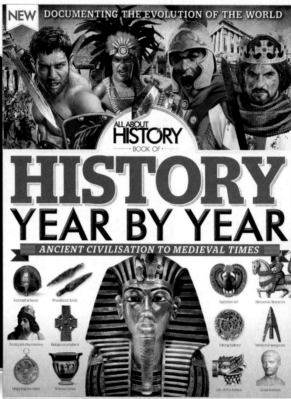
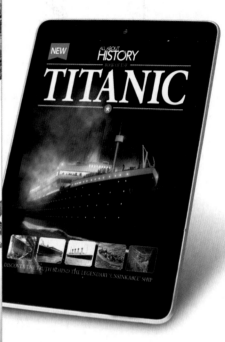